On the Spine of Time

Also by Harry Middleton:

The Earth is Enough: Growing Up in a World of Fly Fishing, Trout, and Old Men
The Starlight Creek Angling Society
Rivers of Memory
The Bright Country: A Fisherman's Return to Trout, Wild Water, and Himself

On the Spine of Time

a flyfisher's journey among
Mountain People, Streams & Trout

H A R R Y   M I D D L E T O N

WESTWINDS
PRESS®

THE PRUETT SERIES

Copyright © 1991 by Harry Middleton
Foreword © 1997 by Ron Ellis

Originally published in hardcover and paperback by Simon & Schuster, New York, New York, in 1991.
First Pruett Publishing Company edition, October 1997

Library of Congress Cataloging in Publication Data

Middleton, Harry.
    On the spine of time: a flyfisher's Journey among mountain people,
    streams & trout / Harry Middleton. — 1st Pruett Pub. Co. ed.
        p.   cm.
    Originally published: New York: Simon & Schuster, © 1991.
    ISBN 978-0-87108-892-5 (pbk.)
    1. Great Smoky Mountains Region (N.C. and Tenn.)—Description
and travel. 2. Great Smoky Mountains Region (N.C. and Tenn.)—Social
life and customs. 3. Fishing—Great Smoky Mountains Region.
4. Middleton, Harry—Homes and haunts—Great Smoky Mountains
Region. 1. Title.
[F443.GM53   1997]
976.8'89—dc21   97–36183
                                                     CIP

Cover and book design by Signorella
Book composition by Lyn Chaffee
Cover painting by Thomas Aquinas Daly

WestWinds Press®
An imprint of Graphic Arts Books
P.O. Box 56118
Portland, Oregon 97238-6118
(503) 254-5591
www.graphicartsbooks.com

For Gil Rogin, for his years of unquestioning friendship

and for Trinket Shaw and Sylvia Martin,

who cared truly through good and bad.

Foreword

WHEN I FIRST suggested to Jim Pruett that it might be interesting to have a dedicated Harry Middleton fan (that would be me) write the foreword to the Pruett Publishing edition of *On the Spine of Time*, I was not sure how he would react to the idea. I mean, it's hardly routine for a publisher to permit someone without a literary reputation (that would also be me) to introduce a book by one of its finest authors. But in typical Jim Pruett fashion—I can hear him saying "interesting"—he saw the idea as unique and said, "Do it." And so I have, ever mindful of the honor its writing represents.

I never met Harry Middleton, not face to face that is, but I did meet him through his writing, month after month, wonderful story after wonderful story in his Outdoors South column in *Southern Living* magazine. Not long after discovering him there, I read Annie Dillard's recommendation for Middleton's *The Earth is Enough* in one of those "what are you reading now" pieces in the *New York Times*. That was on a Sunday, and by early Monday I had placed an order for the book.

Harry Middleton produced five books and numerous articles and book reviews before he died of a heart attack in July 1993. In an In Memoriam tribute in *Audubon* magazine, Nick Lyons calls Middleton "one of the most poignant celebrators of the natural world . . . a young writer of immense promise."

And that he was.

I love all of Middleton's books, but *On the Spine of Time* is a favorite volume, probably because of where the stories are located. This is a special book about a special place: the deep woods and the towns of the Great Smoky Mountains. The book is full of the joys of trout, flyfishing, and mountains, and populated with a delightful burgoo of lovable characters "more real than imagined." I know something of the Smokies and the tourist towns surrounding them, having motored through them many times. I fished for trout there only once, floating (uneventfully) a #14 Royal Coachman for a few hours on Deep Creek in Middleton's honor shortly after his death.

In those mountains, Middleton introduces us to Arby Mulligan, founder of the Owl Creek Gap Church of Universal Harmony and interpreter of "all manner of cranial distensions"; Roth Comers Tewksbury, fellow angler and a Manhattan-based financier who is haunted equally by trout and the beautiful Carlotta, "perfect as sleep"; the Proverb Man who, while filling your order at the Gatlinburg, Tennessee Dairy Queen, dispenses wisdom like "The more you see some people, the better you like dogs"; Jess Napper of Nantahala, North Carolina, who introduces us to UFOs and Fyffe, Alabama, "a cosmic crossroads, a hangout for intergalactic travelers"; and Exie Sopwith who promises the writer, ailing from an abundance of bad potato salad consumed at Miss Molly's Restaurant, that her chicken broth will "nail you back together again."

On the Spine of Time offers enough information about the natural side of the region, without being painful about it, to be valuable as a limited nature and travel guide. Middleton is generous with information about the area's flora and fauna, and he even dispenses a smattering of fly fishing "how-tos," something he rarely does as he always sees to be more concerned with where the fishing is taking place rather than how it is being done. But mostly he tells us of the Smokies' wildness, of the cold mountain streams there, and of the trout they hold: brown trout ("fierce paunchy behemoths that strike out of hell's own darkness"), rainbows ("wary, suspicious, and dyspeptic, all common traits among trout"), and brookies ("native southern highland trout in pools of cold water").

I open my wallet in the town of Gatlinburg annually, as it is directly in the path of the family trip we take each summer to visit friends in South Carolina. It is a mandatory stopover since my twelve-year-old son covets the glitz and games offered there. That's fine with me because, like Middleton, I look forward to a walk around town. It is surrounded by the mountains and close enough to the Little Pigeon River to hear its soothing murmurs. A stroll down Parkway Road leads one to the amusements and to some of the places Middleton profiles in the book.

But the place I like best in Gatlinburg is where the Little Pigeon River rushes out of the national park and crosses "that invisible boundary," where lush green meets bright neon and intense quiet spills into the town, soon gobbled up by the ravenous tourist din. It is here, in a soft, quiet pool that offers different reflections than those he writes about in the book's last chapter (my favorite), that Middleton hooks and lands the biggest trout he had ever caught in the Smoky Mountains, all under the watchful gaze of the Proverb Man:

> The Proverb Man handed me a napkin and I rubbed off my glasses and put the trout on the small meat scale. I saw it clearly for the first time. It looked so inelegant in the creel bag, its body bent awkwardly. It looked as long as my forearm, from the tip of my outstretched fingertips to my elbow and then some. It weighed in at just under 7.5 pounds. It lay there on the scale, the eye facing me black and still like black stone seemingly full of nothing and yet a world of motion, of unrealized tendencies. Eyes that were reservoirs of light and probabilities.

This is a book full of "light and probabilities," written with an angler's passion for trout, cold water, and a love of things green—from the little 4-weight Winston rod the writer uses to probe for dreams in the icy streams to the lushness of the mountains.

This is a book full of good and honest stories, all told with Middleton's special brand of humor and affection. All are punctuated with unexpected joys, like the mysterious sounds of bagpipes played by a secretive piper along a backcountry stream, and heartbreakingly beautiful phrasings such as "First a wash of soft white moonglow, then, on the water, the perfect reflection of stars, specks of light wrinkling in the river's current," and "The soft light of dusk, a trout's rise, the sound of nothing but water over stones."

On the Spine of Time is so beautifully imagined and written that, whether you are an angler, nature lover, traveler, or reader, this is a book that will restore your balance and remain sweetly within your heart. If you're not yet a Harry Middleton fan, the reading of this splendid book will cinch your conversion.

"The Lord's eye on it," as Arby Mulligan would say.

—Ron Ellis
Lakeside Park, Kentucky, 1997

Preface

IT IS AUTUMN and the night is clear and cold. A great
dome of stars stretches across the sky as though pulled
down tight over the worn, dark ridges of the Great
Smoky Mountains. The stars give the night sky a pale white glow, like light
reflecting off melted candle wax.

It was a good day along the creek. Just before noon, the sky turned black
as wet coal and it snowed hard for hours, a great whirlwind of snow, and still
I fished.

Snow was soon piled up on the backs of dark, smooth stones, and the sudden cold, the unexpected turn of weather, stirred me as much as it did the
trout. I had almost forgotten how much fun it is to fish the high country in
a good snowstorm.

I have lit the stove, put a pot of chili on. Staring up at the great sprawl of
the mountain night, my back snug against a broad maple, I realize again that
what I see is like the reflection in a rearview mirror. We see the universe not
so much as it is, but as it was. The light I see in the blue-black mountain
night, even of the stars closest to the earth, is old light, old news, light that
is already more than four years old by the time I see its faint glimmer. Yet, to
me, to my eye and senses, it is immediate and urgent, the topography of the
present moment, a wild dance. Meanwhile, beyond my view, if not beyond
my imagination, beyond this brilliant mountain night illuminated by spent
starlight, the universe continues to reel from its inception, the original Big
Bang, continues to expand like a blind worm probing through dark soil, alive
only so long as it moves.

It is all touch and go, whether it is the insect larvae snug beneath the flat-backed stones at the bottom of the creek or distant galaxies adrift in the dark belly of space. It is all dilemma and no final answers. Thank the gods.

It's all touch and go.

Almost all the leaves are off the trees. They scuttle about the ground, rattle in the cold wind: the year's excess spent, exhausted. Up higher, up above 5,000 feet, there are still the bold greens of the great dying fir and spruce forests of the Canadian Zone, but here midway up the ridgeline of the mountains, winter is a study in the latitude of grays and browns.

From the stony brow above my campsite, out on the rippled lip of the ridge, I can clearly see the lights of Bryson City, North Carolina, down in the valley. The lights look like flecks of mica shining in some fold of wet, dark soil.

Tomorrow, even if the trout rise, I will have to pack up, move on, hike back down the mountainside, and head home, back to the hills of Alabama. I lack Horace Kephart's wild courage and his resolute happy madness. Something compelled him to walk away from one life, including a successful career as one of the nation's most respected and learned librarians, plus a wife and family, and a host of attendant obligations, and into another world and life in these mountains. He never looked back.

While the chili cools down, I look down into the valley and see the lights of the houses and know I must go in the morning. There is a mortgage to pay off, a car with a worrisome cough and balding tires, the usual heap of bills. The radio in my study doesn't work. I need to fix it so that late at night, I can turn the dial to hear how humanity is doing. There is the squirrel in the attic that I haven't been able to evacuate. I've tried everything, even a bucketful of mothballs. I need to get back, put on my headlamp, lay the sleeping bag on the roof, and wait the squirrel out, discover how it comes and goes.

Comes and goes.

I need to get home—for a time, anyway. I have two sons. Both expect to go to the college of their choice. There is a cat that depends on me, too, and a month's worth of laundry to do, and a lawn my neighbors expect me to keep tidy and well groomed. There are taxes to pay and moral commitments and work piling up on my desk.

And so on.

These mountains are fickle and change with each slant of light. The world I see in one range of pale violets is another world entirely in the first pools of morning's hazy blues. Things don't end so much as fade, dissolve, disappear, and reappear as something altogether different. Even the mountains come and go, affirming the wild rhythm of possibility and tendency rather than certainty. Tomorrow at sunrise I will break camp along the rushing waters of the creek, and head down the mountainside toward town. I left my car at the Deep Creek campground. It's the grimy brown one in need of a good wash and wax. When I get to the campground, I will look back up at the mountains as I always do, see them rising up out of the morning's thick blue fog. Sometimes they remind me of lifeboats, there for anyone wanting to feel the palpable touch of solitude and solace against his skin.

A few words of explanation on this cold and windy mountain night. This is not a book about the history—social, cultural, or otherwise—of the Great Smoky Mountains or the high country of southwestern North Carolina, which is where most of the high country trout streams that haunt and soothe me are located. Neither is this some great quest or sojourn, nor a chronicle of some ambitious pilgrimage, angling or any other. It is not an angling guide to the trout streams of the Great Smoky Mountains. There are hundreds of miles of excellent trout streams in these mountains. The best advice I can give is this: come. Park your car. Listen for the sound of fast water, trout water, and start walking.

This is just a story of mountain creeks and streams, of mountain trout, of mountains and mountain people. It's a look at life, its losses and joys, its tragedies and happiness, what is lost in a life and what is found. There happens to be a lot of fishing in this story, as well as certain slants and ranges of light, and time spent well and spent foolishly, perhaps. Mostly, though, this is a story of people—people I have met in these mountains. Some brushed against me like a wind, touched me, and were gone; others have happily become, almost accidentally, a great part of my life.

I began going into the Great Smoky Mountains and into the nearby Slickrock Wilderness and Snowbird Mountains more than a decade ago. I was on my way to West Virginia and got sidetracked. Lucky me.

As a boy I began keeping a journal. I was in other mountains then, the Ozark Mountains of northwest Arkansas. I have been filling up journals ever since. It's an affliction. Writers suffer from all kinds of afflictions. (Healthy and rational people who think they want to be writers should consider some other, perhaps saner, line of work.)

Each night, I scribble endlessly in my journal, putting in everything—stolen conversations; people's appearances and habits, also conscripted without permission; the day's weather; what I've seen and what I've imagined; what I've felt; joys and sorrows; prejudices; the fragile state of my personal economy; wonderings; newspaper and magazine clippings; what I'm reading of late and whether or not it's worth the trouble; grocery lists and car mileage; playing backbone Delta blues in Onward, Mississippi; spending the night at Muleshoe, Texas; the solace of mountain streams, fast water, moving water; trout hooked and trout lost. Everything.

A good deal of what I write comes from my journals. They hold what I want to remember, including my travels among these mountains. Much of this book was first written in the rough form of daily recordkeeping in my journals. The people in this story are real. I have fiddled with them, changed some things about them, such as their names, their appearance, and so on. Nothing more. All of them are more real than imagined.

Was there really a man who played bagpipes along Hazel Creek? Yes, though I never discovered who he was or why he stopped coming to play his music along the creek. I wish he would come back. I miss him.

Was there a man who walked about the mountains carrying a prayer wheel, offering a free spin and hope of a kind to everyone he encountered? Yes.

Rachael Settles's dog is really named Dog. And so on.

This is what Arby Mulligan said when I told him I might put him in this book, "Just say that anyone who's not afraid of a little ice-cold mountain water on their head is welcome in the Church of Universal Harmony, and there's no charge and no obligations. As for readin' and interpretin' the bumps on their heads, well, there might be a small charge."

This is what Tewksbury said, "Make it clear, dear friend, that I find it immeasurably easier to make money than to angle for trout."

Bob Winterwolf Dougal was too nervous to comment. He has a chance to attend the Wharton School of Business of the University of Pennsylvania. But he has nightmares that if he does his soul will turn white. He is full-blooded Cherokee: a fine Native American, a fine man, as complex and delightful, exasperating, and haunting as every Native American I've been honored to know, beginning with Elias Wonder, the old Sioux who lived in the shack along Starlight Creek, down from my grandfather's farm. Elias Wonder was gassed in World War I and everyone thought he was a lunatic who would torch their farms or scalp them in their sleep. He was the sanest man I've ever known.

Truth has a befuddling quality about it, even in the deep quiet of the mountains. It's like quantum physics. Sooner or later you've got to let loose of certainty's hand and leap. Jump. Believe in something, like mountains and mountain streams, trout and mountain people.

Acknowledgments

A WRITER FINISHES a book and is immediately plagued with a great many mixed feelings. After all, a book's end means an end, as well, to many a misery and perhaps a few joys, too. Although a writer may push back from a completed manuscript thinking it is all his doing, it rarely is. Finishing this book, I thought of all the people who were actually involved, especially those who left a touch of kindness behind. Perhaps a smile or lunch, a good word, a cold bottle of root beer, a phrase lingering in the air that I happily stole, or a look I gladly pilfered. Writers are among the world's most insidious thieves. Anyway, there are a few people I would especially like to thank, including Kelso Sutton, Jim Mercer, Jean Smock, Don Logan, Nick Lyons, Tom Morgan, Phil Osborne, Mark Bryant, Linda Hallam, Dr. Jim Casada, and Elias Wonder's ghost. Special thanks to Lilly Yoshida.

There is one other person I want to mention, to single out. His name is Bob Bender. There are, if my math is right, 8,766 hours in a year. Bob sees to it that I waste as few of these hours as possible. He is an endangered species: a true friend.

I'm sure there are others. You know who you are. I thank you, too, all of you, very much.

It is better to be a part of beauty
for one instant and then cease to
exist than to exist forever and
never be a part of beauty

"the lesson of the moth" from *archy and mehitabel*
by Don Marquis

Crossing Over

I T IS EARLY APRIL and the window is open wide. A cool wind fills the small room on the second floor where I keep my desk, a lamp, a chair, and floor-to-ceiling bookshelves packed with books. From where I am sitting, near the room's only window, I can see the moon. It is a little short of full and its reflected light gives the night sky a brooding cobalt-blue coloring. The moon itself is a blend of benign yellows with a muted green mist that hangs at its edges like a ragged halo.

A glaucous moon. That's what I called it yesterday in trying to describe it to a friend of mine who is a disenchanted physicist, a man I often turn to, seeking the answers to difficult questions. I asked him why moonlight and some areas of the night sky seen from the nearby Smoky Mountains sometimes appear tinted by this lovely pale olive-green light. This is what my friend the physicist told me: "Toxins."

"Toxins!" My voice rose in disbelief, a blend of moan and wail.

"Sure," he said in an even-tempered voice. "Airborne toxins. Billions of tons of them. The atmosphere sags under their weight. So do our lungs." He got up from the kitchen table, began searching through the icebox. "Say, does a beer come with this inquisition?" he said. His voice had the warble of birdsong. "All this talk of toxins gives me a powerful thirst. They have such a hard, metallic taste about them."

My friend the physicist has a way of never cheering me up. He used to drink bourbon instead of beer, but he had to give it up, he says, because these days two drinks make him want either to fight or cry. Three drinks and he speaks French, a language he cannot recall ever learning.

"Yep, toxins," he said again, the can of beer hissing menacingly as he popped the tab.

Toxins: the word seeps about my brain, bores into the soft cinerous tissue, laying open tangles of braided nerves. Tonight, staring out the window at the moon, the nerves in my brain rattle and flinch at the dismal irony that such a gorgeous moon, such an alluring light, might be the product of heavily polluted air.

Should one of my sons ever ask me about the color of dying air, I will have an answer, quick and sure. This is what I will tell him: murderous yellows laced with impotent greens.

An hour ago the wind shifted. Now it is blowing slightly north of east, straight out of Mississippi. Odd how things seem to have trouble taking hold in Mississippi, even the wind. I know the feeling, though: that almost inexplicable restlessness of the blood that seizes the muscles, claws at the nerves. Impatience stalks me at every season, settles in my gut—a knot that refuses to give way. It nibbles at my flesh, an emotion like schools of tiny fish whose hunger is insatiable.

Each day's light brings the sudden urge to travel, to undertake some fresh journey. Strangely, exotic destinations do not haunt me. These days my wanderings always lead to the same place, the Great Smoky Mountains. Standing at the window, I strain my eyes hard to the northeast, out over these Alabama foothills, and tell myself I can see the great, worn, rounded peaks of the Smokies, massive shadows rising dramatically in the cold night air beyond the yawning expanse of the Coosa Valley. Even when I am away from these mountains, bogged down in some city, caught up in the frenetic whirlpool of making a living, the mountains are inside me, just below the skin, in the blood.

For years I have tried unsuccessfully to abandon this peculiar need of mine for mountains, for high country and trout streams, for the economy of life that seems to follow a steady rise in altitude. It's a serious malady, a vexing obsession. Cure, remedies, anodynes?—I've tried my share. Sedatives to calm me down; syrups to soothe me; elixirs to steady me; even a therapy calling for the regular use of a poultice made from opossum-belly fur, beechnut paste, and a pinch of ginseng. The poultice was guaranteed to keep my mind out of the clouds and off rising trout. Like all the rest, it failed, miserably. I gave up on the poultice about three years ago. I was staying up at Fontana, North Carolina, and fishing Santeetlah Creek until I slipped, lost a fine brown trout, and decided to give the remedy up.

"What's the problem?" asked Erskine Lightman standing at the door of his two-room cabin down the mountain logging road from Santeetlah Creek near Robbinsville, North Carolina. He ran his long, heavily wrinkled hands through an imaginative crop of thick, unruly hair. Lightman is burdened with a curious array of eccentricities. Smoothing back the hair that isn't on his perfectly bald head is one of them. He turned his attention from his head to the old stove that occupies the middle of the cabin. Breakfast was on.

"It doesn't work," I said. Lightman swung the door wide, motioned me to come in, have a seat.

He walked to the stove, examined a pot of hot, sticky grits. A long moment of silence limped between us like a crippled specter.

Finally, he said, "Okay, you've got me. I'm curious. What in the hell doesn't work?!"

"The CURE!" I groaned, too upset to work up a good shout. I had spent the morning down on the creek above the bridge and lost a fine brown trout. I saw its shadow just before it wrapped the tippet section of my line around a stone and broke it off. I was thinking about that shadow, trying to project it against all the other piscine shadows that clutter my imagination. A fine trout. Another ghost to haul around in my head. Desperate for detail, for a look in its black eyes, I had lunged after the trout, a move that resulted in an acrobatic though momentary pirouette that quickly crumbled and left me chest-deep in the creek's cold rush of water. That's when I packed up my rod and reel, wrung out my socks and pants, and went looking for Erskine Lightman.

Small puddles of creek water gathered beneath my chair. Erskine sat down across from me and put a platter of grits between us, the grits looking like a detailed papier-mâché model of the desolate, icebound peaks of The Himalayas.

"I don't have the mind I had a season ago," Erskine said as he went for the grits. "What is this cure supposed to cure, exactly?"

"Everything," I said. "All this mountain madness of mine. The endless pursuit of high country trout and my courtship of solitude. All of it." The words came somber and heavy, carried by breath that sounded like a gritty moan.

The smile was coming by then, though. I could see the corners of Erskine's mouth tremble as he fought back a loud burst of laughter.

"I thought you said heights make you dizzy, give you one hell of a case of vertigo. Just keep putting that poultice on your chest once a month and you can hang by your toes from the tallest building in Knoxville and still be steady as a preacher. Remember, though, rub it on you in ever smaller circles or it's worthless, and you'll panic climbing up a two-step staircase. And let's not hear any more about this genuine little twenty-five-dollar Smoky Mountain ointment not working."

I sneezed. "Okay, but what about my obsession with mountains and mountain streams and trout?" I asked, trying to dry out my bandanna by holding it near the woodstove.

This is what Erskine Lightman, fifth-generation master of Smoky Mountain folk medicine and trout fishing said, "Only one thing to do: shoot yourself."

And he couldn't hold the laughter anymore and we both let go at once and the morning was filled with it, a noise that seemed to rattle every board and nail of the old cabin. And I told Erskine about the brown trout again, which had already grown an inch in my memory, and beyond the front door you could see that sunlight was filling the narrow valley, a wall of light as wide and flat as a glacier inching inexorably toward the cabin door.

It's true about the poultice. Erskine prescribed it for a fever, which broke just as soon as I got out of my bed at home and drove up into the mountains and fished for a day along the bottom reaches of Hazel Creek. The only cure for a man in love with mountains is mountains; the analgesic for an addiction to mountain trout streams is the sound and feel of them—the low howling of water cascading over smooth stones; the sudden chill of a stream's mist against the skin; the knot in the gut and the adrenaline that spills into the blood on seeing a rising trout; that possibility of wildness that never dulls or wears thin, no matter the press of time, the passage of years.

Lightman called earlier this evening before I went up to the study, opened the window, started packing, before I remembered the poultice, which was really as much for a stubborn cold I had as it was for my trout melancholia. Erskine has a voice with more fits and starts than a temperamental church organ.

"That youoooo," he said, his voice at first siren-high, then trailing off like a train through a long, narrow tunnel. "Here, listen to this." And then the whoosh of water, just water. "Gets to you, eh, flatlander," he said, his voice suddenly booming through the receiver.

"For chrissakes, Lightman, it sounds like running tapwater." I countered his clangorous yell with a reverberating bellow, imitating the guttural growl of dissipating thunder.

And then that calculated, meaningful pause. "Yeah," Lightman said, his voice now soft and harmless as the sound of chimes in a slight wind, "but it's mountain tapwater."

Before hanging up, this is what Lightman said into the telephone, almost in a whisper: "The mountains are here, and the streams, and the trout. Where are you? Where are you?"

Still here, Lightman. Still here. Up the stairs, last room down the hall, sitting at this beat-up, old brown desk, staring out the window and into the April night. Here I am, eager for the morning light and the open road wending its way into the high country.

"Are you coming up?" Lightman asked.

"Of course," I said.

"Come alone," he said, and the words had a coating of urgency to them. "I've put some hens up at the cabin. They're laying now and crowds, especially anglers, upset them."

That was hours ago and the night lingers while I sit here by this open window and feel the night air cold against my skin. I know if I close my eyes all the trout of yesteryear will begin to rise again in all the mountain streams that rush and tumble through my imagination. Every detail is there, ripe and true. My sometimes awkward journeys do not, perhaps, amount to much. They are more wanderings than quests. The mountains keep few secrets. What is there is there. Explorations yield the garnish of details, but the meanings of things lay on the surface and glow in the sunlight. In angling for mountain trout, there is as much exhilaration as sharp solitude. Often have I cheered to an audience of trees and stones. While I am often a man who feels beleaguered, even confined by commitments, I make room for such things and keep those dear to me close at hand. Here is one: to relish the time I have along mountain trout streams and to embrace such moments as completely as though I had walked into a thick wall of heavy morning fog.

Before sitting down in the study to watch the night sky, I slipped another handful of Tabasco-flavored Slim Jims into one of the side pockets of the Dana pack. Trail food tucked in with compass and altimeter and wrinkled topographic maps, all of them worn by time and heavy mountain weather, mud, and sweat, and stained by too many bags of freeze-dried chili suddenly brought to life over the heat of my little camp stove.

I buy the Slim Jims by the box from a convenience store in the valley. I live on the south rim of a hard-luck mountain between Chattanooga, Tennessee, to the north and Birmingham, Alabama, to the south. It is a countryside with more folds than a cheap accordion: the foothills of the Appalachians, rugged and worn: country that is more tenacious than bucolic or pastoral. Sprawling across north Alabama and north Georgia, these hills are the rocky exhaustion of the Appalachians where the high country begins to level and fall, giving way to the wide flatlands to the south and east, a land without peaks or pinnacles, a land far removed from the cool winds that blow at higher altitudes.

The mountain I live on rises 1,100 feet above a narrow valley spreading to the south. To the north rises yet another ridge of hills, shadowy eroded humps pressed against the sky and a horizon as fractured and ruptured as an arthritic backbone. Thick sunlight, the viscous sunlight that marks the first hours of morning and the last moments of twilight, gives this range of low hills the look of a great blue-green sea—swells under a gentle wind, swells rising and falling seemingly without end. Mountains in motion: an image that is more hard truth than comforting illusion. That which we label natural and think of as the natural world cares little for the static, the fixed, the passive.

On good days, days when the air is not thick with the heavy, gray clouds of smog rising up from every city between central Alabama, Atlanta, and Knoxville, I am sure, quite sure, that I can look out this window and see all the way to Tennessee and beyond, all the way to the high dome-shaped peaks of the Smoky Mountains, mountains that appear briefly in the bright light as though they are momentary illusions, tricks of light and shadow like shimmering heat coming off a highway in summer, a heat that seems to turn the roadway into a pond of deep inviting water that like a dream evaporates the instant you move toward it, only to reappear just down the road, just out of reach. When I was a boy, I truly believed I saw these pools of water on empty, hot summer roads, just as I truly believe now that I can stand here and see the vague, wrinkled form of the mountains lifting out of the horizon. They are there and an April wind moves among them sodden with the smell of mountain laurel and sassafras and loam.

I have given a good portion of the evening over to loading the Dana pack. The idea is to carry as few pounds and as few burdens as possible. Hump what you can, what you need, not what you want or what you desire; hump what you must, not what you will. Altitude can as easily break your back as ease your disappointments.

When I was young I spent some time in the Ozark Mountains of northwest Arkansas. I came to those worn-out hills as something of a refugee, a boy looking for more than just escape or insularity. Instead, I found myself in what seemed like the very eye of life's burning chaos. The mountains absorbed me and I absorbed them and lived fully in their geography of light and shadow, stone and root and cascading streams full of mercurial trout. In mountains I first discovered the feel and significance of place, a solitude so rich that at times I felt sure I could feel the earth's pulse, the mountains' measured breathing.

Sometimes I would sleep down by the creek at night. I loved the feel of the stony Ozarks hard against my back, feeling like a layer of living tissue so tight that I could sense its rising and falling. In the mountains I felt at ease, at home. It is a feeling that stays with me still.

There is a raw tenacity that marks the Ozarks and the deceptive lush excesses of the Smoky Mountains, a hard knot of preservation: life everywhere probing air and earth and water, not just hanging on, but reaching out, always pressing the limits. Perhaps this is why I keep cleaning the rods and reels, packing it all up, hauling them up and down mountain streams. At once, angling broadens a man's vision while often threatening to blind him. Beauty comes like lightning, spontaneous, brief, brilliant, dangerous, with a light or a motion or a shape that unsettles emotions. For a sharp instant, everything pulses with an electric-blue glow, a cold light, a light that is stark and casts no shadow. The mountains offer no release, real or figurative, from the fits and starts of modern living. Indeed, they are a clear and often painful reminder of just how wild and intricate life can be where it manages, however feebly, to elude what is often the destructive pressure of man's presence, his influence, his touch. As I go on packing—extra socks, a wool shirt to layer the cold spring nights—I keep thinking how different sunlight feels on the skin in the high country, how, at this time of year, even the dusky shadows below Mount Le Conte are heavy with the smell of rhododendron, and how close the night sky presses against the high mountains, the constellations bent across the sky, their stars like sparks thrown free of some wild, everlasting fire.

This clear night reminds me that there is more to space than cold darkness and clouds of galactic dust. There is wildness, too, primordial and forever expanding.

"I can tell you this much," Jess Napper said, "they've reached the limits of Fyffe."

Jess Napper is a man of medium height and weight from Nantahala, North Carolina. His interests include fly-fishing, mountain grouse, beautiful women tourists between the ages of forty-five and fifty-five who flock to the mountains from Florida in the summer to escape the heat, and UFOs. He believes in aliens, he says, because he has seen one, a creature he refuses to discuss except to say it was connected to its spacecraft by what appeared to be a long, orange, heavy-duty extension cord. Jess Napper is a man who knows we are not alone in the universe. Indeed, as he told me just this morning, our galactic brethren grow more neighborly by the day. And then he told me about Fyffe.

Fyffe is a small town in De Kalb County, Alabama, that has become, according to Jess Napper and a good many others, something of a cosmic crossroads, a hangout for intergalactic travelers. In a single month, residents of Fyffe reported 1,300 sightings of various aliens and UFOs in, above, and around the town, including one astonishing announcement by a town resident that he had had an encounter with none other than Elvis Presley. Mr. Presley reportedly emerged from a craft resembling an immense red-and-blue baler with wings, sang "Don't Be Cruel," and just as quickly jumped back into the souped-up baler and disappeared into the starry Alabama night.

Why Fyffe? Why not? The townspeople are friendly and open-minded and less likely to chase alien visitors off. They are more curious than suspicious. Too, Alabama has a long and surprisingly rich interplanetary history, including the fascinating story of Mrs. Anne Hodges who, while innocently relaxing on the sofa of her Sylacauga home in 1954, became the only known human being to be struck by a chunk of meteorite and live to be thoroughly perplexed by the ordeal. My neighbors down the hill still talk about the whole bewildering episode in whispers. Mrs. Hodges was beaned, they tell me, by a good-sized "piece of the beyond." Actually, the 8.5-pound piece of meteorite smashed through Mrs. Hodges's roof at 270 miles an hour and ricocheted off the walls and a big radio set before clobbering the astonished Mrs. Hodges.

This is all true. The infamous chunk of meteorite that struck Mrs. Hodges is on display in Smith Hall at the State Museum of Natural History. Although her physical wounds eventually healed, Mrs. Hodges never completely recovered from the emotional trauma of being smacked in the stomach by a rock from outer space.

Mrs. Hodges's meteorite came to mind again tonight after I read a story in the evening newspaper of a huge asteroid that hurtled past the earth so fast that we didn't even know of its presence until after it had passed. It took us by surprise, much as Mrs. Hodges's meteorite took her. Scientists believe this asteroid was bigger than a good-sized mountain, one traveling through space at 46,000 miles an hour. It missed the earth by a half a million miles or less— a measurement that in the field of astronomy is a cat's whisker. Had the asteroid and earth collided, scientists speculate that the impact would have been equal to that of 40 billion tons of TNT, a daisy chain of more than 40,000 hydrogen bombs exploding in unison and leaving a ragged wound in the earth far greater than the size of Rhode Island. Something to think about while staring blankly at the stars. Just another near miss. One more fascinating cosmic wake-up call. The universe is more puzzling than we dare to think, much less imagine.

The slender aluminum rod tubes are bound together and tied to the side of the pack. All winter long, every week or so, I took the fly rods from these metal cocoons, unwrapped them, rubbed them with clean soft rags, rigged them up with line and fly, and cast a line out across the backyard and down toward the hickory trees along the edge of the gorge. And with each cast mountain trout would rise in my imagination, all vital and wrinkling with details of motion and color. Emotions dulled by the long winter took on new vigor, pinched against the thin surface of my flesh. Just one cast and I could see and feel myself along the middle reaches of Hazel Creek in a fine pool of pale green waters strewn with ash-gray boulders the size of pianos. And I could feel a cold wind on my face and my fingers going numb; the creek's cold water like sharp teeth tearing through my waders. All of this unreeling in my mind, ribbons of feeling unleashed by a single cast from something as benign yet captivating as a 7.5-foot piece of supple graphite that weighs, without line or reel, less than three ounces. Not much of an object, yet the one with which I go on trying—in desperate fits and starts—to angle my way into the fabric of the natural world, the trout's world: cold, fast, mountain streams. I cast, cajole, flick, toss, dupe, tempt—so many employed gestures so that I might do something as harmless as nap for a while in warm clouds of mountain light. Angling is simply the best excuse I have stumbled onto for investing as much time as possible in the mountains, along mountain rivers casting for trout, throwing my hook into pools of light and shadow. Actually, as a trout angler, I am something of a rather seedy charlatan, a confessed trickster trying, most often in vain, to tempt a trout to gobble down some fraudulent yet alluring fly, not to catch him, but so that he might haul me, if even for one blemished moment, into its and the river's vital wildness, rough-edged, and undiluted. An angler can spend time or invest it; I choose to invest it in the possibilities of mountain rivers and their trout, in the big hemlocks that line their banks, in loam rich enough to still nourish a seed.

Things change, thank the gods, and as the years have passed so has my relationship with trout and fly-fishing. The angling life, for me, anyway, is neither sport nor is it banal recreation. Fly-fishing is neither an arcane art form nor a streamside primer in metaphysics. For me, it is simply the most pleasant and uncomplicated way of living in the mountains instead of just passing through. With a fly rod, I can look foolish, be foolish, and still leap joyfully as a child into the heart of a fast-moving mountain river, into ranges that often seem as though they might reach beyond the dimmest stars. The fly rod not only catches trout; it is a handy fulcrum allowing me to cast to those things that seem so far beyond my grasp.

Of course, each new day also brings the sad prospect that I will leap and find that there is no firm ground under me. Mountains and mountain streams, like people, die, though usually for different reasons. They are ruined piecemeal, used to fuel what seems to be mankind's insatiable greed, the unappeased appetites of progress, development, prosperity. Man's economy, an economy of ever greater accumulation regardless of the price either to his kind or to the earth, seems to demand the destruction of the earth's natural economy. I am caught between the two, an angler seeking a compromise, a chance for man and the earth as well. I carry out my diplomacy in the mountains along trout streams. Mountains urge involvement. They urge motion, a searching not for the distant, but for what is near at hand. My leaps of faith are small matters and though I may cover no more ground than an atom, it's the leap that matters because it has measure and endurance, the force that might illuminate some truth sheltered in the sunlight, hidden in dark earth or twilight shadows. Such things are still possible even where wilderness, true wilderness, is but a distant relic of ancient time.

There is no true wilderness left in the Smoky Mountains. Wilderness must be free of man's taint and his history, and the presence of man marks these mountains well, has sculpted them as surely as has wind and water and every press of weather. These mountains are a latticework of life's scars, a quilt of struggle and defeat, independence, sadness, poverty, humor, and self-reliance, and starched faith. Even in the sad malaise of ruin, mountains are as pitiless as time itself.

The idea is not to fight mountains, but to absorb them. Off and on tonight

I have been thinking of the sometimes difficult trail along Slickrock Creek up in the Joyce Kilmer Memorial Forest. The creek is beautiful, one of my favorite places in the mountains. Thinking of the hard trail, I find that concentration feeds on detail, on every remembered smell, every leaf in the wind, every tree remembered, until the image seems exact and sends a shiver under my skin and fills my blood with sizzling neuropeptides that put a reddish flush on my cheeks and neck, send something like a jolt of electricity through the muscles and nerves. Reality often seems to have a harder edge in the mountains, as though altitude somehow hones it, makes it spare, clean, raw, and honest—an addictive chaos of life that percolates through every atom.

Too often have I turned to the earth for some kind of dramatic statement. What is here is here and yet we search for the eccentric, the bizarre. We dissect and analyze, probe and examine, slide the earth under a microscope's lens hoping to find a code for miracles. Meanwhile, the sun shines and rivers rush and trout rise, and every hour of every day there is a real magic show of light and shadow and the dance of time. Nature is a grand balancing act, life in pursuit of a homeostasis it never quite achieves because its energy is always pushing it further on, tipping the balance, first one way, then the other.

Human beings come equipped with something called vestibular sensors, which are located in the inner ear. They give us a sense of balance, keep us level, if not level-headed. Mountains are vestibular sensors on a grander scale, absorbing the world about them, struggling for balance.

Down here, down on this Alabama hillside, it doesn't take much to upset the fragile disposition of my vestibular sensors. Traffic jams, bills to pay, love gone sour, a leaky roof, a truck with a whimsical starter, and, instantly, my sensors go haywire and I am as clumsy as a drunk haplessly trying to get up a down escalator. This is my body's way of telling me it is time to pack the fly rods and backpack and get back up into the mountains, back up along a good trout stream where I can enjoy the company of trout, which, for the most part, live far saner and more well-balanced lives.

There is a Beatles' song on the radio, music a church down the hillside tells me will get me to Hell a lot faster than I'm already going. I let the music play and recall the last time I heard this song up on Highway 441 driving from Tennessee to North Carolina and thinking that if I drove far enough, gained enough altitude, I would find a good run of water where I might have some say over what assaults my senses. The mountains never let me down.

High among the clouds, the spectacular and the ordinary, the common and the exquisite, all take shape in the same light and disappear in the same common shadows. Ten steps on a narrow mountain trail and the heavy scales of urban life begin to fall away like so much dead skin and I become, almost unconsciously, the honest sum of my parts: a trout angler at loose ends, fishing from first light till last, filling my creel with so much more than trout.

This need for altitude, for cold mountain streams and the possibility of trout, is, I admit, getting more and more impulsive, harder to predict, harder to control. More and more, it surfaces without warning, leaving me happily bewildered and dazzled. One instant I'm putting an edge on a hoe and the next I am an empty sensorium, greedy for a trout stream's endless flood of stimuli, yearning for mountains laced with fall color, desperate for a hollow's rich smells, eager for the sight of a trout flashing just below the surface of the water. It's hard to relax. Every nerve seems a boisterous interpreter of what it feels. The message to the brain is plain, simple: time is not hard, not flat, one-dimensional. Rather, it is fluid, as dynamic and chaotic as a wild mountain river. I want to use it up as fully and completely as it uses me up, feed on it the way it feeds on me—mercilessly.

In the mountains experience is as rich in vital nutrition as chili and sourdough bread. Sometimes I have lived for days on the energy generated by experience. It is filling and satisfying and lingers in every cell. A scientist who keeps track of such things says that each second of our lives we are bombarded by at least 100,000 random impulses of sensory information. A holocaust of electrical information. Against such an onslaught I fumble about desperately like a man who has suddenly lost his sight and is trying to channel the earth—through one less sense.

The mountains dig at my senses, scrape them clean, wash them in cold mountain rivers, and hang them in a mountain wind to dry. Wading in a fine stream, I often try to reduce myself to a cell within its waters, nondescript flotsam riding wildly on the current of time as it spreads without fanfare down through shadow-filled, rocky valleys and finally onto the wide, flat, sunlit sprawl of the piedmont. I let such moments carry me for as long as they can and as far away as they can from that which seems to be doing me so little good—office politics and intrigue, neither of which I excel in, crowds, bad plumbing, polluted water and grimy air, traffic gridlock, the increasingly dreary task of simply making a living instead of living a life. Up in the mountains, I let all this go for a time and let myself drift toward what

I like and enjoy rather than what others believe I need. Be it for an hour or a day or a week, when I am in the high country, I give up and give in, glide with slants of light, dream in cool shadows, cast my line after a good fish.

Once on the mountain highway, once the road rises out of these foothills and serpentines about the scalloped slopes of the mountains, things change, sensations change, priorities change. I change. I gather about me only what seems necessary, fundamental; I delight in what is basic—a cool wind; clean, fast water; the smell of sweet earth; a fat trout in deep water. There is an economy and an urgency to life in the mountains, an immediacy that defies exactness, the defined, whatever is confined by rules. In place of life's clutter, there is daylight and dark and everything from joy and exhaustion to fear coloring the light, giving it shape and substance. You take what is given, even the fear—the fear that the next time you climb this way it will all be gone; the mountain will be slag, trees clear-cut, coves developed, valleys bulldozed and seeded with resorts, streams dammed, all of it tragically transmogrified into the bleary, concrete, shopping-mall sameness I fled from, left down in the netherworld of the civilized lowlands.

The fear is real and I fight it with the fly rod which lets me cast beyond the obvious. Using the fly rod demands a discipline that insists that while on the stream great blocks of life, of time in motion, be allowed to slip by, almost unnoticed. My mind acts in much the same way, casting only to what seems interesting and promising, encouraging me to deal with the small, with currents and eddies and seeps, rather than the enormity of tidal waves. The idea is to concentrate on living rather than merely surviving. The brain is clever and full of cunning defenses, yet for all its splendor and evolutionary magnificence, it leaves me, in some ways, less than the trout which knows its world so thoroughly, so completely, seeing and feeling always the whole, while I feast on scraps of rising sun and setting moon, basins of fissured stone, endless slivers of changing light. When I cast to a trout, there is always that feeling, just below the skin, that I might somehow reach just beyond the given, and feel on my line the full weight of things—the weight of mountain and river laced into flesh and bone by a rising trout.

Below my second-story window, at the edge of the gorge, wild dogwood trees have dropped their faded white blooms. The ground beneath the trees looks like a milky reflection of the night sky, the spent blooms looking like distant points of hazy starlight until the wind stirs and sets everything adrift again. More illusion, harmless, innocent. The earth thrives on it. It's all catch me if you can; now you see me now you don't. Stability is a ruse. Even as I sit in this hard-backed chair here at my desk in this house on this Alabama hilltop, I am spinning, drifting, just as the earth, a less-than-average planet, is spinning on its axis and revolving about the sun, which is but a rather average and insignificant star. And the earth and sun are but two motes in a minor solar system in an average galaxy called the Milky Way that is drifting through the cosmic darkness at 40,000 miles an hour. When last I heard, our galaxy's course was generally east out beyond the stars of the constellation Hercules. As good a direction as any, I suppose.

Meanwhile, I am getting ready to take off in another direction entirely, one closer to home: north and east, up into the spruce-blue haze and fog that shrouds the Smoky Mountains, where I will for a week or so purposely give up chasing time, the futile and exhausting obsession to grasp it, hold it down, mend it to suit me. We give too much of life over to the wasteful chore of trying to undo, resolve, overhaul, resuscitate, and heal what passing time has a habit of leaving on our doorstep. So busy are we with the past, that we never feel or know the present. No wonder the future is always such a cold and ominous surprise. When I go into the mountains I live on mountain time: the warm press of the present splashing against me, filling the narrow river canyons and steep gorges where the swift water sounds like wind through hollow bones and threatens to absorb the very air. When a trout rises there is only a chill on the skin to remind me that time passed at all.

Years ago I spent a fine week hiking and fishing along Forney Creek near Fontana Lake, North Carolina. To reach the mouth of the creek, I rented a boat and made the short run across Fontana Lake and fished the lower portion of the creek. It was early fall, the first cool days of October, and I walked lazily up the trail along the creek, stopping frequently at every inviting stretch of water. By nightfall, I had hiked only as far up the valley as the old logging road where I dropped the backpack and fished the last hour of dim light. I took one small brown trout; the water went opaque, looked as thick and heavy as quicksilver. The wind came up and I reeled in my line, bit off the fly, dried it carefully, groomed it with the diligence of an old cat smoothing out tangled fur.

The wind took on a lasting strength and I shed the waders, unrolled the sleeping bag, and watched ragged clouds, white as eggshell, move quickly across the blackening sky. Barred owls had yet to call from the deep shadows and the only other sound was that of the creek, the gentle slap of water against stone. A vole scuttled through fallen brittle leaves, and I stretched out on the sleeping bag. Overhead, the clouds took on the look of torn rags and the moon was low in the sky. Up on the ridge an owl called, the sound like a low bark that joined with the sound of the creek and produced a new sound, like a symphony of bass drums played softly, a sound that drifted easily on the strong wind and rose quickly up and out of the pinched-in valley.

Twilight: a time for the arrival of cool shadows and familiar feelings, well-worked ideas, which come these days like animals out of the dark. Time raises mountains and attends to their collapse; its teeth marks are in the stone, in the thrust-up, faulted, folded landscape and on me as well. Perhaps that is the ultimate pull of mountains: we share the marks of time. Mountains let go; I hold on, wanting the dance to be everlasting. But the river moves on. There is nothing like a mountain trout stream to undermine whatever new bouquet of trendy neuroses a man might be nursing along.

A few hours more and it will be full daylight. To the east the sky is already luminescent, glowing. I especially like these hours before dawn and have since my years on the Ozark farm with the old men. The farm was in a narrow valley along Starlight Creek. The creek's cold waters were full of trout. Our days began before daylight, the creaking of the cold wooden floors in the soft dark, while from the kitchen downstairs came the smell of hot coffee and sausage and freshly made biscuits. A meal to give the day yet another dimension of character. We would sit at the small, round kitchen table and eat in silence and the sun would finally gain the ridge. Sunlight crept down the hillsides as though it were red-hot, molten iron being poured slowly from a smelter. Often, I would watch the building sunlight from the back porch that had no screen door and where there seemed to always be a cool wind. As the light came over the ridge like a feathering wave, the birds did not sing. Indeed, everything seemed, for an instant, bound by silence, everything but the creek; its waters moved on as always, the sound of mountains being reduced to flecks of stone.

As the years have passed, I've discovered that a good many people find altitude, a rapid ascent of any kind, disagreeable because it upsets their lives, makes them dizzy, light-headed, and giddy—exactly the characteristics of the mountains that I find so pleasing. I have been fortunate and have spent a good deal of time in the mountains, angling and hiking and just sitting along streams, a happy and voluntary exile with time to sort out that which I know from that of which I am only modestly aware. God bless Einstein and the demise of absolute time, the frightening notion of an inflexibly precise universe.

There are several more maps I need to pack. They are somewhere under all these stacks and piles and congeries of magazines and newspapers, bulletins and reports, somewhere here amid these stockpiles of books, heaps of clippings and files. The entire room seems to have become an ongoing and always urgent dispatch on the health and prospects of planet earth. So many strident voices wailing and moaning, protesting, screaming, sobbing, ranting. So many sad and angry and bitter voices, voices speaking the language of doom, the song of the Apocalypse. And I listen to the latest news and file the latest clippings, note the latest statistics. What else is a pessimist to do? Go on clipping and filing, I guess. Files of environmental failures, global destruction, and catastrophe; collections of extinctions, volumes on man's monumental waste. When it comes to the question of the earth's health, bad news multiplies with the rapidity of cancer cells. In every corner of this room there is more disease than cure, more failure than success. The sober facts are here: details of man's pathetic misuse of the planet, his only home, like the story of the madman who burns his only shelter, watches the flames with great delight even as a cold rain turns to ice. And he is naked in the cool ashes, the dying light.

What took the urgent press of life millions of years to create, man, in his endless pursuit of comfort, convenience, and his love affair with the economics of extravagant consumption, has dismantled and brought to the edge of annihilation in little more than a century: a cosmic wink of the eye.

Here in this ankle-deep slough of graphs and charts, this room of serrated words and dreary pronouncements, the earth's forests burn; rains as acidic as vinegar soak and slowly strangle forests and lakes and streams from North America to Europe. The choking exhausts of progress and technology gather daily in eerie dark-edged clouds of bitter smog. There in the east corner of this room, by the window, the earth's ozone layer is dissolving, breaking up under the ceaseless assault of fluorocarbons and other airborne pollutants and toxins. As it dies, the ozone is pulled away like a protective layer of skin exposing the fragile nature of life to the full measure of the sun's rays. In another corner are reports of melting polar ice caps, portents of wrenching climatic changes, rising seas. Anyone interested in beachfront property might want to invest near Philadelphia. The way things look now the Atlantic Ocean could be lapping at its front door in no time at all. In every corner, in every inch of this room's space, mankind increases, and as his population swells into the billions so do his demands on the earth's limited, finite resources. The world festers: a compost for calamity.

Here in the bottom drawer of my desk is a gathering of fewer and thinner files. Words of challenge and inspiration and optimism. Here in this single drawer time has yet to run out. Possibilities wrinkle here like worms in dark, rich soil. Here man's spirit remains decent and noble. Here there is a future worth the name, one in which remnants of wilderness and beauty continue, perhaps even thrive. Here life's diversity prevails. I try believing in what this shallow drawer holds because I cannot grasp the horror or despair of the alternatives.

Hang on, it's going to be a long and harrowing ride. Hold on, it's all touch and go from here on in.

And what's a pessimist with optimistic yearnings to do? What he can. Go trout fishing. Cast a line, set a hook, feel the raw pull of life. Use fewer plastics. No Styrofoam. No pesticides. Less air-conditioning and no spray cans, which means less fluorocarbons in the air. One cat. Two economical boys. My vote and my money, where there is some, for sanity, for what is wise rather than expedient, for the earth, rather than for man alone. A person ought, I suppose, to support his home, and this planet is the only home we have. And, too, there ought to be some time set aside for mountains and mountain streams, and fat, truculent trout. After all, where there is such water and trout, there is, I choose to believe, hope—hope not only for what is but for what is possible.

Bad Potato Salad

THREATENING BLUE-BLACK SKY spread across the flat Mississippi Delta just at dawn on the morning I packed up, headed not for the Smoky Mountains, but for the trout streams of West Virginia. At a gas station near Clarksdale an old black mechanic leaned against my VW van and sipped a hot cup of coffee. He looked up at the brooding sky, shook his head. "Bad day ahead," he said. "Weather that'll surely beat the cotton down, Cap'n. That's the truth of it."

The van had a tired, burdened look about it. Too many fly rods, perhaps. Too many cans of Spam and Vienna sausage, certainly. I had spent the night before burdening the van with way too much. I simply opened the doors and threw everything in. Everything. I packed it all. Boxes of books and folders of undigested time. Time, though, is necessary baggage: something I haul about, visit often, hoping, I suppose, that someday it will all fit, all make sense. Sometimes I believe that's what all this traveling, all these mountain journeys, are about, finally: a determination to make sense out of what so often seems senseless, to press against life and feel only the pressure of it pushing back.

It was spring, 1978, a time to set out for the mountains, for the cold fast waters of mountain trout streams. Mountains where beautiful trout streams spilled down narrow, rocky canyons. I had heard stories, good stories: good enough to put me on the road. Stories of mountain places not yet well known or traveled, places where the trout still outnumbered the people. My last roommate in college had told me these things, whispered them to me as though they were precious secrets, a legacy entrusted to me reluctantly. It sounded like good country, a land of raw energy and high cool forests. And I knew even then I would have to go, see it, fish it, feel it.

I packed the 1968 VW van with sleeping bag, food, canteen, tent, maps, root beer, fly rods, maps on which I had marked the topography of my dreams. In the glove compartment, with a flashlight and snakebite kit, were my college degrees, folded neatly and sealed in a white unmarked envelope. I was an angler at loose ends, getting work where I could find it. A bricklayer in Virginia, a laborer in Florida, a truck driver in Louisiana, and always looking for some excuse to get back into mountain country, back on some mountain stream that would lure me into its cold waters, pull me through some crack in sunlight and time, float me out to the edge of the universe where the real and the imagined shimmer in some slant of deep indigo-colored light.

Fishing mountain streams and the folding, wrinkling currents of time seems a harmless enough pastime. I was still young; the Vietnam war, though it had ended as tragically as it began, was over, hardly spoken of anymore, buried quickly, pathetically in the dark corners of memory. I had just enough college degrees to catapult me out of the job market. Anything seemed possible. Everything was likely. It was May and the fresh, cool air stung the lining of my lungs. I had $108.54 and it was good to be alive and bent on pursuing high country trout. Time in a mountain stream is not time wasted, but rather time fully used, felt, experienced completely. A week before I packed the van, my days were spent in a dimly lit machine shop, smelling of sweat and thick, dark, cutting oil. I swept up, hauled trash away, hardly saying a word to anyone, not even when the lunch wagon came. Each day I would just buy two cold drinks and a candy bar and rest against a rusted-out boring mill, shut my eyes, and dream of the mountains, up where the wind was sharp and cold and the streams were swollen with spring rain and the trout hung at the edges of the fast water, as mercurial as winter shadows. Such dreams made the days into a kind of God, one that offered renewal and possibility, and I would lean hard against the boring mill and imagine a mountain day full and ripe.

The storm that threatened near Clarksdale caught up with me near Chunky, Mississippi. It came fast out of the south and east, at first an innocent gathering of ash-gray clouds billowing like thick smoke, rising high and wide over the hard-luck farmland of northeast Mississippi. A spattering of rain turned the dirty VW van into a metallic chameleon: one moment it was some shade of brown, the next a ruddy, smeared, cinnabar red. The sound of thunder rattled the windows, a sound deep and low, like a convoy of earth-movers rolling over crushed rock. As a boy, I always enjoyed thunder, think-ing it some ancient language, the earth's own patois of sound, a grammar of wildness. The expanding clouds gobbled up the sky with rapacious hunger; weak drizzle exploded into a torrent of rain; in the near distance lightning, great bursts of electric-blue energy, mindless and pure, tore at the blackening sky, and the whole countryside went still, soundless. Not even the raspy rat-tle of wind among the trees or the frenetic cry of birds. And I could not help but think of Elias Wonder, the old Sioux who lived down the creek from my grandfather's farm, and who was, among so many other things, something of a human lightning rod. Wonder was living proof that lightning not only struck twice, but three times in the same place. He knew this because he was the place it kept striking. No matter where he sought shelter from an elec-trical storm, lightning sought him out as though he were solid metal, pure conductivity. In 1966, just before he died of a common cold, lightning found Elias Wonder one last time, long after he had stopped trying to outwit it. He was standing chest deep in Starlight Creek trying to raise a trout when it hit, an instantaneous tongue of intense light as wide, it seemed to me, as a rail-road tie. It shot out of the sulfur-black sky like a snapped whip, threw the old man at least thirty feet, put him on his back up on the soaked glistening grasses above the creek bank. He looked like a misshapen gnome, suddenly crisp and smoldering. Small wisps of smoke rose from Elias Wonder's head and shoulders. He had his waders on and he smelled like burnt rubber. His dark hair stood on end and there was a bright pink burn that zigged and zagged from his left shoulder to his right thigh. He looked, I thought, like a carnival astrologer down on his luck, a teller of fortunes whose own luck had gone bad. This is what Elias Wonder had to say as he sat there in the wet grass, half of a fly rod in his big hand and smoke coming off his shoulders like strands of gossamer. "Son of a bitch! I had a fish on. Son of a bitch!"

After the storm broke, the Mississippi highway became a water slide, a ris-ing branch of the once sleepy, mild-mannered Chunky River. I pulled off the road, killed the VW's engine, gave its oily fifty mechanical horses a rest, climbed into the backseat, listened to the rain pummeling the roof, tried read-ing, tried studying road maps of West Virginia, and dozed as jagged explosions of phosphorous-white lightning probed the dark, ominous sky. An hour later the rain ended and the storm moved on to the north. The dissipating clouds showed a shard of yellow moon sheathed in a capsule of hazy, dim, jaundice light.

The VW's engine caught on the first crank, grumbled, made a noise like a tin can caught in a garbage disposal.

As the years pass, the things I remember fondly become fewer and fewer. A great many trout streams and exasperating trout, of course, a handful of beautiful women I have been lucky enough to know, the endless enchantment of mountains, a fly rod or two, a small gathering of friends, and that 1968 VW van. It had the look of a mutant potato beetle that had gotten out of control. It thrived on trouble—sinkholes, bad roads, no roads at all, my meeting with misfortune. In snow, it seemed to bristle with childlike excitement, just waiting for the opportunity to try acrobatic slips and slides or the wild adventure of a full-fledged cartwheel.

I bought the van in the winter of 1969 for seven hundred dollars cash from a Virginia hog farmer who found that while it was an excellent vehicle for corralling hogs and stray cows, it fell short of being able to haul a cord of firewood, a month's groceries, his wife, and their eight children, all at the same time.

The VW van proved to be an angler's dream: a vehicle that flourished on hard work and never gave in and rarely broke down. It was a machine that kept my pace, slow and steady. Nothing escaped our attention, not a single stretch of a tempting river or the allure of a distant ridgeline. This much can be said about driving an old VW: nothing goes by too quickly and the only thing you are likely to kill is time.

The van came equipped with three long seats—vinyl-covered pews. Under the last seat I kept a wooden vegetable crate full of stones, one from each trout stream I had fished. What an odd pastime, being a gatherer of river stones, odd bits and pieces of wildness. Perhaps it is a way of validating my dreams, giving them substance.

For a young man of modest means (poor) and a mostly befuddled and mechanically incompetent angler, the VW van was a stroke of great good fortune. It leaked one quart of oil every 22,000 miles and it never let me down. Indeed, as the years went on, more and more it seemed to me that it ran not just on gasoline but on some rarefied mixture of gas, oil, and gall.

Across the Tennessee state line, the road began to take on a little altitude, snaking among low, rocky hills, bending and twisting, unable, for all the marvels of modern engineering, to bring the convoluted Tennessee hill country even the semblance of continuity. The map's tapestry of lines marked contours of steep ridges and narrow, hemmed-in valleys, folds of poverty and hardship, cold beauty, self-reliance, pride, and fanatical faith, rivers tinged with anguish and resolution.

Ahead, trapped in a lingering brown haze, Chattanooga, with the rain beginning again, a chilly drizzle that cooled the van's wheezing engine. I plotted the travel of a single drop, watched as the wind pressed it against the windshield, it tumbling like a smudge of jelly along the dirty glass, bending and curving, but in the end, always giving way and moving down toward the rhythmic swipe of the windshield wipers until the blade wiped it from the glass, flicked it aimlessly back into the wind and rain, as another drop found its path and began to slide inexorably down the grime-covered glass. The streams of raindrops on the window mingled, interlaced, one flowing into the next and into the next, so that the windshield took on the aspect of a great map of fast-running rivers. It reminded me of that night my roommate spread the map out on his bed.

"They're there," said my roommate. His name was Ralph Whitlow, an apathetic business major from Elkins, West Virginia. Whitlow had droopy brown eyes and liked chewing wads of cheap bubble gum in his sleep, marking the dreamy hours with the constant wet pop of smacking lips and the merry chomp of gum between grinding teeth. Finally, I started giving him great chunks of gum every night, gradually increasing the amount, convinced that sooner or later fortune would intervene and Ralph Whitlow would choke one night, gasp for air, go bug-eyed and turn blue, forcing me to perform the Heimlich maneuver on him and save his life. He would be in my debt, eager to give up his somniferous obsession with bubble gum. Nothing ever happened, though, except Whitlow's jaw muscles got stronger and our room took on the thick, saccharine smell of cantaloupe gone bad. I got used to it in time, and even got to where I could gauge the power of his dreams by the rhythm of his chewing and smacking.

I left him alone. Why upset his dreams, gum or no gum? Time would handle that, sooner or later. Besides, I reminded myself each night as he drifted to sleep and began popping a fresh piece of gum, Whitlow knew where there were trout. Wild trout, he said. Wild.

"They're there," he said again, spitting a clump of well-chewed bubble gum out the window. He spread the map of West Virginia out on his bed, smoothed the creases as though he were laying out fresh sheets. He kept his index finger stiff as a pointer as he moved it along a rippled blue line that marked the border between Virginia and West Virginia. Of a sudden, the names of towns known and familiar came out of him, as slow and easy as breathing. So many roads home. Hanging Rock, New Creek, Mount Storm, Smoke Hole, Cheat River. Aurora, Bartow, the Greenbrier River, the creeks and streams of the Monongahela National Forest.

"They're there," said Whitlow, his voice soft, the words dreamlike, soaked in the heady smell of bubble gum.

I stood over the map, began circling the mountain towns in blue ink, marking the route I imagined I would take as Whitlow's stubby finger traced West Virginia's mountain country, a knotty spine of hard-luck Appalachian Mountains, and he smiled and kept saying over and over, "They're here and here and here. They're everywhere. Enough trout to see a man through several lifetimes."

Waiting out the storm near Chunky, Mississippi, I unfolded the map and spread it out on the seat waiting for flashes of blue-and-white lightning to fill the sky and illuminate the map for an instant, showing me again the streams I had marked and the roads that would carry me near them. I felt like I was in a cave huddled over some sacred document with a single cathedral candle, seeking some trail to the hereafter, the everlasting, the lost Garden. There were, I had always told myself, worse places to seek than mountain trout streams.

North of Chattanooga the rain slowed, turned to a cold drizzle, and I turned off the interstate and onto Highway 441 North as a chaos of flat-bottomed clouds settled into the narrow valleys, hung there as though moored to the dull-gray mountain peaks. Twilight was wet and heavy and left a chill just under the skin. I kept the van headed north, on past Cleveland and along the fringes of the Cherokee National Forest, across the Hiwassee, its waters dark and fast, the sound like the low groan of wind caught in a deep, rocky gorge. Erosion's voice: a relentless grinding of water against stone. On to Etowah, through Englewood, and Madisonville, the twilight deepening under a portentous night sky, pale clouds scudding to the north and east. The moon hidden deep behind thick banks of cloud and fog, yet a faint diaphanous olive-yellow light rising off the ridgeline of the mountains. Soothing light among brooding clouds and the sound of rolling thunder, a light giving shape and detail to the night, dark forms slumping through the night, up high in the mountains where stone and sky joined, shared the light's common ground. High up along the ridgeline there was a moist, somber glow, a moving light outlining a world mysterious and vast.

By day, the light that hangs just above the Great Smoky Mountains seems anchored over the higher peaks; it is a soft, moody blue. On this night, a wet, stormy glow: another image to tuck away in my mind, in a memory already cluttered with every slant of light that has come off trout rivers at dawn and sunset, off the muscled bodies of trout on the rise. East and south of Knoxville, the lights of Maryville, indistinct in the cold night, like lights seen through a hundred feet of dirty water. Ahead, a rain-slick two-lane highway, the blare of horns, the endless come-on of roadside signs and their deafening silent screams for attention. Even so, the town was a welcome distraction from the numbing sameness of the dark, damp highway, and it reminded me of the fatigue clawing at my brain and muscles.

Too, I was hungry. I had had nothing since the storm stopped me along the Chunky River in Mississippi. Real food, this time. No more Spam and crackers: the angler's burger supreme. Ahead, among a curious pod of roadside billboards, a modest placard announcing MOLLY'S RESTAURANT. JUST AHEAD. GOOD EATS—SOUTHERN STYLE. DONT BLINK OR'IN YOU'LL MISS IT. On the sign a large woman in a blue dress, clogging shoes, and a bonnet decorated with tiny hogs held a huge red arrow pointing more or less due north, more or less toward the direction of Molly's. The figure on the sign tempted me ahead with a gaping smile proudly showing off what looked to be three good teeth. MISS MOLLY'S. A MILE AHEAD. DONT BLINK OR'IN YOU'LL MISS IT. I opened the van's window, let in the cold wind and rain, and didn't blink once.

MISS MOLLY'S: a poorly lit redbrick building sitting just off the highway. Red-and-white checkered curtains across the large front window; identical red-and-white checkered tablecloths on the small fake-wood tables. Around each table, cold metal chairs. On the window a bold portrait of what appeared to be a chicken or some kind of fowl being chased by the same hefty woman featured on MOLLY'S roadside billboard. This time she was swinging an ax. Despite the ax, the chicken appeared to be getting the best of her. There was an obvious smile etched on the chicken's large yellow beak. It was some chicken, orange and green, curious plumage for a chicken, even in Tennessee. The cash register sat on a high table beside the front door and there was a lady hunkered down tiredly behind the table sitting on a tall barstool. In keeping with the restaurant's ambience, the lady wore a red-and-white checkered dress and a large apron mottled with a menagerie of dark, oily stains. SHIRLEY, said her name tag. MOLLY'S was empty; I walked over to the table by the large front window, dropped heavily into the chair. On the dark wall across from the table, another sign. MOLLY'S, it seemed, had not only GOOD EATS, it had GEN-U-WINE SOUTHERN-STYLE EATS; it also had a silence about it that was as thick as iron, a silence broken only by a coffeepot's distant gurgling.

"How-die, there, young man." She had a voice like the sound of a piccolo—high and lingering over each vowel and consonant as though they were dear friends.

"I'm Edith Ann and I'll be your hostess tonight," she said sliding a menu encased in plastic onto the table.

"Our special this evening is Molly's famous bar-be-cue chicken. All you can put away for three ninety-nine. That includes the garden fresh salad bar, Molly's tangy mountain potato salad, and a pitcher of ice tea. It's some meal, honey. It'll put you on your feet."

I put my tired eyes to work reading the menu. Everything blurred after smoked ham and okra, which you could get either fried or boiled. Okra. A perplexing food, one I do not pretend to understand or fully appreciate, any more than I claim to understand the appeal of headcheese or rhubarb. I've tried okra many times and it always leaves me slightly unfulfilled and ill-at-ease, like a weekend in Indianapolis.

Smoked ham and okra? Tangy mountain potato salad?

Edith Ann stood at my shoulder, an exhausted smile drooping across her face, pad and pencil at the ready.

"The special," I said. The words had an intended weariness about them.

"Hep yourself," said Edith Ann, scribbling something on her pad, slapping the check down on the table. "I'll fetch the ice tea. Just go ahead and hep yourself, honey."

And so I did. Two drumsticks, a fat chicken breast drenched in ketchup-red barbecue sauce that had the sharp smell of mustard and honey, three slices of white bread, and a heap of potato salad laced with onion and pickle, swirls of egg and thick globs of mayonnaise.

The ice tea had a disturbing terra sienna color to it and I asked Edith Ann for a root beer instead, large.

"Root beer?" said Edith Ann. Her whistlelike voice dropped several octaves, a sign of despair. Obviously, some ritual of long-standing prominence had been broken. "Root beer—that's not part of the special, darlin'," she said. A deep frown etched across her face uncovering deep wrinkles in her ruddy complexion. I noticed she had her carotene-colored hair teased up in a high, imposing pompadour that was decorated with delicate, tiny blue bows. The whole thing seemed in imminent danger of falling apart, suddenly giving way to gravity, spilling instantly in all directions, a dangerous hailstorm of gooey red wads of hair.

She jerked the check off the table, struck through her initial figures, did some additional math, slapped it back down on the tabletop, grabbed up the pitcher of tea, and in time replaced it with a large glass of root beer, most of which was melting ice.

I had another chicken breast and a thigh, another walloping helping of potato salad. Two more root beers.

"Dessert, honey?" said Edith Ann. My extra runs through the barbecue buffet seemed to have won her respect. She had forgiven me the questionable substitution of root beer for Tennessee ice tea.

"No thanks," I said.

"Come on, now, honey," she said, "can't have a royal gourdmate meal like this here and not crown it. We got Molly's world famous, fresh homemade pies. Apple, cherry, pecan, chocolate. Just fifty-nine cents for a wedge the size of a small pie plate. No lie. Ain't no pies like 'em in the whole country, is there?" Edith Ann yelled to Shirley, who was busy leaning woodenly against the cash register and picking her teeth with the sharp end of what looked like a large sewing needle.

"You betcha," said Shirley, fighting back a deep yawn. "Jess Mueller up at Sevierville says Molly's pies keep his arteries clear. Better than that heart medicine the doctors give him. Takes these pies the way some folks take aspirin. Mondays it's the cherry, apple on Tuesdays, pecan on Wednesdays, and chocolate on Thursdays and Fridays. Hasn't changed in twenty years that I know of. Jess is pushin' eighty. Claims he owes his years to Molly's fresh homemade pies."

"No thanks," I said. My head hurt. Too many hours on the road squinting at harsh car lights and shadowy landscapes. Too much country music played too loudly. Too much icy root beer. I thought again of the map of West Virginia. I was already in the high country. From here on, just more and more altitude. Mountains, at last.

Outside of MOLLY'S the rain had stopped again. High black-lined clouds moved quickly across the night sky from the southwest pushed by a building wind. It was cold, mountain cold. In the near distance rose the dark flank of the Smoky Mountains and a waxen light rose from the high black ridges. My friend the physicist says such light is visible even on the bleakest nights. He says it is vestigial light, light left over from the creation of the universe. Hurled by the force of the Big Bang, it still drifts like stardust through space. Creation's debris. A light that is, he says, like the universe's first full breath, a great exhaling of light let out in the first quadrillionth second of creative energy and force, and motes of it still drift in the great darkness beyond the constellations.

The van's engine grumbled to life, poured lukewarm air into the cab. The seat was like winter frost on my back and legs. I pulled out of the loose gravel driveway, turned north, kept riding higher into the mountains. The heat from the engine got warm and dreamy and I opened the window wide and let the icy wind fill the cab. It felt like needles jabbing my skin, but it kept me awake. I knew this wind: a mountain wind, blowing hard and cold down from the high ridges.

I settled in behind the wheel, put on a worn Muddy Waters tape and the familiar voice came loud, low, and heavy as the heat of a late summer day on the flat, shadeless Delta. There were beads of sweat on my face, but I only smiled, tapping the blues out on the wheel with my fingers. The sweat did not worry me. After all, even the nearness of mountains can cause a rise in my temperature, a low, tempered boiling of the blood. I mopped my face with a red bandanna. The sweat came heavier. By the time I reached Providence, Tennessee, the dripping sweat was joined by deep, aching chills, a shiver that pricked the soft lining of the nerves along my spine, and a feeling of boreal-cold that made the skin of my hands and feet numb as marble. As I reached the outskirts of Pigeon Forge and Gatlinburg, my shirt was soaked in sweat. My hands trembled as my gut fell victim to what felt like abdominal epilepsy—spontaneous aching spasms of muscle being twisted into knots. Gatlinburg's sudden unorchestrated splatter of neon hype and glitz, the cheap and the tacky, seemed to me then, my first trip through the place, barely more than a benign and brightly colored fog, a harmless light show promising something for everyone—beer, pancakes, even God. The sign said SO. CHRISTUS GARDENS. AMERICA'S NO. 1 RELIGIOUS ATTRACTION. And it was right here, at the foot of the Great Smoky Mountains. It was all here: God and the mountains plus indoor skydiving, and beautiful hotel rooms, complete with private fireplaces (firewood, extra). I saw another sign advertising something called HILLBILLY GOLF. The billboard featured red-and-blue gnome-like creatures with orange beards and red freckles, and the wild white eyes of disgruntled lunatics. One of these fellows had a corncob pipe balanced precariously on his bottom lip. One was armed with what looked to be a No. 5 iron; the other was standing over an oversized putter that resembled a croquet mallet, and was looking down at a golf ball the size of a bowling ball. I laughed. Sweet delirium!, what wonders a little fever can produce. I howled like a madman until my fever increased, the sweat running down my forehead filling my eyes, and before I knew it, the van was weaving down the narrow main street of the town and I was hanging half out of the window screaming, "Hillbilly Golf! Hillbilly Golf! A hole in one on the world famous Suicide Par 3 Hamhocks hole wins a free round. Hillbilly Golf! Hillbilly Golf! For chrissakes, someone direct me to Hillbilly Golf!"

Then, as unsuspected as sudden death, I crossed some profound boundary, some slender, fragile line separating the bright lights and cheerful noises of Gatlinburg from the shadows slinking about in the deep mountain night. No gate, no walls of stone. Just a line, a geographical border. On one side, the geegaws and gimmickry, the neon wonder of Gatlinburg; and on the other, wonder of an entirely different sort—the entrance to the Great Smoky Mountains National Park.

Thinking the rain had started up again, I turned on the van's noisy wipers only to discover that the mist was the sweat in my eyes; the source of the damp fog on my glasses was my worsening fever. The wipers squeaked against dry glass and the fog on my glasses and in my eyes got worse and I drove into the Great Smoky Mountains National Park for the first time laughing hysterically, wondering what illusion, what fit of fever and dyspepsia and momentary madness, could account for what had danced past my eyes and through my mind, images as troubling as Hillbilly Golf.

Off to the right was the park's Sugarlands Visitor Center, near the west prong of the Little Pigeon River. I had entered another kind of place altogether, a place where the preservation of nature is more a matter of law than of will. I have crossed such boundaries hundreds of times before and since and always I pass over with the same feelings of dismay and reluctance, as though I am visiting a sick friend, a friend I can do little to save. Even so, the compulsion to act, to be there, is too strong to deny. I keep crossing boundaries into the country's remnant wild places that we have roped off and set aside like museum pieces, exhibits in some last great zoo, extolling not just the earth's natural history—not only what was, but, as well, what might have been. Although isolated and often misused or at least misunderstood, these places, these extant pieces of natural wonder, still bristle with wild energy. Their message seems clear and certain: that life will not be denied; that it is, in one form or another, as inevitable and unstoppable as daisies rooting under slabs of concrete.

As it gained the mountain highway, the VW van took on the aspect of a long-haul seaman trying to fathom the tricky reality of stable ground. My intermittent fever had become decidedly remittent, even eruptive, and the cramp in my gut performed grand acrobatic twists followed by deep, fulgurant pain, as though slow-burning acid were being injected just beneath my skin.

More effective than a glob of Nembutal, more accurate than a mortar round, Miss Milly's tangy mountain potato salad finally dropped me just beyond Newfound Gap across another invisible line, the one that separates Tennessee from North Carolina. The highway rises to the gap, more than 4,500 feet, then descends quickly, following alongside the Oconaluftee River, to 3,000 feet. Somewhere on the downhill side, I managed to get the van off the narrow highway. My muscles felt raw, exposed, covered with a glaze of cold night air; my head throbbed; my stomach seemed caught up in some torturous and doomed struggle with gravity; my eyes were nearly swollen shut. The van off the road, I groped about its insides and found the sleeping bag. I remember hearing the sound of water and thinking how good it would feel to splash facedown in it. Instead, I wrapped the sleeping bag about me and fell to the ground and started giggling again, thinking how appropriate it was that I should be done in at last by nothing grander than several dollops of mountain potato salad gone bad.

Moonlight shone through frayed clouds. The moon itself looked moldy-gray, the look, I thought, of a weathered tombstone. I imagined an inscription that said, "Bad Potato Salad." That and no more. Below me, down the hillside, I could hear the soothing sound of the river and I could see nothing in the dark sky save quick glimpses of moon behind moving banks of mud-black clouds. Rising all around me were the dark, monolithic forms of mountains, murky shapes, every detail obscured by the deepening night. The rain had left every surface smooth and moist. The landscape looked as if it had somehow been smudged in lampblack. The fever in my brain took me on incredible journeys, while salmonella, that nimble-toed emetic, danced a kind of digestive salsa or gallopade in my blood. I drifted into a burning half-sleep and found myself on a mountain stream working a morning rise of rainbow trout or just resting in the light blue tent on some high ridge, the last of the day's sunlight seeming to gather behind the billowing edges of a single massive cloud in the western sky, so that the sky looked like a field of smoking lava, the light a thick liquid moving irresistibly across a vast expanse of sky. And then I was wide-eyed, on my hands and knees in the wet grass away from the sleeping bag, groaning and puking, the wind cool as new porcelain against my hot cheeks. I crawled back to the sleeping bag and waited for sleep, kind anodyne, to take me again, walk me down yet some fantastic slant of light and time where dream takes on, for a time, the tint of reality, hard and firm. I eased into sleep, a tentative traveler, knowing that the legions of salmonella would be back to again send me scuttling crablike across the cold grass and into the woods.

Perhaps an hour before dawn the night sky began to clear. The wind changed direction, shifting almost due north. To the east, above the dark, rounded peaks of the mountains came a light at first no brighter than a stand of mountain fox fire glowing in the dark, but spreading, becoming a frail shadow-blue stretching beyond the moon, deeper into the sky, beyond the stars. It was a blue light that increased rather than diminished, a blue flecked with shades of absinthe and sorrel. At dawn this somber blue light went pale for an instant, then pressed closer and closer to my face, a dark central whirlpool surrounded by widening circles of cornflower blue. I realized at last that I was staring into what turned out to be a woman's soft blue eyes.

The eyes were set deep in a face marked by a delicate chin, thin, firm lips, high cheekbones, long, perfectly straight, pearl-gray hair that fell well below the woman's narrow, slightly rounded shoulders. Brighter light brought sharper focus, greater detail. I noticed the lovely watery blue eyes had a mettlesome look to them. My face still ached deep below the skin and my teeth hurt, even down along the roots. The woman's face looked directly into mine and I wondered if it too was but Molly's potato salad transformed into some other guise. Hallucination portrays the lovely as often as the horrid. Yet this was too pretty a face to be but the waste product or side effect of a whopping case of food poisoning. The face pulled back from mine, the soft gray hair falling freely from the woman's shoulders. I saw her hands and arms, the skin heavily freckled but tight against the bone. She had a pianist's long and slender fingers.

She lowered a cup of warm chicken broth to my lips. Again, I concentrated on the eyes: warm blue were the eyes of my savior and soft gray the color of my redeemer's hair.

The broth warmed my lips. I sipped, then slurped. Finally, the woman spoke. Her voice had only slightly more volume than a whisper. Her name was Exie Sopwith and she lived, she said, "down the gap on toward Smokemont, but I ain't naturally from there, exactly. Fact is, I ain't naturally from no town at all."

She tipped the cup toward my lips again. "Drink up, now. This stuff'll nail you back together again," she said.

I felt the warmth of the broth on my tongue, against the roof of my mouth, on the swollen tissue of my throat.

"My kin came from up at Proctor, on Hazel Creek. Used to be a lumbering town. I did some of my growin' up there. Then one day I got a notion to wander down the mountains. I got as far as the Tennessee line once, saw to my satisfaction that Tennessee, at least the piece I saw of it, wasn't much different from North Carolina, so I came back. Hard times is hard times. Ain't no state line I know of ever changed the truth of that."

The broth felt good in my stomach and there was a fine cool breeze through the trees. I moistened my lips, managed to talk, though the words at first felt like sharp pieces of stone in my throat.

"It's unusual . . . your name," I said, my voice sounding like a cheap penny whistle.

Exie Sopwith stood up. She was tall and slender and wearing a dress of pastel blues and bright red high-top sneakers. Her long, milk-white fingers nimbly brushed her hair off her slender neck.

"Sopwiths been in and out of these hills for some time. They're even down as far as Knoxville, I hear. Ain't a name that's all that unheard of, really."

"No, I'm sorry," I said, "I meant your first name. Exie."

Her hand was too slow to cover a grin. "Ah, that. It's said EX-IE and that's the way I spell it, too. My baby brother had trouble saying his s's. The more of them, the more trouble they gave him. Really, my given name is Essie. Brother couldn't say Essie; it always came out as Exie. It's been that way since I was six and he was three. He's dead now. Been dead for years. Drowned up at Cherokee. Found him facedown in the river. Maybe two feet of water. Drowned. Dead drunk, if I can put a play on words. Dead drunk."

As she talked, the small breeze picked up suddenly and furled her faded blue dress about her tall, thin frame like a flag. I inched my tired, cramped shoulders out of the sleeping bag, tried sitting up. She handed me the cup of broth. It warmed the palms of my hands. I asked her about Hazel Creek.

"Not all that much to tell," she said. "It's a lovely creek, but that's an old woman's opinion. I've walked up and down most all these mountains hereabouts and seen most of what there is to see and I can tell ya this . . . there ain't no prettier place than Hazel Creek. When I was a girl, I used to bathe in the creek on hot summer nights. How I loved the feel of that icy water on me. I'd brace myself up against a big smooth rock and sink down till the creek water covered me up to my neck. And I'd just lay there for hours listening to the water coming down that valley, coming down, down, washing over me. Some nights I even wished the creek water would turn up my stone and wash me away with it. Creeks gets to you. There's something about them that makes it easy to let go, let go all at once.

"Lord, but listen to me go on like a addled mockingbird and you just coming back from the dead and all."

"No," I said. "Really, I'm feeling better." Her voice was wonderful. Like the broth, it and the news of Hazel Creek, warmed me. Indeed, my forehead felt cool and I wondered when the fever that had seized my brain had broken. I looked around carefully and realized that somehow I had managed to drag myself and the sleeping bag about forty yards off the highway to a small terrace of lush grass that slanted downhill to a stand of thick hardwoods, mostly oaks and hickories. A scoured wall of blasted stone flanked the far side of the highway. Morning shadows and tiny streams of water no wider than my thumb slid down the face of the craggy rock wall, making it look like a massive black lake. Below me, down the hillside and through the trees, came the sound of a river. Arcs of flashing sunlight came off the water like sheets of summer heat lightning. Fortune had treated me kindly; the place I had picked to die from Molly's potato salad was beautiful.

Finally, I tossed the unzipped sleeping bag off me, stretched my sore back and legs. Looking hard through the trees, I could see the river. It looked neither manicured nor managed. In look and sound, at least, it had a wild edge to it. Indeed, the morning echoed no other sound save that of the river and it was a sound like a small symphony of kettledrums and cymbalists.

Exie Sopwith was hunkered down tending a small camp stove. She took a pair of small, round spectacles out of her dress pocket, put them on. She turned, offered me more hot chicken broth. The glasses magnified her blue eyes. I shook my head, asked her about the river below us. She stood, walked a few steps, her small feet leaving dark stains in the wet grass. She kept her back to me.

"It's the Oconaluftee," she said, saying the name slowly, her voice surrounding each letter the way a steady rain runs down among stones, eventually covering each one completely. The way she said the name made it sound poetic, an effect that seemed natural.

"An Indian name. Cherokee," said Exie Sopwith. She wrapped the river's name in deeper sounds, sounds of genuine reverence. "All these mountains were theirs until we took them and kicked the Cherokee out. Sent them all out to Wyoming or Utah or Oklahoma or California. Some godforsaken land. Not mountain country like this. No great forests, no cool creeks, no deep, quiet hollows. Just a lot of dust and hot wind from what I heard of it. My mother told me about some of what happened to the Cherokee. An injustice, she called it. Said most of them got out there, took one look around, and dropped dead on the spot. Fell over dead. Course, some of the Cherokee ran and hid out in these mountains. Their people live over on the Qualla Reservation. Like the folks over at Gatlinburg and Bryson City and up at Asheville, Indians at Cherokee depend mostly on flatland tourists for a living rather than the mountains. Times change, I suppose."

Then she said the name again, "Oconaluftee," and turned and walked back up the hill. "Kinda slides off the tongue, don't it? My mother thought next to Scripture, Indian talk was the most beautiful language she'd ever heard."

I tried saying it, a clumsy effort that left me stuttering and lisping uncontrollably so that what came out sounded like "O-come-And-Luf-Me."

Exie Sopwith's shoulders shook and I knew she was holding in a good laugh. She turned and walked back toward the river, sunlight mixing with her long hair, giving it a delicate dove-gray coloring. Through the trees I could see her at the river's edge climbing among huge wet boulders tucked away in shadows that covered the stones and gave them a smooth, oily-looking blackness. She moved easily over the slick rocks toward midstream. I stood up, took a few tentative steps down the hill toward the river. I could feel the blood flooding into my thighs and calves as I walked to the river and leaned against a huge chunk of lead-gray granite and watched Exie Sopwith move like a dancer among the stones farther out in the river. Despite her age, she moved with a young acrobat's confidence and ease.

I tried the name again. This time a sudden dysphonia gripped my larynx and I tripped over the second and third syllables producing an amusing corruption that came out as "Oh-kon'a'la-tree."

Standing near the middle of the river, Exie Sopwith stood straight up and laughed long and hard and loud, holding her blue dress at her knees, trying to keep it dry.

"No, no," she said, "it's 'O-con-a-luf-tee.'" She paused between each sound the way a sculptor might pause between the bite of his hammer and chisel. She said the name again slowly, and I could see all the muscles of her jaw go tight as though she were grinding out the sounds, saying each with precision, giving each one a deliberate shape and sonance.

"You got to say it fast and loose," she said, "like it was a good Bible verse, something with a little Amazing Grace to it."

I tried it again, trying not to think too much of the fearful gauntlet of irksome consonants and vowels, but just saying it all in a single mouthful of air. "I-kinda-fluff-tee."

Speech class ended when Exie Sopwith spotted the first rainbow trout holding high in the slack water behind a good-sized boulder just upstream of where she was standing. The rocks there were many and broke the river's fast current and the fish could hold easily, its blunt nose to the current, as though it were moored there. It waited patiently, taking whatever the fast current washed its way. It lunged at the current, striking fiercely at drowned insects. Trout are driven by an unmitigating hunger, a hunger as incontinent as their perplexing character.

Trout. And near at hand. Through my fingertips came a sudden spreading chill, as though I had been handling ice cubes. First confusing signs of a relapse, I thought. Siren call of a lingering knot of aerobic bacteria in my bloodstream? Some portentous warning of more pathogens on the loose inside me? No, I decided, just the slow burn of excitement, a familiar tremor just under the skin that comes when I am faced with the prospect of cold, fast-moving trout water.

Quickly, I walked back up the hill to the van parked by the roadside, gathered up my R. L. Winston rod, a reel loaded with a No. 4 weight-forward line, the small metal box that held my collection of dry flies, and two warm root beers.

Back by the river, I submerged the bottles of root beer out in the river down between two large stones, then rigged up the rod. The cold water pulled irresistibly at my feet. Exie Sopwith sat on the big rock out in the main channel and held her face up to the warming sun. Meanwhile, the cold river water soaked through my boots and socks, chilled my skin, turning it raw pink up to my knees. The water was like ice against my sore muscles, bringing them quickly to life.

Wading into the deeper water, I worked out maybe thirty feet of line and cast behind and across the rock where Exie Sopwith sat and let the No. 18 Elk Wing Caddis fall upstream of the rock and drift down with the current. The little dry fly floated easily on the leaf-green water, no more conspicuous than a tiny piece of shed tree bark, just one more piece of life's debris mingling with the stream, the moving water, something so slight that it looked, I hoped, as if it had just slipped temptingly out of the shadows.

The cast had felt good, despite the deep ache in my shoulders. As the fly drifted toward the big rock, toward the irresistible pull of current swirling about that great slab of stone, I picked up line, leader, tippet, and fly, and in one quick motion, cast again.

Exie Sopwith was standing again, watching me closely, shading her eyes with her hands. She was still laughing a high nasal laugh, more like sneezing than laughter, I thought. The late morning sunlight moved in broad strokes down the mountainsides, tracing every form, filling every space, highlighting what had been shadow, revealing a landscape of incredible diversity, a choking excess of greens. Slabs of light came off the river, fractured, leaving tiny motes of polished silver light lingering in the old woman's silky gray hair. In that light she looked young, like a child playing on a slick rock in the middle of a cold Appalachian mountain stream.

Exie Sopwith stopped laughing long enough to inform me that I would never catch a respectable North Carolina trout with "no more bait than a piddling woolly-looking bug made out of leftovers and whatnots." She told me that getting a trout out of the Oconaluftee was no easy matter. These trout were sensible fish and catching them required a genuinely tempting offering.

"My daddy caught these trout, plenty of them. My oldest brother, Frank, too, until he took to chasing good fortune and prosperity from city to city. No matter where he went, where he ended up, seemed like good times had just up and moved on and was always just one town ahead of him. Frank went through cities the way Henry Meagher up along Bent Hat Run went through pints and fifths and quarts and half-gallons of sipping whiskey. Before Frank fell under the wheels of a westbound freight train headed for Salt

Lake City, he would send us postcards from every city he'd tracked prosperity to, every city that built up his dreams then crushed them. Asheville, Knoxville, Richmond, Charlotte, Nashville, Memphis, St. Louis, Kansas City. Last one we had was from Lincoln, Nebraska. It said, 'Good times ahead in Utah. Everyone says so. I can't miss.' Poor Frank. A fool. I never been a hundred miles from these mountains and I would say I probably get more reward in a day than poor Frank got out of all them cities, traveling fifty-seven years, checking out every city he came to, looking for Easy Street."

A sudden pause, deep and wide, a moment of bewildered silence as though her words had taken her to a part of her mind that was little visited, that made her uncomfortable, that touched emotions she meant to keep in the deep, dark folds of memory.

"Frank could fish, though," she said. Her eyes fixed on mine. She had pulled Frank back over time, through the faded light, yanked him from under the freight train's gleaming steel wheels, brought him to this river, brought him home. "Fished every morning on Hazel Creek or over at Forney Creek. Never came home empty-handed. When he'd let me, sometimes I'd watch him, sit on a big rock near the creek just like now. Frank looked so natural standing in the creek, that old fishing pole of my daddy's in his big hands. Caught nice trout with worms and fat crickets and fresh pieces of corn from the garden, niblets as big as a thumbnail and shiny yellow. Never saw him ever use nothing like that funny little thing, though. It's so pitiful-looking. I can't understand why a fish as uppity as a trout would bother with such a trifle."

Exie Sopwith was already concerned about my health and I saw no need to draw doubt to my sanity as well by trying to explain the tenets of fly-fishing to her. I simply gave my shoulders a gentle, harmless, understanding shrug, cast again, putting the fly farther across the current. This time the trout hit the fly hard and leapt once, its flanks flashing in the sunlight. It was a good mountain rainbow, perhaps a foot long.

Exie Sopwith regarded me as I worked the trout as though I were some kind of carnival sorcerer employing magic she suspected was all fraud. She took to the rocks again, moving among them as effortlessly as the river. Before noon she had spotted four more nice rainbows, each time saying nothing but only pointing excitedly to the sudden rise of a feeding fish. And as the sun got higher in the sky and the sunlight came off the river in hard angles, I took two more trout.

A diaphanous blue haze hung low over the high peaks and ridges of the gap, an easy blend of form and light, and to the north the sky reminded me of the first time I saw the deep blue liquid wilderness of the Gulf Stream off the Florida Keys: blues that seemed without end, beyond description. One instant the absolute of a burning methylene blue fading into a blue far wilder and bolder, as though the stream were actually striving for some perfection of blue, some shade of it as yet unknown or unseen.

Just after noon, I bit off the Elk Wing Caddis fly, reeled in the line, set the rod in the warm grass. I gutted the three nice trout in the shallow water at the river's edge and Exie Sopwith put the fillets in a small black skillet and heated them over her camp stove. I found a small lemon in the van, along with salt and pepper, and a bottle of Tabasco sauce. All in all, ingredients for the making of a fine sauce. Exie Sopwith put it all together in a cup and poured it over the fillets. I found the forks and knives, a half-used pack of napkins, some cheese crackers, and a can of Vienna sausage. The bottles of root beer I had buried in the river hours before were cold to the touch.

Exie Sopwith watched the trout with care, making sure not to burn them, adding several more dashes of Tabasco sauce. I brought two small paper plates from the van. On hers, Exie Sopwith put all the trout fillets, the cheese crackers, and Vienna sausage. On mine, she placed a handful of saltine crackers.

"A meal like this would lay you low again for sure," she said, motioning me to pass the Tabasco sauce.

"Why the slightest hint of spices would set your innards to revolting," she said. She ate hungrily, washing down big mouthfuls of trout and Vienna sausage with the cold root beer. She stopped only once to lean over and touch the R. L. Winston fly rod.

"Who'd of thought a body could catch a trout with such a weak-looking contraption?" she said. "I wonder if Frank knew about such a thing? I bet he could have emptied Hazel Creek in a day with one of these things and a handful of those odd-looking woolly bugs."

She told me the trout were good, almost as good as Hazel Creek trout. "It's the water makes the difference," she said. Her voice fell into a curious, but knowing métier. "Hazel Creek's just a better creek, that's all. Been blessed, I suppose. God knows there were enough baptisms in it. Why the whole creek's practically one long stretch of holy water, except, of course, that pool where Eliott Ray Porter all but drowned. Circuit preacher from town came over to welcome the born again and sprinkle them. Everybody gathered down along the creek. Preacher found a place that pleased him, a handsome pool of still, shallow, cold water. Plenty of shade. By that time Eliott Ray was having a right proper religious fit, even talking in tongues, only with Eliott Ray it was hard to tell 'cause he kinda talked that way all the time. He got so carried away he went running into the creek, heading for the preacher. He hadn't taken five steps and he flat vanished as though he'd fallen through a trapdoor. Last thing he said that anybody could understand was 'I'm yours, Lord!' Words came out mostly as a gurgle. The Lord had ol' Eliott all right. My daddy laughed till he hurt. The preacher waded real calm-like to the spot where Eliott Ray had disappeared, reached his long arm down into the water, kinda felt around, and finally pulled Eliott Ray up by his hair. His eyes were squeezed shut and he was still praying. 'I'm yours, Lord. Amen,' he said, spraying water everywhere. About then, someone in the crowd shouted out, 'Put 'em back, preacher, he's too small to keep!' And everyone laughed, even the preacher who blessed Eliott Ray and then ushered him out of the creek."

The freshly cooked trout had a heady smell. My crackers were gummy and tasteless. I started layering them with Vienna sausage and Tabasco sauce. Better. The wind came up, cool and changing again, blowing more out of the west.

By late afternoon the rising moon was already visible in the clearing sky. It looked as fragile as a communion wafer.

Exie Sopwith took up the plates and skillet, walked to the river's edge, washed and dried the skillet, then began to pack her things in a small brown sack. She asked how I was feeling, wondered if maybe I ought to go into town, see a doctor. I thanked her for everything, said no, I really didn't want to go into town, remembering it was the town where I had gobbled down Miss Molly's potato salad. No towns. Not for a while, anyway. My luck always seems to go sour in towns and cities. These mountains and the river were medicine of a kind, I speculated. While they couldn't save me, perhaps they could soothe me, heal me for a time.

Exie Sopwith nodded. "When I was thirteen," she said, "my mother carried me to Bryson City to see a medical man. I'd coughed nearly the whole winter through. The doctor listened to my chest and gave me some kind of clabbered syrup to take. Smelled like kerosene. Tasted worse. Cost my mother fifty cents. I threw it in the bushes the first chance I got."

A bashful smile eased across her face. She said, "I cured the cough by eating little bits of spiderwebbing rolled into tiny balls. Looked like little white pills. My aunt Lucy gave the stuff to me. She said everybody knew spiderwebbing was the best thing for a stubborn cough. Everyone, that is, excepting my mother, who was an open-minded woman and wanted modern medicine to succeed. Aunt Lucy loved my mother but said she'd been to town one too many times."

Her small sack all packed and tied tight, Exie Sopwith asked again if I would be all right. I nodded. She asked where I was headed. West Virginia, I told her. A genuinely quizzical look took hold of her face.

"West Virginia!? Ain't much of nothing up there," she said. She told me of an uncle who had left the mountains to look for work in the West Virginia coal mines.

"His name was Jarvis. Saw an ad in the Bryson City paper. 'Prosper With West Virginia. There's a future in our black gold.' Some such nonsense. Anyway, Jarvis just kept on repeating and repeating it like it was some sacred prayer. So he went. Stayed until his lungs went black and every breath was harder than death and soon he just quit breathing altogether. That was 1959, I think. He's buried up there somewhere. Mining company wouldn't pay for the funeral, not even a cheap coffin. Got word from some funeral parlor that they'd put him down in a pauper's grave. They wanted fifteen dollars for digging the hole, shoving Jarvis in, then covering him up."

"I hear there's trout up there," I said.

"There's trout twenty-five feet from where you're sitting, and better trout still in the mountains at your back. And if you get up on Hazel Creek and go up the valley some nights, there's voices on the wind. I've heard them. Plenty of times."

Again, Hazel Creek. Not only trout, but now voices on the wind.

The late afternoon sunlight was warm on my skin. I lay out on the unfolded sleeping bag and soon fell asleep. When I woke up again the sun was behind the mountains and the sky flared with deep purples and soft blacks, and Exie Sopwith—healer, nurse, storyteller, angler, companion—was gone.

It has been more than a decade since Molly's potato salad hurled me from the VW van at Newfound Gap, since I opened my eyes and saw Exie Sopwith mopping my hot face with a cloth soaked in the cold waters of the Oconaluftee River.

I never made it to West Virginia, not for a long time, anyway. That night after Exie Sopwith left and before the last of the daylight had gone from the sky, I spread out a map of North Carolina on the sleeping bag, and in that fading light found Newfound Gap. I began tracing the high ridges of the Smoky Mountains: a rugged spine of eroded, ancient rock, time's debris lingering high among the clouds.

Bagpipes on Hazel Creek

EXIE SOPWITH WAS RIGHT about Hazel Creek—about its trout, its beauty, even about the voices. About everything. I traveled to the creek more than twenty times before I came across another angler camped along its cool, fast water. That doesn't include the shadowy, mysterious person who moved up and down the creek's narrow valley during every season, playing the bagpipes.

When I heard the bagpipes for the first time, I thought nothing of it, dismissed the music as some enchanting combination of wind and rushing water that produced a soothing litany of liquid notes up along the higher reaches of the creek where the valley narrowed and the creek moved through membrane-thin shadows.

I heard the bagpipes again the next morning. A truly Great Awakening, more startling and invigorating than frightening, as though the notes were attempting a musical interpretation of a chicken coop caught up in turmoil and rebellion.

I sat at the open flap of the blue tent and listened. This much was certain: whoever the hidden troubadour was he believed strongly in vigorous and uplifting streamside music, something that mingled with the creek's tricky rhythms. At first I thought the sound came from above my campsite, up on the worn, rounded ridge along the trail that led up from Fontana Lake. A half hour later, though, like a fickle wind, the music had shifted and now seemed to seep out from a huge gallery of lichen-mottled stones the size of bank vaults just where the creek bent in a gradual arch to the left and fell into the silky light of early morning.

Whoever filled the dawn with music kept it up until well after first light, fitting the morning with a cycle of haunting music, a humble painting of notes and harmonics: images of tone. Like the creek, both the musician and his music were ever changing, mixed cadences of tremor and the unlikely hurdy-gurdy sound of bagpipe jazz.

Exie Sopwith had promised voices, but nothing so grand as some lunatic mountain balladeer who greeted each day along the creek, each renewal of light glowing off the water, with a celebration of rough-edged music.

I ate cold cereal and made hot tea over the camp stove and the elusive bagpipe virtuoso played on. The smooth gray morning light broke up, dissolved like thin clouds rising in warm air, and the music took on a stronger beat, sounding suddenly like a chorus of pipe organs playing madly, wildly, all stops open wide. I washed out my bowl, stowed my few belongings inside the tent, and did not bother to tie the tent flaps closed, and went about easing into my pair of old waders. The thick rubber still held the night's deep chill. And the music came now from the far side of the creek, from among wild dogwoods and stands of oaks and maples. The change in location brought a change in sound—softer, the low, reedy, melancholy sounds of wind high among the trees, notes as solemn as prayer. I thought how easy, how nice it would be just to crawl back into the tent, roll back into the wrinkled comfort of the sleeping bag, and slip into dreams as I listened to the sound of the music drifting down the narrow valley toward the lake, toward open skies.

The chilly night air left the 4-weight line stiff. It felt as tense as cramped muscle as I threaded it through the little R. L. Winston rod's ferrules and worked out about thirty-five feet of it, massaging each inch of it thoroughly, stripping it hard and fast through my fingertips as though trying to rub off the night's cold. I worked it until I felt it pinch, bend gracefully, take on the physical characteristics of good tooth twine: supple yet strong, unobtrusive yet enduring.

The day I set up camp I purposely ignored a wide pool of alluring water just downstream from the small rise above the creek bank where I put up the blue tent. It was good water, a good place to play a hunch, cast line and hope for the unexpected—wide and smooth and deep water, the kind of creek water where a streak of good fortune might fill an angler's creel with as much solitude as brilliantly colored, hard-muscled, belligerent mountain trout. It was a stretch of water worth saving, for tomorrow or the next day, or a morning such as this.

I sat on the big stone by the tent. The rod was ready, as was the angler, and the creek ran fast and cold. Daylight widened along the creek, giving a flat shine to the stones and the damp ground littered with a chaos of fallen leaves heaped by the wind into low swales, against outcrops of stone, in weathered coverts, ravines, and cuts, scattered like winnowed duff about the deep shadows of the forest floor. With each breath of wind the landscape shuddered, became almost liquid, a geography of colors rather than of fixed landmarks and boundaries, colors endlessly mingling one with the other. On the far west ridge, damask reds and vermilion giving way to softer Chinese reds and the blunt reds of aged wine, and these, in turn, mixed with leaves of moody sallow and the dull yellow of sulfur and raw cream, and among these were newly fallen leaves still bright as jonquils. Lower down the slope, down among the sturdy oaks, amid the random sprawl of reds and yellows, were scattered leaves of pumpkin-orange, trees looking like daring blotches of apricot, and now and then the wrinkled browns of the oaks with leaves the color of tarnished copper and well-worn leather. All along the upper ridges, the thick deciduous forest glowed in the hazy autumn light. Under a press of wind, the trees and their fashion of dead, brightly colored leaves bent and swayed like great coils of undulating ribbon, bolts of warm, rich color.

Sitting on a large, flat, comfortable stone, I took a No. 18 Royal Wulff from my small metal fly box, examined it carefully, decided it looked too well kept, too tidy, too much the imposter to entice a fish as suspicious as trout, especially at this time of the morning. Instead of putting the fly through the expected routine of preening, making it presentable, I intentionally mussed it up, giving it a rumpled, tacky, almost ruinous look, like an insect truly fallen on hard times and in deep trouble, a morsel ready for the taking, a temptation tied invitingly about a fine, well-sharpened hook and knotted securely to nine feet of 6X leader and tippet. A tippet's thickness is measured down to the thousandth of an inch. The end of a 6X is like spun gossamer, yet it is strong enough to stay with and haul in two to three pounds of wild-eyed, twisting, flailing, unrelenting trout. I remember confessing then, in a delicate whisper, as I have often confessed in such private moments, "Okay, okay. So technology can sometimes be a wonderful thing."

Rod in hand I walked up the creek. Brittle leaves crumbled underfoot. At the instant of my first cast above and across the deep pool's smooth dark surface, the bagpipes fell silent and a kingfisher across the creek squawked harshly.

Two days before, I had taken a small boat from the boat dock at Fontana Village (now the Peppertree Fontana Resort) and crossed Fontana Lake to the mouth of Hazel Creek. The only other convenient way of reaching Hazel Creek is the hike down from the summit of Clingman's Dome.

It was October and the brown trout were on the move and I was anxious. Brown trout have an unsettling effect on me. Despite the calendar, the weather was mild and had been for a week. I had fished the creek before in such pleasant weather and taken some nice trout both near the mouth of the creek and high up near Bone Valley. On a Friday the weather began to turn: the temperature dropped and the wind blew cold out of the northeast, and I knew the browns would be moving. By Friday evening I had rented a small boat and loaded it with tent, sleeping bag, fly rods and reels, and enough food for two days along the creek.

The boat's motor cranked on the first pull. Moving away from the floating dock, I drew my collar up high over my ears. The cold left my fingertips numb, feeling heavy and useless, as though they had been injected with Novacain. As I nursed the motor's throttle easily, the boat eased through shredded wisps of wet fog. The mountains rose up and in the sunset's faded light, fall's colors burned like thick tongues of flame across the high wooded peaks. I remembered how dead leaves had scuttled about the wooden dock giving off a low, raspy sound. Death's tune, one of them, at least, and the sound, sure and true, of winter's approach, of life burrowing in, settling down, conserving itself in seed and warm ground, in hidden warrens and in cloisters of stone, wherever it might hold out, hold on, wait. In the mountains come autumn and winter there is an overwhelming sense of waiting, waiting out the cold, even though the life that waits cannot know that the cold will end, that the sunlight will again warm the land. Instead of assurance, in place of certainty, there is only the silence of the cold, the long, emotionless waiting.

Along the creek, dropping temperatures put a shiver into already cold water and brought the moody, rapacious brown trout out of their dark watery holes and into flat shadows that spread across the creek like opaque planking. Autumn's sober light, the livid light of morgues and funeral homes, a light that is abstract and tender, just the right light to shield the fickle, often mysterious movements of the brown trout. The brown trout is a brutish fish, the great piscine carnivore of cold mountain trout streams. As a predator it is deadly yet fair, eating everything with equal resolution and enthusiasm.

Despite the wind, the surface of Fontana Lake the day I crossed over to the creek was flat and smooth and looked of old, unpolished glass. I put my left hand in my coat pocket, maneuvered the small motor with my right, and with my head tucked in turtle fashion, I leaned my shoulders forward into the wind. The bow rose up and moved ahead, bouncing only slightly, and I remember settling down onto the cold plastic cushion and thinking how time in the mountains seems thicker, heavier, slower, insulated. The cold holds its own fascinations, its own delights. For one thing, it tends to thin out the traffic that can sometimes clog the narrow winding roads that snake through these mountains. It sends the tourist packing, heading for home, comfort, and warmth. Meanwhile, the brown trout stir and I stir with them, eager to move in that same pale gray light and watch for them in the creek's cold, deep pools, wade in the icy water and feel winter hard against my skin, and, if my luck holds, feel a good trout's great weight on my line, bending the little Winston rod even before I have fully set the hook.

So I put on extra clothes, filling the old rubber waders with layered warmth, and tried not to think too much of the cold hours because there is that chance, no matter how remote, of being among or near trout, a fish whose company has never failed to thrill and astonish me. Trout never cease to surprise, to fill the blood with great soaking doses of adrenaline. For a moment, as they rise, they see, all at once, fish, image, illusion, symbol, wildness suddenly fleshed in substance: color, character, the power of sleek, raw muscle and undiluted energy.

The trip across Fontana Lake to Hazel Creek is several miles. Each time I pull into the slender cove where the creek empties into the lake, I shut the boat's motor off, drift slowly into the shallow water listening to the sound of the creek hissing and percolating over jumbled piles of stones. Rocks completely submerged in the swift water look almost alive, like something desperately attempting to shed a thoroughly worn-out skin, something sloughing off an ancient burden, grasping for release. Above the sound of the water is the sound of the wind rattling in the trees and the trill of birdsong. Over my shoulder, out over the spreading lake and rising mountains, only a deep and abiding silence, the kind in which a child imagines hearing the sea's roar in the hollow, dry chambers of a spent seashell or the kind in which an angler imagines seeing the shimmering shadow of a trout moving in clear, cold water, rising to strike violently, relentlessly, at insects hatching off the surface of the creek.

I pulled the boat up past the big rocks, up past the mud, up onto dry, hard ground, tied it firmly to a chunk of granite the size of a VW, grabbed the backpack and fly rods, walked up to the trail that shadows the creek, follows its rock-strewn twists and turns. The relationship between trail and creek is conventional, traditional, one of cordial, even-tempered tolerance rather than intimacy or some essential symbiosis. I walk the trail as I do most mountain trails, in some mild, harmless trance, pleasant and lucid, brought on by the rattling sound of the creek just down the ridge, just beyond the trees and tangles of creeper and greenbrier, honeysuckle and deer laurel.

High up beyond the ridgeline, the day's light was fading. Only a gauzy pale light lingered among the branches of the trees, high up on the humped and swollen summits whose silhouettes are pressed hard against the horizon. Once, from high up in the Blue Ridge Mountains looking south and east, I saw just the charcoal shadows of the Smokies, a ridgeline that looked at that distance like a diseased backbone, a long, ragged scar of violent breaks and fractures worn smooth by time.

The trail following Hazel Creek up the mountain from the lake is good, hard-packed, easy to follow. I know it well, so well that I walk it measuring not its mood but mine. The trail is not bothered with destinations; it goes on and so do I. I walk until there is reason to stop, and in these mountains almost every footfall kicks up a dozen reasons sane and sound enough for stopping. No imperative manipulates these harmless trout journeys of mine except the desire to be where trout are. Too, there is something in me, something deep and inescapable that needs the rush of mountain streams, the nearness of trout, the possibilities of both, the honest feel of root and stone and mountain wind.

Trout are excellent company, creatures of noble and admirable and perplexing qualities, much like human beings only more honest and sincere. They are totally unpredictable and therefore totally bewitching, at once brutal, beautiful, suspicious, graceful, and powerful, fastidious and wary, cautious and aggressive. Raw instinct burns like electric current through their cold, wild flesh. There is a charming snobbery about mountain trout, a stubbornness that is absolutely unbending. Their needs are specific rather than arbitrary and capricious. They know nothing of compromise. Life means moving water, fast water, clean water, water rich in prey and with at least a measure of wildness, meaning a solitude free of the whirl of cities and civilization. These are not luxuries or whims. To the trout they are necessities, the basic elements of life—a life worth living, struggling after. It's wildness or nothing.

Some things are worse than death, at least to a trout. Clear-cut the forest up the valley from their stream and they die. No compromise. Pump toxins into a stream's watershed miles away and the trout go belly-up. No compromise. Dilute the balance of their streams with acid rain and they bloat and float to the surface. No compromise. Among mountain trout, wildness is more than a notion, a principle, or an attribute; it's a matter of blood and bone, the instinct of cold, hard, inexorable refusal to accept less of life than what they need.

Night on the creek came easily and smoothly, like a dark silk shirt slipping down slowly over the hands, arms, head, shoulders until there was a complete and comfortable soft darkness covering everything. In the hour since anchoring the boat, I hadn't walked half a mile up the trail. I stopped, put up the blue tent quickly near the Proctor campsite, one of the handful of designated primitive campsites along Hazel Creek, tied my backcountry permit to the tent flap. Permits are required for backcountry camping in the park. Park rangers issue the permits to keep track of who is wandering about the mountains, off the main roads, off the well-used trails. There is no fee, yet. It's all done by way of the honor system. The rangers let you go and you promise to use only designated trails and campsites and generally leave the backcountry as you found it. Just in case you don't make it, in case you end up facedown in some deep pool along a creek, in case you lose your footing along a ridge, in case some irascible trout gives you heart failure, the permits also come in handy as body tags, with two thin strips of wire easily twisted about a naked big toe or through the black zipper of a body bag.

As the light retreated it seemed to leave a slight warmth against the skin. Just enough daylight to rig up the little rod, attempt a cast or two. Fall trout fishing on Hazel Creek calls for daring among fish and angler alike. The cold urges the experimental, the unexpected, the improbable, even the provocative. No need to match flies with nonexistent insect hatches. For the trout, the cold means a lean diet. Anything goes. The idea is to tie on a fly that is both alluring and believable, something that might strike incorrigible trout as honest, something that will stir their blood, pinch their deep winter hunger. My autumn collection of flies is modest, but bold: some dry flies, sizes 12 to 20 and a handful of nymphs and wet flies, all tucked safely away in empty film canisters. I tied on a slightly frazzled McGinty, forgot the waders, walked up the trail to just below the Proctor Bridge, then walked into the river, wide and cold, a glacial cold, deep and numbing. Below the bridge, on the far side of the creek where the bank curves sharply, small oaks bent grace-fully out over a large pool of quiet water. My line, leader, tippet, and the old McGinty fly unfolded inches above the pool's surface. It was so flat and calm that the water had the dull, thick shine of quicksilver.

For two years, through every season, there was a fine trout that lived in this big pool. An old fish, I imagined, fat with experience. Not wise, just knowing. Just the sudden ripple of its great charcoal shadow across the pool would raise atavistic hairs on the back of my neck and put a shiver on my skin. That undulating shadow got to me, obsessed me, possessed me. All I wanted was to somehow get to that trout, tempt it, get it to not just take my fly, but swallow it, hook and all, so that I might haul its massive shadow into the light, feel its great weight on my line, watch it jump in pure desperation twisting violently in midair, the wide stripe along its flanks as pink as flesh laid bare by a sudden wound. If even for an instant, I wanted to see the glint of daylight in its limpid black eyes. I wanted that trout, not to keep, not to hang on the wall, not even to eat, but only for the assurance of its reality. I dreamed of it, lit candles for it, courted fortune for it, even took a chance on Ambrose Noel's prayer wheel for it.

Ambrose Noel wore simple brown shorts and a red flannel shirt, worn leather hiking boots, and a permanent smile. He had the features of a small-town po-lice blotter description—cheerfully nondescript. He was a man of average height, average weight, average looks, abiding concerns and convictions, and a Thomistic belief in a divine logic lurking just under life's chaotic skin.

I heard him before I saw him. He was up near the headwaters of Hazel Creek where he had stopped for lunch and was singing a single line of lyrics from an old Doors' song. "When you're strange, faces come out of the rain, when you're strange." The words never varied, although his style and deliv-ery did as he crooned, yodeled, screamed, even hummed the lyric as ballad, anthem, lullaby, psalm, requiem, and rhythm and blues.

I walked down along the creek to where Ambrose Noel kneeled patiently over a pot of shimmering butter beans, pinto beans, field peas, kidney beans, shallots, and squash, all of it covered with a hash of bean sprouts.

Introductions were made.

"Sit," said Ambrose Noel. "Let's break bread together."

I cringed at the notion of some kind of hideous bean bread, but it turned out to be harmless whole wheat.

We talked and ate beans and bread and divided a ripe tomato that sat temptingly on a bright blue bandanna. Ambrose Noel told me he was on a mission to bring hope to these hard-luck mountains.

"God came to me at 1:03 P.M. in the parking lot of the McDonald's in Pigeon Forge and told me to pack up and get into the mountains," said Ambrose Noel severely, with absolute sincerity. "God is invisible, in case you're wondering. He's just a voice. But, man, what a voice!"

I helped myself to seconds on the beans.

"No trumpets," said Ambrose Noel, "not even electric violins. Just a voice, as unemotional and flat as an insurance salesman or the midsummer drone of an irritating insect. I kept hoping it would just go away. It didn't. In fact, it kept coming back, always to the parking lot at McDonald's. Some recruiting station, huh? God has one lousy memory, man. He had to keep coming back because He couldn't recall what He'd told me. Hell, He wasn't even sure I was the guy He had let hear His voice. We met in the McDonald's parking lot four times, then He stopped coming. Believe me, man, I stumbled onto this gig.

"Glad I did, though, ya know. Great job, having a mission and all, and these mountains are way beyond mellow."

"Why the wheel?" I asked as I imagined God and Ambrose Noel exchanging small talk outside McDonald's over hamburgers and Diet Cokes.

"To make things fair and to make sure that everyone has a chance," said Ambrose Noel. "The Man told me to peddle hope, not assurances or guarantees. The wheel gives everybody a spin, a chance at hope. This is what God said to me: 'I have given hope some thought and have nothing against it, though My principal means of employment is Life and Death. Life is the root, Death the leaf.' That's what He said to me. You go and figure it. Mostly, the whole thing's a gamble. Everybody likes to gamble, man, take a chance, risk something for something more. Hope is the something more."

It was well after noon and the May sun was warm against my face. I leaned back against the cool, smooth surface of a huge outcrop of granite.

"How about the odds?" I asked. "What are the odds these days for hope?"

"Lousy," said Ambrose Noel, the smile on his cherub face growing wider, a perfect slim upturning curve of lip and cheek. "But the wheel's bound to hit it sometime, bring some lucky soul more hope than he's bargained for. Meanwhile, brother, everybody can spin, turn the wheel."

Like Johnny Appleseed sowing seeds, Ambrose Noel walked about the

Smoky Mountains offering hope, a chance to spin the wheel. Just a spin of the prayer wheel and your luck might change. In these mountains stranger things happen all the time.

I sat up, brushed off my hands, put my lucky worn-out bush hat back on.

"Okay, Noel, set the thing up, I'll spin."

"Dollar first." He said the two words crisply, evenly, as he took up the prayer wheel, set it firmly on his crossed knees.

"What dollar?" I asked, suddenly realizing the source of Ambrose Noel's permanent smile. "What was all the talk about everybody getting a free spin?"

"Truth," said Ambrose Noel. His eyes were closed now as he rattled the thick wooden wheels stacked on the wide wooden cylinder that made up the prayer wheel. Each of the wheels on the long center peg were heavily engraved with strange symbols, characters, it seemed, of some alien alphabet, rubbed smooth by legions of chance takers, crowds of the hopeful and hopeless.

"Everyone spins for free as long as they're willing to make a dollar contribution to my Mission of Hope. Just a dollar to keep one of God's pilgrims alive and in the pink."

Using his left hand, Ambrose Noel spun the wheels which turned noisily, making an unsettling heavy clacking sound. Above the noise of the rotating wheels was Ambrose Noel's voice, suddenly like that of a heroic tenor giving a pained and somber importance to the Doors' lyric, "When you're strange, faces come out of the rain . . ."

Just one chorus.

"Hope's worth something, isn't it?" he said. His speaking voice, like his features, was featureless—smooth, lackluster terrain. "And the dollar goes toward the work of the mission, toward keeping hope alive. And the spin's for free, as long as you believe enough to contribute to the mission."

While he talked, I kept looking down at the tin bowl of beans and sprouts, what was left of the single tomato. A dollar for the mission: a fresh sack of beans and a prayer wheel of hope.

I put my dollar down by his knee, spun all of the wheels at once, prayed for enough hope and fortune to hook the big rainbow trout in Proctor Pool, bring that hulking shadow up through the deep olive-green water and see how the mountain sunlight and its deep-water wildness mixed, how the light might come off its body like electricity and ripple in blue waves across the smooth surface of the pool.

But the prayer wheel fell short. While my luck stayed sour, I went on hoping that I would somehow connect with that trout. It was some fish. Often I dreamed of the worlds of sensation, of reality and image, through which its muscled weight might pull me, set me to wandering.

I saw the shadow of the big trout that moved warily about the edges of Proctor Pool off and on for almost two years, then it vanished. Even in that deep green water the trout's shadow had a dark blue cast, as all shadows do on cloudless mountain days. Shadows gather the sky's reflected light, an array of blues, rather than the sun's stark golds, hard yellows. Light—every man's magic show—the extraordinary swaddled in the common. It warms life, feeds life, sustains life, fuels life, seems a sea of inestimable size, a sea choking with particles and waves that considered separately are of almost no consequence or importance. The magic is not in the pretty cold colors, but in the warmth. Wherever light is denied, even partially, there are shadows and every shadow is a mystery, whole and true, because it portends the unrevealed, not only undiluted beauty but, as well, unspeakable brutality.

Other shadows, other fish, other mysteries, have moved in and out of the pool's rich water and soft light. But the old trout is gone. Dead, surely, rather than caught, because that is the way I want to think of it, a natural end: water to fish, fish to water. Death and life are the energy of the same process, one preoccupied neither with beginnings or endings. The first breath of life is also the first step toward death. Time flies on death's wings.

The big trout's shadow is gone, but its energy is here yet, moving in the creek, in this rush of fast mountain water mingling with the day's moody light.

Like the big trout in Proctor Pool, Ambrose Noel disappeared. For a long time I would stop along mountain trails, rest along stream banks, listen deep in the mountain nights for the telltale wooden clacking of his Himalayan prayer wheel and his voice rising above its spinning wheels singing the Doors' lyric as though it were part doxology, part canticle. But he never comes, Ambrose Noel, peddler of hope. Nevertheless, I always carry a wrinkled dollar bill, a humble contribution to keep his mission alive, just in case. The spin for hope, of course, should I ever get another chance, is free.

It seemed that I had only just allowed myself to think of the trout's big shadow and Ambrose Noel and the day's light went dull, lost tone and texture as night rose with the moon and eased over the mountains and onto every leaf and stone. I stood at the edge of Proctor Pool for a long time watching the widening night and the first smudges of starlight on the surface of the creek, light thin and cold. I reeled in my line, walked back to the tent, and the darkness was like an artery in which I felt, at once, safe and secure and yet, too, poised on the cusp of unimaginable wonder and adventure.

Dinner: cheese and crackers, hot chili, and lots of water. Dinner music compliments of Hazel Creek, barred owls up on the far ridge, and what sounded like a coyote to the east. In all, a heady blend of mountain chamber music, the coyote's melancholy yowl balanced by the endless syncopation of rushing creek water. I closed my eyes and featured an ensemble of oboes and jazz piano.

Clouds drifted over the mountains from the west, hid the moon, diffused the night's deep blue light, and I crawled into the tent and lay still on the sleeping bag listening to the night stirring. Predictably, since I am a member of the Information Age, a fact broke loose from my brain, swung loose as a hammock in my mind. It was this: the average person sleeps 220,000 hours during his lifetime. Time flies, it seems, not only on death's wings, but on sleep's as well. I decided to stay up and enjoy the mountain night, put a wrinkle in at least one average man's lifetime statistics. I spread the sleeping bag on the cold ground outside the tent, crawled in, watched the night sky until it seemed to press on my chest, overwhelming every thought, every feeling, until my only connection to the earth was the sound of the night's cold wind high among the trees and the hiss of the creek's waters over wide beds of smooth stones.

Over the last decade, I have discovered, to my pleasure, that the Smoky Mountains delight in paradox.

Irony and the waters of Hazel Creek surely mingle, at least in my experience. When it comes to reputation and popularity, Hazel Creek is one of the most famous Smoky Mountain streams. Although the Smokies are marked by hundreds of miles of prime trout streams, few are as loudly heralded, frequently praised, or widely loved as Hazel Creek.

But here's the good part. There is rarely anyone along the creek, much less actually fishing in it. Some years ago, as I walked down the creek from Clingman's Dome, I came across two other fly fishermen and immediately grew sullen, morose, disillusioned. Here were two other anglers on a creek I had more or less fished alone for years. In trout fishing, and especially in mountain trout fishing, one angler and trout borders on the idyllic, or some version thereof. Two anglers and trout is a crowd, claustrophobic and unbearable.

I hiked on down the mountain, well beyond the second angler, who tipped his hat and sent me on with a cold stare. And when I had walked a mile and had not seen another human being, I shed my pack, took up the Winston rod, and waded out into the creek's cold, fast water. The sun was high in a clear sky and its warmth felt good against my face and eased my building sense of doom, the lurking, dreadful thought that tomorrow there might be four anglers on the creek or five. Not just a mere crowd, but a chaotic, jarring horde.

I fished until well in the afternoon, then shed my waders, put up my rod, and stretched out in the cool shade of the tall trees along the bank, eating a firm apple, mostly not concentrating on a book I had brought along, and just thinking about the creek. The afternoon hours are as good as any for taking stock, massaging memory and experience.

From where the creek empties into Fontana Lake, the main Hazel Creek Trail climbs toward Siler's Bald and Clingman's Dome, a rise in altitude of 3,500 feet. It's a pleasant walk, especially with frequent stops for fishing, enjoying the creek's great beauty and tranquillity. The creek can also be reached by hiking down the valley from Clingman's Dome, which is an easier proposition: mostly downhill. The cold mountain springs that make up the creek's headwaters are up on Siler's Bald. From there, Hazel Creek meanders generally southwest down the mountains toward the lake. The creek's beauty and intrigue are deepened and increased by its many branches, especially up around Sugar Fork and Bone Valley Creek where a side trail goes to Pickens Gap, crosses the Appalachian Trail, and continues on to Eagle Creek, another fine trout stream.

Bone Valley is memorably quiet. The valley supposedly got its name after a late and especially cruel winter storm hit the mountains killing cattle already put to pasture in the high country. The spring thaw exposed their bones. Death of any kind has a way of marking a place, giving it a name soaked in memory and meaning. Bone Valley. Too, last year, not far down the valley, an angler took a brown trout that weighed in at more than six pounds, not the biggest brown ever taken from the creek, but quite a fish to be found so high up the valley.

It was here along the creek, up around Bone Valley, that whoever had been playing the bagpipes along the creek for so many seasons stopped for good. Maybe it was the crowd, the two other anglers, the sudden appearance of so many people at once, the startling, but undeniable press of civilization. Whatever it was, like the big trout down in Proctor Pool, the bagpipe player along Hazel Creek simply vanished. The music stopped.

I heard it for the last time not far from where Cold Spring Branch enters the creek. It was early morning, the pale blue light easing down through the valley like a low-hanging fog. There was tea warming on the camp stove and fresh apples and dry cereal for breakfast.

I had started hiking down the creek some days before and was in no hurry. The day before I had taken two fine rainbow trout. Both fish hung high in the water at the edge of a wide, fast section of shoals. The trout fought hard, betting all of their power and energy against the hook and line, and I set them loose in the calm water below the shoal where they regained their strength and moved off quickly into deeper, darker water. How slowly that absorbing hour on the creek passed, like a glacier over hard ground. I wore that hour of thin sunlight and widening shadows, of water and the two good fish, as though it were my skin.

I had that same sensation sitting up on the old railroad grade in drifting clouds of fog, waiting for the tea to warm. Rivers flowed all about me, through me: rivers of water and air tinged with the smell of wild onions, rivers of sky and changing light, moving water, rushing time. The creek raced by giving up so much more than fish—a morning of revelations and sounds, and, finally, a river of music. The bagpipes pouring out mountain folk songs, bluegrass bagpipe tunes coming from down the creek, down where the Sugar Fork Trail splits off, goes up Sugar Fork. Like Bone Valley, Sugar Fork and the Little Fork of Sugar Fork have their own fascinations, most of them bound up as much in one man as in the delicate beauty of the small creek and the mountain country it moves through.

The man was Horace Kephart.

Among those whose lives have been entangled completely with these mountains, Kephart remains an intriguing and haunting figure, as much legend and myth as fact, mere crumbled bone. Although a great many writers have tried to figure him out, Kephart, so far, has mostly eluded every writer who has tried to interpret not only his dreams, but what fueled them.

The music along the creek lasted until the warm May sun rose above the mountains, until the fog had lifted, dissolved, except from the low places along the creek where it hung like lacy clouds of bone-colored mist fringed in yellow sunlight.

While the music went on, changed from country swing to down-and-out blues, I walked down the creek and the cool morning wind pressed gently against my face. And I thought I saw him, finally, the bagpipe player, well back in the shadows of the trees, tall, thin, leaning against a big sycamore tree. He was wearing a red baseball cap.

I sat by the creek, watched, listened, and stayed quiet, as though I were watching some wild animal as yet unaware of my presence. I studied the man's every move, his manner. Like the big trout in Proctor Pool, here was yet another beguiling mixture of water and light, mountain and shadows, something obviously real and yet compellingly incomplete. He stopped playing and the disembodied notes of the last song hung on the air for a long instant, drifted on the wind. The man in the green shadows of the sycamore tree took up his instrument again, began playing an old gospel hymn, a tune that was familiar to me, a melody out of the shipwreck of memory, and yet its name escaped me. The bagpipe player turned and walked back toward the thick woods along the creek, never missing a note, and I kept on listening until the only music was that of the creek, the slap of water against flat stones. All that day I fished the creek and mindlessly hummed that half-forgotten gospel hymn whose name I still can't remember, though I flip through church hymnals when I can hoping to find it. It is important. It was the last song the bagpipe player along Hazel Creek ever played. It is fitting, perhaps, that the bagpipe music stopped in May, the mountains newly green and wrinkling with the wild energy of renewal, both the anticipated and unexpected.

There is a mountain story I first heard in Robbinsville that goes like this—when Horace Kephart showed up in these mountains he had reached the interesting and vexing point of intoxication where the body goes happily numb while the mind hungers for immediate adventure, anything that smacks of lawlessness and daring. Since he was well past the point of navigating with his legs, so the story goes, someone managed to slump Kephart over a mule. A sudden surge of energy supposedly rippled through Kephart and he raised his head, took off his rumpled hat, bent close to the mule's ears, and said loudly, "Take me to paradise, you ass, and quickly." Eventually, the good-natured mule deposited Kephart near Dillsboro. From here he would later move up Hazel Creek. The remains of his old cabin are still there, off the Sugar Fork Trail along the Little Fork of the Sugar Fork up toward Pickens Gap.

True or embroidered, the man who ended up on Hazel Creek had been all but unhinged by city life. He came to the mountains both to be healed and fulfilled, to celebrate in his own way these mountains and those who lived in harmony with them.

Kephart wanted resolution and balance more than escape or complete solitude, refuge. He did not come to the Smoky Mountains to hide, sink away into the cool shadows, but to sing their praise. Like Muir, Kephart wanted to call his fellow man's attention to what he considered the greatest of temples, the world's richest cathedral: the mountains, where God was not over the earth, apart from it, but of it, inexorably—in all the dispassionate beauty and power and process of water and stone, wind and forest.

Kephart, the often bitter old drunk up on Hazel Creek, was a man of firm beliefs, unshakable principles, and opinions concerning man and wilderness, ideas that finally cost him everything, one way of life lost and another gained.

Kephart was born in East Salem, Pennsylvania, in 1862, the son of a stern God-fearing father. The Kepharts moved from Pennsylvania to the back-country of Iowa, where wildness and wilderness became the young Kephart's passion, one he was never able to kick. The still rough-edged Iowa country-side filled young Kephart's every need, his every wish. As he grew, he had two great passions—books and the outdoors. These loves stayed with him always, even though his father took a position with the United Brethren Mutual Aid Society and moved the family back to Pennsylvania. More and more, Kephart turned his great energies to scholarship, attending Lebanon Valley College, Boston University, and Cornell. Horace Kephart quickly became one of the most respected young librarians in the nation. He studied and worked in Italy, worked at Rutgers, then accepted a position at Yale, and married.

A life greatly blessed, or so it seemed. His good fortune continued until his deep interest in the American West landed him the position as librarian at St. Louis's much respected Mercantile Library. By 1897, he had a prestigious position, the respect of his academic peers, a growing academic reputation, a successful career, a social position of importance in St. Louis, a wife and a family of six children. Horace Kephart had it all, save what he wanted: to live the life he spent his days and nights reading about, a life in the wilderness, a life devoted entirely to the outdoors. He began, more and more, to shun his duties and responsibilities at the library and ignore his family as he slipped off into the Ozark Mountains, often for days at a time.

Instead of scholarly works, he began writing articles on woodcraft and hunting for the popular outdoor magazines. He drank and went off into the mountains. And when he came back to town, he drank more and more until he could go into the mountains again. There was talk of his wife having an affair, of Horace finding her with the other man. Whatever happened, his need for drink and wilderness increased dramatically.

Wilderness absorbed Kephart's anger, eased his bitterness, took the edge off his rage. Finally, he decided to leave the Mercantile Library, St. Louis, even his wife and family, live the life that threatened to suffocate him if he did not embrace it—a life in the mountains, a life lived for the most part alone. Depending on who you read about Kephart, his last days in St. Louis were either marked by a nervous breakdown or complete alcoholic exhaustion. Whatever the condition or the reason, Horace Kephart was in bad shape when in 1904 his father showed up to carry him home. The next anyone heard of him he came falling off a train near Dillsboro, North Carolina, in the Smoky Mountains. Drunk again, but happy. Actually, his first camp in these mountains was on Dick's Creek and from there later in 1904 he moved up Hazel Creek. Of this new journey into the Smoky Mountains, Kephart wrote: "When I went south into the mountains I was seeking a Back of Beyond."

The "Back of Beyond" he found was among mountains that knew man's presence and touch, mountains heavily logged and mined, mountains whose summits looked out not over great wild lands stretching to the horizon but over some of the most populated and polluted cities of the Southeast. Here, Kephart came in search of his wilderness and here he found it.

Another intriguing Smoky Mountain paradox. A man consumed by wilderness ending up not among the sprawling open lands and great mountains of the West or Alaska, but in the Smoky Mountains, lands that had stood up to nearly everything man and civilization had thrown at them and still hung on to their wildness. Kephart admired these mountains and the people who lived in them for their tenacity, self-reliance, and resolve. Here, deep in Southern Appalachia, Kephart lived, worked, and died. Sometimes he would spend days, even weeks, in the mountains, hiking, hunting, writing, living the life he loved.

In the end, another Smoky Mountain irony: Horace Kephart died in an automobile accident on a mountain highway. It was the spring of 1931. He died pretty much the way he came into the mountains: happily drunk. He and a visiting writer were on their way back to Bryson City from a local bootlegger's place outside town. Both died instantly. Only the car's driver survived.

Kephart was buried on April 5, 1931, up on School House Hill in Bryson City, North Carolina. His grave is marked by a huge piece of Appalachian greenstone. There is a simple plaque fixed to the face of the stone with this inscription: HORACE KEPHART 1862–1931. SCHOLAR, AUTHOR, OUTDOORS-MAN. HE LOVED HIS NEIGHBORS AND PICTURED THEM IN "OUR SOUTHERN HIGH-LANDERS." HIS VISION HELPED CREATE THE GREAT SMOKY MOUNTAINS NATIONAL PARK.

The cemetery on top of School House Hill is a fine place to wait for the Hereafter. It is a hill with a clear view out over town toward where Deep Creek joins the Tuckaseigee River. Kephart had his last camp along Deep Creek. In the far distance are some of the high peaks of the Smokies, in-cluding Mount Kephart, named in Kephart's honor just weeks before his death, and dominated by Clingman's Dome.

Kephart's great love for these mountains and their people produced two books that have measured well against the passing years—his *Camping and Woodcraft*, a classic among a dull crowd of often bland and useless outdoor field guides, and *Our Southern Highlanders*, Kephart's personal paean to the Appalachian Mountains and the Appalachian way of life, both of which he not only celebrated but struggled to preserve and protect. At the time of his death, Kephart had turned from his writing to fighting for the establishment of a national park in the Smoky Mountains. He also championed what later became the Appalachian Trail.

I go up to the School House Hill Cemetery often. It is well tended and crowded with silence and people joined even in death by their sincerity, their fierce determination and spirit. Most of the extinguished lives in the School House Hill Cemetery are marked by hard luck or no luck at all. They were and are a people of hard, unflinching faith, a faith that allows for humor and lets them love the mountains while praying for a way out of them into some kinder fate, gentler heaven, higher glory. Whatever their fate, though, they are, like Kephart, still here, of this ground, these thankless mountains, bones blended back into the rocky dark soil, the pungent loam, deep down among the roots, home at last.

My first visit to School House Hill came a year after meeting Exie Sopwith down near Newfound Gap along the Oconaluftee River. I had fished Hazel Creek three times and Deep Creek once. I knew of Kephart and had read his books. A friend from Bryson City, where Kephart lived when he felt the need to come to town, sent me a quote from the *Asheville Citizen* dated April 3,

1931, the day of Kephart's death. The headline read AUTHORS DIE INSTANTLY IN WRECK NEAR BRYSON CITY, and carried these words from Kephart: "I owe my life to these mountains and I want them preserved that others may profit by them as I have."

"I have," I said aloud, sitting on the massive stone marking Kephart's grave, "I have, indeed." It was twilight and the scattered lights of Bryson City looked like cheap strings of Christmas lights, every other bulb burnt out. The wind was up and the night was cool. I had set up camp down along the bottom end of Deep Creek, but I decided to sit a while longer on the hilltop and watch night settle in the valley and the lights of the small city shine soft as moonglow.

Why?

Of so many mountains, why these?

Why the Smoky Mountains? They seem such an unlikely destination for a man like Kephart, for anyone looking for true wilderness. There is, scientists and earth watchers tell us, no true wilderness left, at least not here. Recently, two scientists set out to determine just how much of the earth's wilderness is left. The study lasted eighteen months. No region could be accepted as wilderness that showed roads, buildings, airports, railroads, settlements, pipelines, dams, even power lines. What, then, is left?—almost nineteen million square miles, or roughly one-third of the earth's surface, is still wild, at least by this study's definition. Where is this wilderness, where are these last of the earth's pristine wild lands?—Antarctica, remote parts of the Soviet Union, and North America, large parts of Africa and South America, smaller parts of Asia and Europe.

In North America the prime remnant wilderness lands are located mostly in Alaska and parts of northern Canada and the Arctic. Of all these patches of wilderness barely 20 percent are now protected. Each year a little more of the earth's great diversity and richness slip away and with them go not only beauty and solace, solitude and renewal, but much of the planet's possibility and potential. With them our desperate hope for the future grows fainter, fainter.

If there is less and less wilderness, there are still those places, even among the roads and dams and towns and power lines, where wildness hangs on. There are such places in these mountains, remnants of a land that is as tenacious as it is bucolic, as hard as it is beautiful. Tucked deep in these narrow valleys and shadowy coves, life goes on, luxuriant and unyielding, a broth of water and wind, stone and root, seed and bloom.

On summer afternoons on my grandfather's farm in the Ozarks when the heat sat on the land like hot iron, we gathered on the porch at noon and traveled through the well-thumbed pages of the old man's big black world atlas. There were few rules or limits: we journeyed to every land that seemed to offer cool rivers full of fat trout. Innocent fantasy, harmless dreams of old men and a young boy. Thoughts of such places cooled us, helped ease the heat, helped get us through afternoons that sizzled like the heavy walls of a blast furnace. No matter how pleasant and exciting our back-porch travels were, though, no other mountains, no matter how exotic, moved us as deeply as the hard-luck hills we lived in, for they were our lives—what was real, immediate, honest, the source of our joy and pain, our small gains and endless failures. If they were not the limits of our dreams, they were the boundaries of what we knew, the world out the back door, the wildness beyond the trees.

There is something in me that needs mountains and fast mountain streams. The rough-edged Smoky Mountains remind me of the Ozarks. Like the Ozarks, they are enough, all I need, time moving in the rush of a fast mountain stream, caught in the glint of light off rippled water or in a trout's cold black eyes, iridescent flanks, a single red leaf spiraling in the press of an autumn wind. There is no true wilderness here, but there is wildness, honest and deep and as much as a man could hope for. These mountains are sincere. They are a place of margins rather than pristine grandeur. There is as much ruin along these ridges, deep in these valleys, as there is natural glory. In these thick forests man and the land have collided again and again, battled for hundreds of years, and still there is no clear victor. Like the trout in these rocky streams, the mountains know no compromise. Consequently, the Smokies are a land marked more by loss and bankruptcy than prosperity.

Mountains are the scribblings of time on the surface of the land, a good place for a man to rub life's immediacy and its Jobaic persistence. Mountains absorb life yet do not hide it, either its fecundity, beauty, or its cruelty. In the high country every ridge seems a lodestone. Touch a great, smooth chunk of granite, wade a river, sink into a heavy sleep beneath hemlock trees—everywhere the feel of undiluted process, motion, raw possibility. And you are just another part of it all. Here man does not matter, does not count. Here he is just another expression of life, neither feared, envied, acknowledged, or especially needed. The stream, the trout, the mountains, go on with or without me, dancing, as they have for so long, to time's madder music, rhythms older than interstellar dust.

Life in the Smoky Mountains is hard, often luckless, impoverished, yet there is to these mountains richness of another kind, hard to measure, a legacy of holding out, holding on to a wildness deep in root and seed, blood and bone.

Sitting on the big stone over Kephart's grave up on School House Hill, I remembered a line of his, words full of celebration and wonder at these mountains. "There is not," he said, "a cranny in the rocks of the Great Smokies, not a foot of the wild glen, but harbors something lovable and rare." More high country irony—that mountains so thoroughly used, even abused, can still lay claim to some of the most sublime mountain country east of the Mississippi River.

No matter where I might be, these mountains stay with me, always. In any city, at any time, during any season, I can shut my eyes and see these summits dark and brooding against an indigo-blue sky and hear the low rumble and roar of swift trout water down rocky gorges and feel the weight of a good trout on my line, the tug that hauls me into the world of stream and water, mountains and trout. These mountains persevere, hang on. And every time I wake and find that I too am suffering from Kephart's disease, the unsettling feeling that I have everything that I want and so little of what I need, I go to the mountains, wade a fine stream, fly-fish until there is only the pure feeling of honest exhaustion and a light in the sky like that of a bed of embers, a perfection of reds, reds without names or definition or description. Coming to these mountains has nothing to do with pilgrimages, with looking for some piscatorial Holy Grail. Such adventures are luxuries and require large sums of what I don't have: money. I am only interested in the company of trout and the beauty they demand, a wildness that is as essential to their way of life as fast, clean water, life of a different kind for a time, a life as true and spare as smooth stone, as uncompromising as trout or wild orchids blooming in the cool shade along a mountain stream. The reassurance of no assurance is the medicine I need, the convenience of no convenience, the soothing order buried at the heart of chaos.

These mountains are enough. Here, on the Carolina side of the mountains, along Hazel Creek and Deep Creek, Snowbird Creek and Slickrock Creek, the years pass and the trout rise and the country is good. There is quiet and beauty in abundance. A brown trout on Slickrock Creek, a fish sometimes marked by a telling bloodred back, hits my fly with raw ferocity and Slickrock is all the holy water I require; it is the Afjord in Norway, the Te Anau in New Zealand, the Sustut, the Lower Talarik, the Big Horn, the Madison, the Bow. Wildness is rare and beautiful, moving, valuable, and profound whether it is experienced in the outback of British Columbia or Iceland or thigh-deep in a cold Smoky Mountain trout stream running unseen through the fingers of ten million visitors a year.

Along a few of the trout streams of the Smokies I have mingled with fish and water and light and I have felt the press of time, the great power of the present, the energy that fashions both the past and the future. It is not how many experiences we pile up in our lifetime, but what we make of them, how they mix with blood and memory, how they enrich our lives. Mountains and trout streams sustain me, are the handles through which I have glimpsed the slight and the immeasurable, the vast and the small. Being among them is never disappointing, even when there are no fish. For there is always the sensation, so deeply satisfying, of belonging, of being genuinely connected.

Estimates vary on just how many visitors a year pass through the Great Smoky Mountains National Park. Some say six million, others put the crowds at closer to eight or ten million. However many there are, most of them keep to the roads, the paved highways. They are eager to see whatever a road passes near. We have come to the point where we like our wilderness the way we like our food—fast and easily digestible, served up on the go, through the car window. The Great Smoky Mountains National Park's great appeal is that it is a drive-through park, that great good place where you can have a wilderness experience without ever having to leave your car. And the road does twist and turn through some magnificent countryside. There are frequent pull-offs and overlooks of great mountain vistas suitable for snapshots and a quick picnic. If the trash cans are full, it's all right. Wilderness, it seems, is for a great many of us just another handy place to dump beer cans, dead cars, plastic garbage bags full of chicken bones, and used plastic diapers. Along its main roads, even along the pastoral, often inspirational Blue Ridge Parkway climbing out of the Smokies and into the Blue Ridge Mountains, these mountains are like any other major national park, more trash than treasure.

Off the roads, off the main trails, back up in the thick woods, down steep slopes, along rock-strewn streams, these mountains have an admirable mean streak to them. Despite the hard-pressed towns, the creaky old dams, the telephone poles and electric lines and pipelines that climb and fall with nearly every ridge, despite every attempt to tame them, domesticate them, these mountains refuse to be easy, charitable, friendly. No compromise, none at all. Way off the roadways, deep in the hollows and stream valleys and in the thick forests that are not virgin but second, third, even fourth growth in some places, wildness persists, thrives. I am in wonder of these mountains for many reasons, but none more than their capacity for absorbing abuse and their capacity not just to hang on, but to endure.

I come for the beauty and the good fishing rather than grand truths, though these too are here scattered about the creek bottoms like weathered stones. The soft light of dusk, a trout's rise, the sound of nothing but water over stones are glamour and excitement enough. Mountain solitude is deep and wide and abiding and yet coiled tight as a snake, something alive, ready to give way at any instant to something as ordinary as birdsong or as confounding and bewitching as a trout's sudden inexplicable leap out of a stream's cold waters and into the sun's bright, warm light.

On a fresh, cool Sunday morning in March I met Allie Carlyle down the hill from one of Bryson City's many churches. The service was ending and the choir was on its feet, full of robust, uplifting song. We sat on big stones near large oak trees. Allie Carlyle looked to be in her forties, maybe more. Whatever her age, she was beautiful. The years and the mountains had been uncharacteristically kind. Long, soft, braided red hair, deep green eyes, skin the color of new butter, still cool, soft, fresh. As striking as her looks were, though, it was the old cane fly rod in her hand that caught my attention. Her voice was no louder than a whisper that blended with the church organ's inspirational chords. She, too, told me of nearby mountain streams full of trout.

"I don't know why I'm trusting in you, but I am," she said. "Keep all this to yourself. There's knee-deep silence up on those creeks, quiet that hasn't been broken just yet. Leave some when you go. It's a policy I try to keep." She turned then and looked up at the redbrick church up the hill and hummed along with the choir as it sang. In song her voice was loud and bold and there were uneven streams of sunlight moving wildly through her hair. After the hymn closed, after a weak chorus of amens, Allie Carlyle leaned close to the stone on which I sat, told me she had moved to town to teach after her father died some years back.

"There was the old farm," she said, and I noticed a definite roll to her whisper, like the rise and fall of emotion, "but I sold it. Unfair odds did it.

Too many rocks, a soil way past hope, even luck, and just me. I have a son. Can't feed a boy on beauty, can't pay the bills with scenery. So I moved to town and called it a compromise. I earn a living for me and the boy and we get to stay in the mountains. Mountains can get to you, you know. I mean only that for me there's just no finer place to wait out Judgment Day."

You could hear the shuffle of robes and feet and chairs as the choir rose to sing again, put fire to sin with a powerful gospel song. Organ music wrinkled out of every chink and crevice in the old church, gave the wind a rich new tone and texture. Allie Carlyle picked up the melody, hummed along, smiling, absentmindedly twirling the old cane fly rod in the fingers of her left hand. I said good-bye and walked down toward the river and then out toward Deep Creek, thinking that time spent in the mountains is indeed well invested and how lucky I have been to have invested so heavily: when I am old and bent and my mind is dim, the dividends of mountain time will nourish me still.

Crossroads of Time

BRYSON CITY USED TO BE called Bears Town. I
like that name and wish it had stuck. ❧ In the early
1800s the place was a nervous gathering of log cabins
along the Tuckaseigee River not far from the aban-
doned Cherokee town of Kituwha that once sprawled
along the lower reaches of Deep Creek. There were plenty of black bears
then. Not anymore. Now there are more people around Bryson City than
bears, though black bears continue to survive up in the high country, and
Bryson City, despite its brush with technology and prosperity, still has the
slightly frayed, rough-edged look and feel of Bears Town. There used to be a
sign just outside the city, out toward the turnoff that follows the Nantahala
River down into the rocky, wasp-waisted Nantahala Gorge where shadows
still drift through the valley well past midmorning and where, on cool autumn days, just before moonrise, the gorge bristles with a thin-spun eucharistic light.

This is what the big roadside sign said: JESUS SAVES. WHERE WILL YOU SPEND
ETERNITY? HEAVEN OR HELL? As good a question as any, I suppose, especially
for a fly fisherman with time on his hands. The first time I saw the sign, wide
and tall up on the hillside, two lines of Milton's *Paradise Lost* broke out of
some chamber in my head, whispered in my ear—

The Mind is its own place, and in itself
Can make a Heav'n of Hell, or Hell of Heav'n.

The last time I passed the sign it was a warm and balmy Thursday and on reading the message I decided to heed it, sort of, and go for a sampling of both—a couple of days up along Slickrock Creek in the Joyce Kilmer Memorial Forest and Slickrock Wilderness Area that sprawls across parts of Monroe County, Tennessee, and Graham County, North Carolina.

Although the Great Smoky Mountains National Park covers more than 500,000 acres, I tend to keep to the North Carolina side of the mountains. My reasons are strictly self-centered, self-serving, and practical. The Carolina side of the Smokies has fewer roads and fewer towns. Fewer roads and towns means fewer people and less use which means a harder, rougher, more isolated countryside, wilder streams, and spookier trout.

The border between Tennessee and North Carolina twists and turns, folds and pleats, for more than 50 miles through the Smoky Mountains. Geologically, the Smokies are considered part of the Blue Ridge province of the Appalachian Mountains, a massive 1,600-mile spine of weathered and worn mountains that reach from the Gaspé Peninsula in Canada to the exhaustion of rounded hard-luck foothills that spill across northern Alabama and Georgia. Most of the great mountains of the Appalachian range are in the Smokies, including Clingman's Dome (6,643 feet), the highest point in the park, and Mount Guyot (6,621). T. L. Clingman and Arnold Guyot were geologists who both undertook exhaustive studies of the Smoky Mountains in the 1860s. More than twenty peaks in the Smokies rise to or above 6,000 feet. Enveloped by clouds, the mountain summits look like dark islands in an endless broth of cool, misty fog and low-slung clouds.

Although the Smokies anchor the southern edge of the Blue Ridge province, they are 2,000 feet higher in elevation, on average, than the Blue Ridge Mountains to the north. The southern end of the Blue Ridge province is marked by the narrow, well-defined stony backbone of Virginia's Blue Ridge Mountains that begins to crack, split, and widen below Mount Mitchell, letting out a broad marrow of mountains along its eastern edge—the Smoky Mountains: broad-shouldered, dark and brooding in nature, wearing a burly hide of forest and tangles of laurel and rhododendron. The high country and dominating peaks give way to deeply pleated foothills as dark and dull as old spurs that rise and fall northwest toward the Appalachian Valley in Tennessee and southwest through parts of North Carolina and into north Georgia.

If dark colors are soothing, the moody Smokies, then, are hypnotic, a geography of deceptively uncomplicated shape and forms and forms within forms, great undulating seas of color and light all pressed hard against the sky. But it is a landscape marked as much by its diversity of life as by its topography. The Smokies are a land of almost claustrophobic excess, fecundity gone haywire, life probing every possible expression. It is a place where diversity moves and thrives in floods of water and mild climate, endless ranges of sunlight. No matter summer's oppressive heat, here in these mountains water seems to cling to every surface, swell every root and seed. The Smoky Mountains are often as wet and humid as the rain forests of Central America. Whatever the season or weather, there is rain in these mountains, even if it is but a mist barely light enough to moisten the lips. In the high reaches of the mountains, up above 4,500 feet, these mountains can get more than eighty inches a year. Even the shadow-filled, narrow valleys, which can be as much as 20 degrees warmer than the summits, can get as much as fifty inches of rain each year. Up on the ridges, the air is heavy with a cool mist and thin clouds that sometimes hang about the high ridges and peaks as though tethered to the tops of weather-gnarled firs and spruce. The Smokies seem almost shy: dark mountains slightly hidden in damp blue shadows—veils of blue moisture, layers of blue, soft, soundless explosions of blue. Curtains of cerulean blue light drift low over the ridges, a heavier mildew of beryl blue hugs the dark ground back in the dark coves and pinched-in valleys, and the haunting dark blue of uncut lapis comes off the high boreal forest, the stands of Fraser fir and red spruce, just at twilight.

Shaconage, the Cherokee call these mountains enveloped in blue hazes. Translation from the Cherokee varies. I like the one given me by a young Cherokee I met up on Raven Fork, one of the streams that flows through the Qualla Reservation. While most of the trout water on the reservation is for the Cherokees alone, part of Raven Fork is open to any curious angler.

His name, he told me as he worked on his fishing rig, was Bob Winterwolf Dougal and he was 100 percent Cherokee.

"Some crack-brained ancestor took hold of the name Dougal from a white-bread ground-buster thinking it might help. Lift our burden or something. It didn't."

He sat on the edge of a wide gallery of stones that tilted out over the stream and fished with a simple cane pole and line and a small Eagle Claw hook baited with what he called the "Sure Thing"—a bright red salmon egg sandwiched between two meaty niblets of fresh sweet corn. He had on jeans and a gray sweater and had his thick, black hair tucked up under a blue-and-white Duke University baseball cap.

After perhaps a half hour of edgy quiet, he hauled up what looked to be a fine rainbow trout, at least a pound of fish, maybe more.

"We can talk now," he said suddenly, turning my way, facing me. "Had to keep my tongue on the trout's account. They're not much on conversation." He baited up his hook again, flicked the line back out into the stream.

"I'm easy to talk to because I don't hold a grudge. So you're a white man. So your ancestors drove my ancestors from these mountains. So they stole our lands and herded us like broken-down cattle to Oklahoma, the dung heap of the world. So they told us fat, wonderful lies and made treaties with us that were worthless. So you have gathered us up and tucked us conveniently away in pretty little internment camps like this one and forgotten about us mostly. So you give us too much money for liquor and too little respect, too many handouts and not enough education and hope. So what? Ain't your fault. Ain't mine."

Bob Winterwolf Dougal fishes and hunts and works sometimes in his uncle's souvenir store in Cherokee. He held up a stringer of handsome Smoky Mountain rainbow trout, jiggled them at me smugly.

"Nice, aren't they?" he said, plopping them back in the cold stream with a loud splash. "Got 'em back up on tribal water. Sacred water. Whites can't fish there. You get education, jobs, housing, all that stuff and we get our own trout water. Fair's fair."

I've fished with Dougal many times. He fills my creel with Cherokee stories, myths, memories, with dreams and nightmares and with honest laughter. Last fall, up on Raven Fork, he gave me a rubber tomahawk with a fake red-and-black feather tied poorly to its plastic handle.

"For you, white brother," he said, "I make heap big deal, give you heap big break. Yours for one dollar, no tax. A real steal. We get these things by the gross, by the ton, by the truckload, from Korea. Pay 30 cents apiece for 'em and stick it to the tourists with a three hundred or four hundred percent markup. In time, my son, victory will be ours. Economic victory, political victory, that is."

As if to emphasize his point, he bopped me on the head with the little rubber club. It wobbled harmlessly like so much Jell-O.

"You scalped, white eyes. You hoodwinked, flimflammed. You been had. Heap big sap. Ultimate yokel."

Not long afterward on a cold November afternoon we were along the stretch of the Oconaluftee River that runs through the Qualla Reservation.

Most of the tourist shops and stores in the town of Cherokee were closed, and all of the chiefs had gone south to Florida for the winter. Even the bears that are sometimes kept as tourist attractions along the main highway, token bits of wildness held captive, controlled and harmless, bait for travelers patrolling the town for safe adventure, had disappeared. These bears are not supposed to be Smoky Mountain black bears. There are laws protecting them, laws mostly ignored. A cold wind rattled store signs, messages with no takers on this icy November day. Bob Winterwolf Dougal pulled an envelope the color of damp walnut from his red-and-blue wool jacket, shoved it toward me. It was from the Wharton School of Business, Office of Admissions. Bob Winterwolf Dougal had been accepted into the school's MBA program.

"Of course," he said, "you know this means I'll be slipping off the reservation, going on the lam. An act of defiance, revolt, revolution."

"What will you do? After school, I mean."

"I'll scalp the white man by importing rubber tommy hawks and cheap headdresses made of fake eagle feathers from Korea and selling them to my white brothers at a hefty profit. That and walk these mountains and fish for trout, Indian trout. As everyone knows, Indian trout are much bigger and nobler than any other trout."

Bob Winterwolf Dougal seemed uncharacteristically optimistic and I thought of Ambrose Noel and wondered if he had been this way, if perhaps Dougal had gotten his spin on Noel's tempting wooden prayer wheel.

We walked down the middle of the highway in great slants of cold November sunlight and then made our way back along the river. We could see the Blue Ridge Parkway climb out of the Smokies and toward the darker, distant Blue Ridge. Toward the hinge of the softly lit sky, up toward Asheville, the light came off rounded mountains in sheets of indigo, and I asked Dougal about the Cherokee word "shaconage."

"As good a word as any," he said. He looked hard at the water that was as black as obsidian in the waning light, looked hard for any sign of brown trout on the move. We sat at a wobbly picnic table near the river. Spent leaves were pressed by the fast river water against the smooth stones and looked like blotches of damp color, blood reds and decayed yellows. Dougal told me that one of the nice things about the Cherokee language is that it isn't all that specific. Like the river, the language is endless in its mood and character. It is never fixed and is nearly impossible to pin down. Translating it, he told me, was rather like interpreting dreams. So many possibilities, so many answers, each as correct and right and true as the other.

"To many old men I have known," he said, "those that have been in these mountains all their lives and remember and believe the stories their fathers and grandfathers told of this place before there were whites and towns and tourists and the tacky things that tourism hauls with it, shaconage was a word the Indians used that tried to express what was special about these mountains. The unknowable, I guess. Biggest magic of all. But things change, even words and what they mean, what they say or do not say."

He pulled the collar of his coat up over his ears and tucked his long dark hair under a wool ski cap.

He lay down on the top of the picnic table, staring blankly up at the dissolving light and went on talking.

"I have heard it said many ways, a word of different meanings. Blue Heaven. Land of the Blue Smoke. Blue Mountains. The Dark Place. Rising Smoke. And so on and so on. I liked the way my uncle said it, the meaning he gave to it. Land of the Blues. Land of the Blues.

"He was the one that gave me my Indian name. I grew up thinking it was that of a great Cherokee warrior, a sacred chief. When I asked my uncle about my name he laughed. This is what he said to me: 'Lupus est homo homini.' Man is a wolf to man. That's what it means. Comes from Plautus's *Asinaria*. Uncle Broken Stone had a library card as well as a fishing pole."

South of Roanoke, Virginia, the mountain rivers cascade down the eastern flank of the mountains and drain to the Atlantic, while those running down the western flank drain toward the Gulf of Mexico. Most of the major streams of the Smoky Mountains generally drain to the west and northwest, then south toward the Gulf. Up at Newfound Gap nearby mountain slopes still wear the puckered scars of great landslides that ripped and gouged the mountains after they had been clear-cut. Time has obscured the scars, but not dissolved them. These are insistent mountains, absorbing even what harms them, turning scar tissue into luxuriant excess. Most of this mountain country, at the turn of the century, was owned by lumber companies. Horace Kephart and many like him came to believe that the mountains' only chance for survival lay in federal protection. Only a national park could save and protect the grandeur of the Smoky Mountains. As early as the 1920s, members of the Southern Appalachian National Park Commission selected by the secretary of the interior climbed Mount Le Conte and concluded that the Smokies offered the only lands left in the Southeast wild enough for a national park. Legislation was passed and moneys raised both in Tennessee and North Carolina. The most critical funding came neither from Congress nor from the states but from John D. Rockefeller, Jr., who contributed five million dollars to the proposed park in honor of his wife. Finally, in 1940, the mountain park that had been envisioned as far back as the 1890s was dedicated at Newfound Gap by President Franklin D. Roosevelt.

A large crowd followed the president's party from Knoxville into the mountains, sensing that perhaps a truly important moment was at hand, and so it was. The president's words and Congress's laws merged to attempt the preservation and protection of this monumental new park that sprawled over 800 square miles of hard-edged mountain country still wild enough to support 1,500 species of wildflowers, 50 species of mammals, 200 resident species of birds, and 80 different species of reptiles and amphibians. Crowding the thick ridgelines and steep, narrow valleys, the broad, crenellated slopes, are more species of trees than in all of Europe. If diversity is reduced to numbers, to charts and graphs, then the Smokies are a statistician's fantasy, a glory of numbers that fail even in their volume to reveal fully the press of life in these mountains. Here there is a dispassionate beauty that marks every cove and stream, a richness that is part of every rounded hill and stony meadow.

Shaconage say the Cherokee. Land of the Blues. Blue Refuge. Perhaps. Like skin, the Indian word fits tight about the mountains. This is what Bob Winterwolf Dougal told me: "Cherokee is this place put into language." These mountains nurture life in time and through time. Each grasp of altitude determines the limits of survival, what will make it, what will give way. Altitude settles, calmly, without strain, without remorse, the question of living and dying. Each cold summit, each balmy valley, is a broth of life often mixed in unimaginable profusion.

Near the end of the last great Ice Age 10,000 years ago vast sheets of ice inched deep into what is now North America, as far south perhaps as St. Louis and Louisville. While the peaks of the Smoky Mountains were not crushed by walls of ice, they were buried under great weights of snow. Where lush stands of spruce and fir would take hold, galleries of stone glinted in the dim, cold sunlight. As the earth's climate warmed and the great ice sheets retreated, the seas rose, forcing plant and animal species to higher ground. Mountains became islands where life dug in, hung on, survived, and eventually flourished.

Above 5,000 feet, up among the cold winds and icy clouds, the boreal forest took hold, while below 5,000 feet one of the planet's great deciduous forests dominated every slope and hillside, every valley and cove. Like an immense blue-green ribbon, spruce and firs clogged the Appalachians' seven highest peaks. At one time this wide and imposing Canadian Zone covered millions of acres. Today, however, the Canadian Zone has been shrunk to a modest ragged strip running perhaps 150 miles along the backbone of the mountains, and it is in danger of disappearing altogether. Life ran as widely and wonderfully amok in these mountains as though it were as isolated and protected as life on the Galápagos Islands. In the cold shadows of the Canadian Zone grow more than twenty plants endemic or restricted to the high reaches of the southern highlands. Up among the icy clouds is the mountain habitat that is rare and wild, home of mountain ash and Fraser fir, of bearberry, Indian plantain, and northern red raspberry, whose leaves need to feel the wind's cold touch, its icy reassurance. Among the dark limbs of the spruce and fir, the wind smells of balsam and takes on a new chorus of sound—lilting, haunting sounds that blend with the call of the dark-eyed junco, winter wren, southern brown creeper, and the shy Cairns' black-throated blue warbler. Farther back in the purple shadows is the mountain vireo, whose call is the very sound of what is solitary, alone, and at ease.

I like driving into the Smokies from the high country to the north, following the twisting folds of the Blue Ridge Parkway until it finally climbs through the Plott Balsam Mountains to the weathered, battered pinnacle of Water Rock Knob rising 6,292 feet off the valley floor and into the thin, chilly clouds. Water Rock Knob is an exposed fist of stone that allows for a grand view. Every point of the compass is crowded with mountains. The sky itself seems endless scraps of stone—pleated, folded, rising and falling, cluttered against the fractured horizon. To the north, the blue-black domes of the Balsams and to the south toward Saco Gap in the Great Smokies, ridge after ridge rising like great humped whales out of a dark sea. The sky is wrinkled with worn domes of stone: dark, profound, massive. From Water Rock Knob it is but twenty minutes or so to the splashing cold waters of the Oconaluftee River and the Cherokee entrance to the Great Smoky Mountains National Park, the junction with Highway 441, the mountain highway that indelicately bisects the park, zigzagging from below 1,500 feet at Gatlinburg to more than 5,000 feet at Newfound Gap, then dropping quickly along the Oconaluftee River to 2,000 feet.

Seen at a distance, as a range of peaks and ridgelines and shadow-filled valleys, the Smokies look as though they have been violently compressed, an accordion of worn-crested peaks and thin, gnarled valleys. Many of the knuckled ridges covered with great slicks of mountain laurel give way suddenly, precipitously, to nearly vertical slopes that tumble at air-gasping angles into valleys and gorges so narrow that even shadows find scant comfort there. A missed step along these slicks and it's a one-way adventure down the mountainside, beat-up and bruised, down among stones and weak light where only the toughest roots sink in and hang on.

Along the entire ridgeline of the Smokies large, garish outcrops of stone are rare. These are thick-coated mountains, heavy-browed with forest and undergrowth, tulip trees and white oaks, lush cucumber magnolias, hemlock in the damp shadows and glorious sugar maples, knots of goatsbeard, dog hobble, wood sorrel, and mountain laurel, galax looking like polished greenstone, irrepressible thickets of Catawba rhododendron, while higher-up sunlight goes gold among stands of yellow birch. The liquid sound of calling black-throated blue warblers gets lost in the rush of mountain streams, and the wind high up among the trees smells of spruce and hemlock and wild onion, sharp and fresh. Higher still, up along the ridgeline, the sky shimmers, a thick liquid of blues as the light comes off bent Fraser firs, their needles flat and blunt and unforgiving, like the worn summits they occupy.

The highest peak in the eastern United States, the apex of the ragged Appalachians, is Mount Mitchell. Its summit has the look of a heavy fist, jutting through smoky-blue clouds and perpetual chilly mists. Mitchell, like all great mountains, is a place of wrenching extremes. Its summit makes up the firm belly of the high Appalachians' intriguing, haunting Canadian Zone, a land that is closer in character to parts of China than to North Carolina. Life in this high country, in this land above the clouds, is perpetually pressed by hard times, hard, unforgiving weather. Another mountain paradox: a place that is at once exceptionally fragile and yet doggedly enduring. Like trout in wild mountain streams, what survives above 5,000 feet does so on its own terms, without compromise. The press of civilization, of man's coughing, wheezing, pneumatic world, brings death more than adaptation.

A raw cold wind blows hard atop Mount Mitchell. A constant wind, merciless. Trees are gnarled, twisted, stunted, bent in grotesque attitudes like galleries of violent sculpture. The summit is a place of harshness, an environment where death is a common resident. For as long as I have been coming to these mountains, the crown of Mount Mitchell has always been marked by dead trees, great stands of them, hard, honest evidence of the vagaries of life above 5,000 feet. They were part of the fabric of the mountains and I paid little attention to them until the winter of 1984 when it struck me that their numbers were growing, that the small stands of dead and dying trees had become a bulging, swelling host. I studied the summit of Mount Mitchell through powerful binoculars and the dead and dying trees piled up before my eyes like massive gray shoals of dust-colored bones. A sweep of the binoculars showed that almost the entire crest of the mountain seemed to have taken on the aspect of a long, rippled, grimy scar pinched against the sky.

And the trees, the great stands of spruce and fir on Mount Mitchell, go on dying. The mountain today looks like death's gray land, wearing the despair of a plague's vile kiss. The once thick forest that crowded the ridgeline lies fallen and falling, as though laid down by some sudden killing wind. No matter the month, no matter the press of weather, Mount Mitchell knows only death's touch and its dull gray color.

The death atop Mount Mitchell has fueled argument among scientists and environmentalists for years. The common explanation for the great number of dead trees along the summit was the mountain's severe climate and the sudden appearance in the 1950s of a number of insects, especially the woolly balsam aphid, that feed on the spruce and fir trees. The woolly balsam aphid, it turned out, is a recent immigrant, just another insect that had been accidentally imported into the country. After its arrival, it eventually made its way to the Appalachian Mountains and found there its favorite meal, Fraser firs. Nothing has as yet stopped the aphid. It, too, knows no compromise. It seems as irrepressible as the chestnut blight. But Dr. Robert I. Bruck, a plant pathologist at North Carolina State University in Raleigh, refused to lay all of Mount Mitchell's troubles on a single aphid. There was just too much destruction. He sensed that the mountain's deepening ruin went further than the appetite of the woolly balsam aphid. After all, the aphid ate mostly fir trees, yet the destruction on the mountain swept through all the trees above 5,000 feet. Indeed, in many places the red spruce were dying out even faster than firs. Bruck believed that something else was killing the trees, or at least contributing to their deaths, and he believed that that something else was airborne pollution and acid rain. He studied the mountain's air, soil, and its water, and his findings portray an atmosphere atop Mount Mitchell that is more toxic than the worst smog-bound summer days over downtown Knoxville,

Nashville, Charlotte, Birmingham, and Atlanta combined. Yet another irony: the lure of fresh, invigorating mountain air, the clean winds blowing over the rim of the highest point of stone in eastern North America, when in fact the air swirling about the summit of Mount Mitchell is only slightly less foul than the brown, congestive, ruinous automotive emissions floating stiffly above Los Angeles.

According to the Environmental Protection Agency, concentrations of 120 parts of ozone per billion parts of air at sea level even for an hour a year is cause of serious concern. In 1986 Dr. Bruck measured such alarming ozone levels atop Mount Mitchell ten times during a single month's worth of readings. Ten times. The summit is literally wrapped in pollution. A gauze of clouds and mist and fog shroud Mount Mitchell more than three hundred days a year. This cloak of moisture, Dr. Bruck has learned, is saturated with toxic substances, whopping doses of heavy metals and acidic moisture. Even more alarming is the mounting evidence that the dire effects of air pollution above 5,000 feet are beginning to show up at lower elevations. Once thought to be the problem solely of the northeastern United States and Canada, the pall of acid rain has now spread over the entire continent, a rain that is an efficient killer, neatly leaching minerals like magnesium and calcium through the leaves of plants and trees, strangling them just as it quietly and efficiently strangles mountain lakes and streams. On the summit of Mount Mitchell the destructive wet cape of acidic moisture is compounded by increasing levels of toxic metals present in the thin soil—traces of cadmium, zinc, lead, mercury, and aluminum. Bruck's studies show that the moisture at the top of Mount Mitchell is from eighty to one hundred times more acidic than that of normal rainfall. It is as if the top of the mountain were daily submerged in a great, sour-smelling sea of pure vinegar. Dr. Bruck, of course, is no soothsayer. He brings neither good news nor bad, only the facts that make such news, one way or the other. Even he remains hesitant to say firmly that pollution alone is killing the Canadian Zone of the high Appalachians. What he does contend is that the high country is under extreme environmental stress caused perhaps by a weave of interconnected causes from insects to airborne pollutants. But he does say, without reservation, that the high country is dying.

I still go to Mount Mitchell, though it is not easy. I hesitate, grapple for excuses to stay away the way I might hesitate about visiting a dying friend because I know that going will seal the truth of things, make me hold death's hand yet again. So I go to the mountain and stare at the dying trees that now cover nearly its entire summit and below, and I understand that even setting aside a wild land, a mountain or a river, any piece of remnant wildness does not guarantee its survival. Against winds heavy with ozone and toxic metals and acid rains, laws that call for protection cannot begin to ensure preservation or survival.

Sometimes as I walk along the bony ridge of Mount Le Conte, I am reminded of Mount Mitchell the way I first saw it more than a decade ago—crowded stands of fir and spruce dripping with tattered wisps of cold mountain clouds, tendrils of fog, sudden icy mists. Often I will taste this cold rain, let it sit for a time on my tongue, waiting for that first bitter metallic taste of acidic rain, while the rain runs off my face and hands and down among the layers of spongy moss that spread among the rocks and fallen trees looking like lush green islands in a vast and bleak gray sea. Still the view of the Smokies from the summit of Mount Le Conte, especially looking north from Cliff Top and east from Myrtle Point, when the daylight is nearly spent and is the old red color of faded roses, is like looking into great sheets of red rain pouring out of the sky and slanting off Clingman's Dome and Thunderhead and the worn hobble-headed crown of Siler's Bald where the headwaters of Hazel Creek gather. The knotted dome of Mount Guyot is clearly visible, too, and beyond the vaporous shapes of the Plott Balsams and Great Balsams, even the rocky thumb of Water Rock Knob.

Enjoying this country's remnant wild places is a touchy issue. The Great Smoky Mountains National Park covers more than 500,000 acres. In the half century since the park's creation, conservationists, state governments, the federal government, lumbermen, and developers have argued about the proper use of the park. In 1988, in a unanimous vote, the House passed a bill that would have permanently set aside 419,000 acres of the Smokies as primitive wilderness area. So far only Senator Jesse Helms of North Carolina has stood in the way of the bill making its way through the Senate.

If the bill does pass it will only more or less validate what has been happening to the park for a long time. There is not enough money or manpower to keep the entire park tidy and groomed, ready to embrace the public at all times. Making most of it wilderness would mean the Park Service could stop spending its time maintaining trails and other facilities that so few people use. Most of the park, and especially the great wild North Carolina sections of the park, is already wild and has been for years.

Let the trails go to hell. Don't improve the roads. Make anyone wanting to expose themselves to the hard beauty of these mountains get a permit. Keep all cars at a distance. Pass laws that will stop anything like a Gatlinburg or Pigeon Forge from happening on the North Carolina side of the mountains. Do all of these things. I am for all of it, and more, selfishly so. These are the kinds of things that will keep the streams open and wild and the trout alive and uncompromising and me trying with fits and starts to hook into them both, hoping they will pull me into the soft, warm cathedral light that comes off mountain streams just at dusk.

I walked the trail down along Slickrock Creek in a hard rain that tasted cold and clean, innocent, free of toxic metals and the sharp taste of acid. Knowing that the creek made a wide bend ahead and that there was a nice pool above a gallery of stones, I stood in a thick grove of sheltering trees, rigged up the Winston rod, and noticed a tiny pool of rainwater gathering in a green fold of my jacket, the drops of rain as firm and regular as cells. On the creek, the light eddied and spilled and rushed with the water and the water took on the moody character of the light until they mingled so completely that I could no longer separate water from light and light from water. Everything drifted in a warm, rainy harmony of motion. I worked the green 4-weight line out through the guides of the willowy rod and tied on a fetching nymph. I cast and watched the small nymph go down in the fast, cold water.

On the sixth cast a small brown took the nymph and ran. I could feel its weight and its anger and its determination as it bent around stones and submerged roots and limbs trying to free itself, to escape line and hook. It spent its energy in a great rush and I pulled it close, bringing the line in with my hands, not even using the reel, and as it rose just out in front of my rod tip I could see its head and eyes—eyes raven black, a blackness as wide as a clear night sky and drenched in wildness, a wildness of trout and creek and rain; everything seemed liquid, a welcome stream that reached for me like a spring tide, flooded around my calves and thighs, pulled at the muscles of my legs and stomach. I felt the full weight of the fish in my hands and arms and I gave it line, not wanting it to die as it fought. Near the surface I saw it still tossing its head violently, folding and unfolding its deep brown body like a coach whip. Its muscled back was mottled with dark blotches of deep red, the red of dried blood, dark and melancholy. Call it Slickrock Red because there is no other name for it, because I have seen it mark no other trout save the big browns of Slickrock Creek. I lifted the fish slightly, just so its back would break the water, and the rain on its back flashed red, ran down its flanks like tiny streams of claret. I held the trout only for an instant, then freed the hook from its lip, let it go, slowly, gently, carefully. For an instant there, knee-deep in the creek with the rain falling and that brown trout's seared-red back disappearing in the deep water, I was absolutely certain of the interconnectedness of all things, the cold touch of time against my chilled skin.

The rain came down harder in great pounding sheets, grinding torrents that churned up the creek bottom, made it look like some storm-tossed sea, hell's own boiling ocean, and still the red-backed brown trout took the little nymphs and wet flies and fought fiercely, more aware, it seemed, of their lineage than their size. Trout. *Salmo.* No compromise. None at all.

I took two more while it rained, neither any bigger than the first, their dark backs laced with jagged pools of bitter red. As I let them go, I could feel the heavy rise and fall of their flanks and bellies, the deep pull of their near total exhaustion. They had held back nothing. Nothing. Part of the great allure and fascination and temptation of mountain streams is that everything about them seems so fully alive, so completely caught up in the rush and motion of life. Motion twitches against every flash of light, no matter how dim, just like the speck of light widening in a rising trout's endlessly black eyes.

The last brown slipped out of the landing net I had eased under it to hold it steady in the water while it regained its strength. It moved off slowly, deliberately, and sank like a wet leaf into deeper, darker water. Mountain storms have a tendency to reach biblical proportion, pounding and ripping at the sky and earth, vibrating the very atmosphere, but by midmorning the apocalyptic-looking storm clouds had broken up, moved on, pressed by a fresh wind out of the southwest. Sunlight came up off the creek like a sudden mist, and the creek seemed a whirlpool of process and form, time and energy, a whirlpool that feeds the imagination and gets it good and drunk. Moments like this are wild and rare and are, like just the thought of trout, what lasts, endures, lines the membrane of memory rather than the fleeting excitement of rod and reel, the near-perfect cast, the set hook. The best experiences are those that are earned, even if, like me, you happen to be but an angler of modest skills.

A mist fringed in tendrils of green light drifted just above the trees, and the wind smelled of birch and hemlock. Large drops of rainwater hung languidly from leaves of wild hydrangea, falling, finally, and exploding against the backs of dark stones. I packed up the rod and reel and sat in the middle of the trail and made lunch—a can of Spam, crackers, and cool root beer, all bought that morning up at the Crossroads of Time grocery, gas station, and motel up on U.S. 129 at Deals Gap near Peppertree Fontana Resort.

Slickrock Creek is part of the Slickrock Wilderness Area tucked back in the hard and devastatingly beautiful reaches of the Joyce Kilmer Memorial Forest, a stretch of woods that covers 11,000 rugged acres of the Little Santeetlah Creek and Slickrock Creek watersheds defined by the high ridgeline running between Stratton Bald and Haoe Lookout. From Stratton Bald, the crenellated backs of the Smokies are to the north just across the Little Tennessee River. To the west is the great expanse of the Cherokee National Forest.

Established by law in 1935, the Joyce Kilmer Memorial Forest is dedicated to the memory of the young soldier and poet Joyce Kilmer who was killed in World War I. I cannot say I care much for Kilmer's poems, but his forest is beautiful indeed, wild and unsettling and heartbreaking as any enduring rhyme. Although lumber companies logged vast tracts of these woods before 1900, there are islands of virgin timber here, groves of giant trees that give the woods a dark and alluring character. Like fragile stands of spiderwebbing, more than twenty-six miles of them move through this magnificent forest. Many of the trails are rocky, unkempt, difficult, poorly marked. Slickrock is not a place that is easily stumbled on; rather it is discovered, slowly, gradually, like a distant star carefully brought into focus through the powerful lens of a telescope. Here I walk slowly, deliberately, taking it one step, one trout, one sunset at a time. Shadows drift about the woods like a dark fog and there is mystery under every stone.

There is a strange comfort in a forest, along a trout stream, where mystery hangs on, where not everything sits out in the bright sunlight completely revealed. In these woods I fight the urge to define and order what is about me, what is in and out of the light. And I attempt only to raise a trout or two, and accept what each moment brings, even what pants and growls in the dark shadows at dusk, what moves beneath the water, what thrives beyond man's rules and categories, his expedient designs and explanations. Too often we explain the world to suit us, to ease our own uncertainties, even though, in truth, it often suits us not at all. Watching the creek run hard with the afternoon's rain, feeling the olive-colored mist on my face and arms, listening to the trill of warblers far back in the thick trees, looking hard at the creek's surface for any sign of fish, it seems to me that I am fated always to see the world as it rushes by and that I can never outrace the moving universe, feel it moving toward me rather than forever sweeping over me, by me, through me, leaving me behind, seeing not where it's going but where it's been.

My view, it seems, is that of every modern man—the sight of the so-called natural world, the natural earth, in full retreat, like watching the faint glimmer of an exhausted comet's tail. Time, like certain ranges of light, is not fully appreciated until it's spent, a mend of memory instead of reality's immediate ache. Which is another reason for my journeys here: to be closer still to the ghosts I willingly carry about of the old men I spent some of my boyhood with in the Ozark Mountains. The present is the past impacted, swelling moment by moment. Here my moments, all of them, are clear and fresh, energy, light, and wind, and every trout a reminder that I am, for better or worse, only what I choose to remember, what I choose to haul about.

There are several ways to walk into the Kilmer Forest and the Slickrock Wilderness. I like going, when the weather holds, by way of Big Fat Gap and the old Cheoah Lake Dam bridge. The Slickrock Wilderness offers anything but a genteel and accommodating character, which is one of the reasons why the place is so completely admirable. Well into these woods and a man is pretty much on his own.

The rain eased and sunlight threaded through thin clouds and I followed the sound of the rushing creek, refusing to worry about destinations. In the mountains, I am bound only as far as the next step, the next pool of sunlight, the next stretch of good trout water, the spreading woods, the edge of the immediate universe.

Come fall along Slickrock Creek, though, I do have a destination of a kind: a large pool near the old railroad grade. Here, each fall, a rendezvous takes place, an old one. For years now, every autumn, near this wide pool of dark water, I have met Roth Comers Tewksbury—financier, anguished lover, passionate angler, who loves the Slickrock Wilderness because it scares him to death.

"There's never anybody here," he said to me not long after our awkward first meeting. "No one. And listen." Which I did.

"No, I mean really listen," said Tewksbury. "There's nothing metallic in the air, nothing grating, oily, greasy, pounding, sucking, crunching. It's unnerving. It gives me the creeps. I can't stay away from it."

He had been coming to the Smokies and to the Slickrock, he said, for more than fifteen years. He came for two weeks in the fall and he fished for the creek's moody brown trout and at the end of each day hiked out and stayed in Robbinsville or up at Fontana or in Bryson City because, he told me shyly, "among my simple needs is that of a night-light. I'm spoiled, I suppose. Manhattan never turns off the juice. I need neon the way some men need tobacco."

I first saw Tewksbury in the fall of 1982. October had settled easily over the tangled rhododendron thickets above the creek, and the woods looked like a mad painter's mix of colors. So many leaves lay upon the creek that the water had about it the pink glow of salmon flesh. Coming up the trail from the mouth of the first falls, climbing over a precipice of slippery, gray-green stones mottled with blotches of gray lichen, I thought I glimpsed a man up on the old Babcock Lumber Company railroad grade, but thought nothing of it, dismissed it as just another thrilling marriage of shadow and light, forest and stone. But this shadow not only persisted, it grew, took on detail and shape. The closer I got to it, the more it took on the physical characteristics of Ichabod Crane: a body composed almost completely of vertical lines, ripple free, nearly, save the sudden outburst of nose and what appeared to be a perpetually vacillating Adam's apple, and disproportionately large feet ensconced in hip waders. All this was gathered not in one glance, but over several nervous minutes of observation, because the shadowy, stiltlike figure with the conspicuous nose, bobbing Adam's apple, and clown feet was at the time leaping desperately, violently, up and down on some object. Throwing his spindly arms up as if to gain ever more momentum, the figure all but launched himself into midair, uncoiling so that at the apex of his leap he was straight as a freshly ironed pleat; then, in an instant, in one revengeful motion, he drew up his knees and drove them onto whatever it was that had obviously driven him insane.

Cautiously, I walked on up the trail, quickly flipping through a mental file of the unspeakable horrors that might wait ahead. I had read the latest editions of both the Bryson City and Asheville papers just that morning and recalled no mention of escaped mental patients, disgruntled tourists, dyspeptic farmers, edgy lumbermen. There had been no mention, either, of any recent sightings of Arby Mulligan, a self-appointed minister who travels the mountains baptizing the unsaved, redeeming troubled souls. Unfortunately, few if any of Arby Mulligan's swelling flock were willing converts. Mulligan had a habit of simply grabbing hold of anyone he thought looked in need of God's mercy, dragging him to the nearest creek, and holding him under while he read the Twenty-third Psalm, slowly. Mulligan then hauled him up, gave him a faded white towel, kissed him on the cheek, and greeted him back into the family of God. But I knew Arby Mulligan, and the figure ahead looked nothing like him. I supposed that it could be just a man who liked to leap and hop his way along mountain streams. After all, trout streams can lead a man to bizarre outbursts of behavior. Then I saw that this tall, thin man with the black hip boots was leaping on what looked to be the remains of some kind of hat that had been reduced to several ragged, muddy, soggy lumps of cloth, most of them smalt green. And he leapt again and bounced furiously on the crumpled remains of the hat and began talking, yelling, howling—not at me, or himself, but at the hat.

"We had him, you faithless charm!" he said. His voice had the snap and power of a bark. "You traitor, blackguard, scum."

He stopped jumping, his small, concave chest palpitating wildly. He settled down, and when finally at rest he took on the smooth, almost graceful look of a ceremonial dagger.

Shedding the Dana pack, I sat down by a rotted bone-white trunk of a sycamore tree, poured a long, cool pull of root beer from my army canteen.

"Its crime?" I asked, nodding at the hat on the ground. The root beer fizzed in my blood, stung the walls of my arteries and veins.

By now the man had collapsed like a length of spent straw and sat coiled on the damp, green grass, still gasping for air. He grabbed a nearby day pack, began digging through it desperately, pulling out, at last, a battered gray-blue fedora.

"Scurrilous cap," he said. He pointed a shaky, bony index finger at the pummeled, crushed hat half buried in mud and trampled grass.

"Losing a trout like that. Such a fine brown it was, too. What good is a fellow's luck then, once the charm's faded?"

The hat's transgression, then, the one that did it in, was that it had lost its luck and with it a good-sized Slickrock brown trout.

"A noble fish," said the man across the small opening of woods, the man who looked like a bent knife-blade. The dew on the grass gave the soft reflected sunlight a smoky-blue cast. A cool wind came off the creek and moved through the deep woods.

I introduced myself and offered him some root beer.

He got up, hobbled tiredly toward me, giving the crushed hat one last kick.

He took the big, pea-green plastic canteen, its contents still cool, the last of the ice bought up at the Crossroads of Time grocery not yet completely melted, put it eagerly to his lips, then spit the contents on the grass.

"Chilled paregoric?" he asked. His face had the pinched look of a squeezed lemon.

"Root beer."

"Root beer?"

"I.B.C. root beer."

"Got anything harder, something with hair on it? Something like scotch or a handy bottle of vodka? That's V-O-D-K-A, the potato's sweet nectar."

"Just water and root beer and a packet of cherry-flavored Kool-Aid."

"Why couldn't I be rescued by some mountain alcoholic St. Bernard, a fifth of the local mash chained about its neck?" he said in a low voice, adding, "Okay, water, easy ice.

"The name's Tewksbury," he said, "Roth Comers Tewksbury." He extended his hand and I noticed how the skin was elastic-tight over the bones, and pallid.

He liked Melville, that I knew, because he kept saying he came from the great island of Manhattoes, which made him, he said, something of an escaped Manhatto. Back in Manhattan, he said, he was nailed to matters financial, clinched to a life sadly lacking in mountains or trout. He thought it was somewhat nutty that there he was on what is probably the most famous island on the planet, a spit of land that seems to shoulder mankind's every want, every desire, express his great greed, beauty, and brutality, the wide sea so near at hand, and yet he was tormented by these mountains and these trout. The sunlight reflected off his bright blue eyes was soft, a light full, I imagined, of telling memories.

"What's with the hat?" I asked at last.

The blue of Tewksbury's eyes deepened measurably.

"Had a brown on up the creek. Best fish I've hooked into in days. Put on that old green hat this morning. Luckiest hat I owned, or so I thought. The brown went deep, twisting among stones. I saw its dark jaws rising with the line, then it jerked its head once and broke the tippet. I would have had him if the damned hat hadn't gone sour."

He looked back at the remnants of the crumpled hat, shrugged his narrow, slightly bent shoulders.

"In its prime," he said, "it was a good hat." His words seemed caught up in a sigh of true regret. "It oozed good fortune. I could put it on in the morning and raise trout all day. Then it went bad."

"That is too bad," I said.

"Yes," he agreed, "it is too bad, even tragic." He poured himself another cup of water. "But they are something here, though, aren't they?"

"Who is?"

"The trout, the trout," he said. His voice went up and down with the spent and tonal range of a Wurlitzer. "Trout," he said again, his voice quickly dropping what seemed a full octave, giving it a sound like water working its way through clogged pipes. "Trout," he said again, his voice sounding more dismal still. "Trout . . . Can't we talk about something less upsetting, less controversial, like transubstantiation or the question of papal infallibility?"

Over his narrow shoulders, I could see the creek threading its way over a shoal of smooth stones, and I remembered how when I was a boy I used to imagine creeks as liquid scrolls, watery history moving through time, endings and beginnings, both forever ancient and immediate.

I noticed that Roth Comers Tewksbury had reflective eyes, sandy-blond hair, and sunken cheeks. He came from a good family, a family of means. His father was a stockbroker. They lived in comfort in midtown Manhattan. As Tewksbury says, "I have the world spread around me. Anything and everything a human being could want. Everything but trout and a good woman. I found a good woman on West Fifty-sixth and I come here for the trout. Call me contented."

Early in his life, Tewksbury evidently inherited his father's genius, turned into another financial magician just out of Harvard who made a fortune convincing investors that time really is money.

"Actually," he told me later, "the equation comes closer to their time turning into my money, which seems a fair exchange. The idle rich deserve a pastime, too, a hobby, and my financial future is as good a hobby as any, don't you think?"

I nodded.

We talked for so long I didn't notice that the sky had cleared and a soft, warm light was coming off the creek like a golden haze. Tewksbury took the rumpled fedora off, jammed it back into his day pack, retrieved a wool seaman's cap, pulled that down tight on his head.

I went on talking, tried to find out what Roth Comers Tewksbury did when he wasn't making a killing with other people's money. For one thing, he obviously collected hats. It wasn't that he especially liked hats or even enjoyed them, but they had become essential to his life as an angler. They were the repositories of luck.

"I've never hooked a fish while hatless," he said. The wind came up stronger. It had turned colder. He pulled the wool cap down tight over his ears.

"Never for me has there been a trout without a chapeau. Some anglers remember special rods or reels or fly patterns. With me it's hats. My angling memories are mostly bound up with beat-up clancy hats, bold sombreros, low-slung cowboy hats, practical slouch hats, salty wind-cutters and sou'westers, eloquent homburgs, bowlers, and derbies. It's a terrible affliction, I know, but there you have it. Sooner or later every man involved with trout ends up courting some superstition or another. Sometimes I wonder if I'm the only trout angler that is obsessed with charms."

He started breaking down his cane rod, shoving his gear into his day pack, suddenly, quickly.

"The daylight," he said, "it's going fast." A hint of panic marked his reedy voice. And I remembered about the night-light. It isn't that Roth Comers Tewksbury is afraid of the dark, he just doesn't trust it.

"So many things can go wrong in the dark," he said, "and usually do. People can disappear and never be heard of again. Where I come from, it happens all the time, starting right at sundown."

I've known Tewksbury for years now and for as long as I've known him, for as long as we have fished Slickrock Creek together, he has always fished so he can make it safely back to his avocado-green Range Rover before the belly of the mountain night settles in. I walk with him down the trail back toward where he left the truck. Often we walk in a heady mix of moonglow and deepening twilight. The creek hisses through a net of thick shadows. I always ask Tewksbury where he's staying. I think he likes Robbinsville best of all, especially since the Hardee's opened.

This is what he says about Robbinsville: "It's such a warm, comforting little night-light. From a distance it seems to just barely glow, like a light about to go out, like a dim forty-watt light bulb. Just enough light to keep the night at arm's length."

When he doesn't stay in Robbinsville, Tewksbury holes up at Fontana or over in some cheap motel room in Bryson City.

And what does Tewksbury do with his nights? How does he pass the time?

The one night I stayed with him, the night it rained ice and I decided to go into town, and he told me I could curl up in my sleeping bag in his room, he spent the hours fiddling with a small, portable shortwave radio, dialing far-off lands, enticing the world into room 10 of the Bryson City Motel, filling the place up with static and broken-voiced news reports of famine in Ethiopia, heartbreaking filth and disease in Pakistan, disappointment in Hungary, want in Poland, disillusionment in East Germany, depression and moodiness in Los Angeles, epidemic angst in New York City, an outbreak of flu in Hannibal, Missouri, a wife in Broome, Australia, who did her husband in with a heavy pot because he wouldn't powder after his morning shower. The radio spilled the war in Afghanistan on the room's cheap carpet, left it there like bloody stains. Our nighttime hours were filled with ballads from Ireland, touching Schlummerlieds from Bonn, West Germany, the "Old-time Gospel Hour" fading in and out of Jackson, Mississippi, madrigals from Tuscany, anthems from Moscow, chanteys from Britain, hot Paris jazz, and dirges from everywhere. Calypso rhythms from Tobago, the low-down blues from Memphis, hyperactive zydeco from the humid streets of New Orleans. Prayers and orations, atonement and amends filtered through radio waves from Rome and up the highway at Boone, North Carolina. There were offers of redemption, expiation, penance, purgation, and reparations from the followers of Buddha, Jesus Christ, the Christian Scientist Divine Mind, Allah, the Hindus' Brahma, the Supreme Soul, pleas for funds to pave the road to heaven from German Baptists, the Gideons, Erastians, Shintoists, Mormons, Lutherans, Zen Buddhists, Anabaptists, and the followers of Henry Cratis Duls and his followers, the Dulists, who evidently believed that God would take form in the kitchen of Duls's Iowa farmhouse just as soon as they collected $164,000 to pay off Duls's farm loans and get the place ready for the Second Coming. And Tewksbury would keep turning the dials, exposing the cramped little room to rattling earthquakes from Japan, mud slides from California, sweeping floods in India, fog and cold drizzle in London, balmy winds along the Aegean Sea, heavy, damp heat of Myanmar's jungles, the cool, fair skies of Montana and Wyoming, a pleasant cold front moving no faster than a breeze over the eastern Appalachians. Finding the world under a press of heavy weather always seems to upset Tewksbury and he turns the radio off, then the light in the room, but only after pulling the curtains wide and letting the faint streetlights of downtown Bryson City leak harmlessly into the room.

Before snuggling up to the shortwave radio, Tewksbury likes to have dinner at the Holiday Inn in Cherokee. I like to join him on buffet night—all you can eat for a reasonable price, and we always eat more than our fill of fried chicken and mashed potatoes with gravy, fresh lima beans, and glass after glass of unsweetened ice tea.

Not long ago, after going through the buffet line, our conversation swung from Tewksbury's increasingly tragic love for Carlotta, to our addiction to mountain trout. Between arguments on the behavior of trout and the nature of angling, we agreed on many things, particularly our deep obsession with these mountains and the highlanders who call it home. While the old mountain culture seems to hang on only deep in the mountains, the way some forms of life continue to survive only on islands of wildness completely isolated from the modern world, we agreed that the virtues of that culture, what made it strong, abiding, unique, still survive in many of the mountain people. As one old-timer told us at the Crossroads of Time grocery, "One good thing about progress in the mountains, gentlemen, is that it progresses slowly. Turtlelike. Mountain folks are naturally suspicious of change, especially prosperous change. Good times are mostly foreign to us up here."

Even while change and good times inch up the high country, the people, especially the old folks, hang on to what they know, a life bound by honesty, an almost inexhaustible self-reliance, unyielding independence, an unswerving devotion to God and family and their neighbors, and a nagging distrust of strangers—that is, any flatlander—a firm belief in themselves and their history, and a deep attachment for the land. The land is hard and thankless, but there is a bounty to it for the man who will bend his back and work for it.

"I been wrestling with these mountains more than sixty years," Letha Moss told Tewksbury one day on the main street of Bryson City, "and so far it's still a draw. I ain't broke them and they ain't broke me. I got me a house in a cool holler, a garden, a roof that don't leak, a warm bed. I got a neighbor up the hillside, which is too close, but I ain't complaining. And I've been dreaming of my wedding of late. Married in 1920, I was, to Garland Moss. You know, of course, that dreams are God's messenger. Old woman like me dreaming of a wedding means death's near. I'm so close to heaven's gate I can feel the cold gate-knob in my hand. Truly."

Letha Moss died the next year, the day after Tewksbury and I met at the trailhead into the Slickrock Wilderness. I had water boiling for tea when I heard him on the trail.

"Hi-ho," he called out cheerfully, and I turned and saw him standing against a wide oak tree. He was dressed in a faded-green smoking jacket, tweed pants, hip boots, and a tattered Stetson.

"You feel an iron gate swing wide this morning?" I asked.

"Miss Moss," he said. "She did tell us she had her hand on the gate didn't she? May she get some rest."

We had tea and apples and raisin bread and Tewksbury said, "When the gate swings wide for me, I hope these mountains are on the far side, and a little cabin with Carlotta waiting for me tenderly, gently pulling a hundred-dollar bill from my hand in that loving way of hers."

As he talked, Tewksbury animated his speech, punctuated his sentences with great sweeping gestures of his arms and hands so that he looked like some troubled creature trying frantically to take flight.

We cleaned up, packed, walked the trail until we came on a stretch of water we both liked, water rich in possibility. Tewksbury headed upstream, cane rod in hand. He believed graphite fly rods to be a serious transgression of angling ethics, as serious in magnitude as cutting serious bourbon with tapwater.

"Anyway," he explained, "I'm allergic to synthetics of any kind whether they be blended in my underwear or my fly rod. Dacron, polyester, nylon— all those things are a danger to my health, happiness, and peace of mind.

"Cane is an honest material, reliable. It is loyal in the same sense that a fine leather jacket is loyal. Both improve with the elements and passing time."

Tewksbury and the cane rod had been together many years. Once he admitted to me that actually the rod knew he was a pitiful trout angler and not suited for its great angling legacy, and yet it never tired of his company, the possibility that one day his skill might equal its craftsmanship.

He worked the rod well, though, that morning and every time I have fished with him. Though we were separated by 40 yards of water, Tewksbury, as is his habit, insisted on carrying on a conversation while we fished. Among his many angling tenets is this: the best way to get a trout's attention is to ignore it.

So he began to cast and work the current and eddies about the rocks upstream from him and to shout.

"Say, do you ever get to a place that is completely foreign to you and find that you are immediately at ease? You are suddenly filled with the eerie sensation that you fit into the place. That's the way it was with me here in these mountains. Like with Carlotta. Love at first sight. Here I am all instinct, no frills, just more wind and water. How odd, yes? A sense of belonging, nonetheless, rather than the feeling of being just another ball bearing in a ball-bearing factory. It's so silly, isn't it? How we grown men take up trout angling not simply to pursue trout but to find some place, some special place, where we feel at ease. A place to belong."

Roth Comers Tewksbury really talks that way. He has a European soul and the English he speaks is almost Elizabethan, rich and full and unafraid to court meaning. He talks constantly and without fear or reservation. One fall, years ago, while we were fishing the middle stretch of the creek, he yelled downstream to me, the words crackling among the trees like dead leaves rattling in the wind.

"I've joined a Manhattan chapter of Alcoholics Anonymous," he said. His voice boomed louder still. Another of his angling principles is that enough loud noise will sooner or later pique a trout's curiosity, get the brown trout off the bottom, out of the shadows, raise them, not with a great fly or a telling cast, but by sheer force of will.

He went on: "I know, I know. My drinking is social and modest, but this group is a fine group of people and a place to go on Tuesdays to talk to other troubled human beings. And if I ever feel like a drink, which is every evening, all I have to do is call and there's friendship and support on the line. An angler, you know, always like to have something on the line. Standing up and saying 'Hello, my name is Roth, and I'm an alcoholic' seemed like such an innocent and harmless little lie. As soon as I said it an older woman with brown eyes and Dresden-blue hair took my hand and told me not to worry and I didn't because she was there. And who knows, maybe I am a closet alcoholic just waiting for something to set me off, shove me toward that first inevitable double scotch for breakfast.

"It's nuts, isn't it, what lengths a man will go to share the company of another human being? The whole question of loneliness worries me, friend. It's the part of eternity that scares the hell out of me. The next time we see Arby Mulligan we should question him about loneliness and the hereafter. Why for chrissakes is life so short and confusing and why is eternity forever and cold and lonely?"

Then the steady yell turned instantly to a glorious scream.

"Ha! Got the bastard!" He had taken another handsome Slickrock Creek brown, well over two pounds.

That was the day we stopped fishing at noon and settled down along the creek and ate Spam and saltines and drank cool water and Tewksbury told me as he wiped down the cane rod with a freshly pressed white handkerchief that he really didn't think he was much good at life, at least in Manhattan, where the great press of humanity so easily and totally ignored him. The mountains and the creek, though, did not judge him at all and the lights of Bryson City and Robbinsville were soft and warm, almost compassionate. This is Tewksbury's sobriquet for the Smoky Mountains: "They are my Blue Himalayas. My lovely smoky-blue Nepal."

We sat on the cool ground near the creek and ate and he talked in a hush, as though he were telling great secrets. He told me he wasn't as happy as he looked. And I said to him, who is, Tewksbury, who is? He confessed that he worried a great deal. What better place for a man and his troubles than the mountains, feeling the pull of a cold mountain stream, the possibility of trout? He napped for a time there by the creek and Tewksbury, I thought, looked like a great question mark lying there in the grass, a man bent over by worry and doubt, a good man, kind and lonely, and deeply afraid of the dark.

And I lay down, too, after washing out the cups and packing them away. I lay my head against the backpack and felt the cool October sun on my face. The chemicals that are me enjoy the sunlight, this mountain world of plants, of so much greenery, this world free of bone and muscle and nerves, this world of chlorophyll, process and tendencies and altitude.

We slept until midafternoon and felt good when we woke rather than guilty or angry that we had let an afternoon slip away without squeezing a profit from it.

This is what Tewksbury said from under the deep blue derby he had pulled down over his eyes, "Sometimes up here I'll go into a sleep where I think I have fallen through myself and the feeling is absolute ecstasy and I never want to come back, never want to resurface, come crawling back to consciousness."

His voice sounded as sad and distant as a trio of violas. Yes, I told him, sleep in the mountains is good and sound, restful and welcome. He whispered that he had a dream that came to him only in the mountains, a simple dream of landscape and form, of sounds and beauty.

"I told my psychologist about it, asked what it might all mean. Are you ready for this? He told me it was a message from my genius. The message was, invest in the work of American landscape painters. The psychologist did and made a killing. But I think there's more to it. This is what I think the dream means—that what is important on Wall Street doesn't count for diddly here. I can't buy, trade, finagle, or finance a mountain trout onto my hook. That's nice."

"Yes," I said, "that is nice."

And we fished until the daylight began to recede up along the dark ridges of the Smoky Mountains and Tewksbury reeled in his line, wiped off his rod, slipped on his green smoking jacket, and walked down the darkening trail toward his truck, back toward his small motel room and the crackling static of the shortwave radio and the small handful of lights in Bryson City that burned through the night giving off a hazy glow like candlelight from behind thick windows. An hour after the last streaks of light had gone out of the sky, I walked along the trail to the campsite and the darkness was soft and damp as wet velvet.

I look forward to each fall, to my time on the Slickrock, to my time with Tewksbury. He is a fine talker and I am a good listener. Sometimes as we wade the creek and talk and fish and the light is just right and the wind is cool and soft, I find it hard to tell where we end and the creek and the mountains begin. The rushing water carries the sweep of time, mingling past and present and future, and every moment is a lifetime. And Tewksbury will stand up straight in a fine riffle of moss-green water and yell out, "Welcome to the Enchanted Forest. Enter and please behave. Be good, be kind. Leave things as they are. For my sake, because there are so few places like this left."

He says the words full and round, like a speech from a play, like a grand soliloquy. Conversation gives a certain rhythm to Tewksbury's casting, a smooth cadence, an unaffected grace. He handles the old cane rod with more joy than reverence, working his long leader and tippet effortlessly, dropping his dry fly on the surface of the creek as naturally as though it were some bit of spiderwebbing that has suddenly fallen from the air. Indeed, the rod often tempers his words and ideas the same way a conductor's baton qualifies an orchestra's every sound.

Once, after three days on the creek, when we had finally worked our way past Wildcat Branch, Tewksbury, who had already taken seven good brown trout over the three days, told me that mountains provide the perfect climate for philosophy. Mountain light, he said, engages the mind. Just then he hooked another trout and it took line and made a mad run downstream for a pile of rocks and sunken limbs, and Tewksbury went to his reel and finished his thought, saying that thankfully trout tended to neutralize an angler's attraction for the abstract. Indeed. For the whole two weeks the trout of Slickrock Creek kept him so busy that he had no great repository of thoughts at all, much less deep ones. I stood by the green Range Rover as he packed it up. He slid in, rolled down the window, and said this: "About all I know for sure is this, friend. There is nothing thicker than an atom's waist between isolation and wisdom and isolation and madness." Maybe, maybe not. There is a certain purity to the isolation of these mountains, though, something hard and true rather than merely symbolic. Tewksbury got in the Range Rover, drove off, I went back to camp, crawled into my sleeping bag, and listened to the trill of the creek and felt the earth hard against my back.

It is hard not to admire Tewksbury, to wander cheerfully between the wide latitudes of his humor and humanity. Some men simply fit their geography, but he complains of feeling limited, even somehow deformed by the press of the city, and for two weeks each year he lets go, comes here, and fits these mountains and streams and coves as though he has known no other place.

Walking back to his truck that night, he turned, grabbed my arm, said, "Here I am full and round and true. Nothing more or less. Here I am fact rather than parenthesis."

Sometimes I think I know what he means—that feeling of genuine solace rather than purchased adventure, negotiated thrills, the illusory romance so often pinned to wildness and wilderness. The Smoky Mountains hold fast to their character, unbroken, still apart from our desperate want of a great American generic landscape, a common natural nostalgia, the stuff of murals, postcards, and nature films. Life holds fast here. It rattles noisily on every wind, on every cascade of tumbling water.

Tewksbury and I agree on this: it is important that sometime in a man's life he get to know a place, become bound up in a special piece of geography. Such a place need not be vast, exotic, brutally wild. It need only be a place that increases him, nourishes him. For us, the Smoky Mountains are such a place, and their geography of ridge and gorge, hollow and cove, roaring streams, shadowed forests, fickle trout abide in us as much as we abide in them. We carry the mountains with us, as we do the range of light that falls on them, and the press of the seasons upon them. Just coming here, making our yearly journey, arriving with pack and rod rather than bulldozer and chain saw is our contribution, a small act of defiance, of anarchy, two votes against the trend toward development, the loss of yet another piece of unique geography. It is our way of renewing our bond with this place, this smoky-blue land of cold rivers, shadow-filled forests, and belligerent trout.

Tewksbury believes mountains broaden his definition and his possibilities. It is because they defy measure themselves. Life wrinkles in leaf and stone and water, is brutal as well as beautiful. What these mountains are not is the image of just more and more public recreation and entertainment. The experience of mountains cannot be bought, it can only be lived, a lasting tie of blood and bone, a fever that once contracted cannot be cured, a sensation along the spine that endures long after the transitory adrenaline high of packaged thrills and advertised adventures.

"It is important to be from someplace," Tewksbury said to me on the trail along the creek at sundown, the light in the sky a wash of soft reds and the wind a reedy rattle in the trees. "I mean I love New York. It's the world crammed onto my island. Everything a man could want within walking distance. There, everything I could want. Here, everything I need. I am fortunate that I can call both home and mean it."

A man becomes an environmentalist when the issues of development and pollution, destruction and exploitation, threaten his geography, his home, the land that defines him, when it all becomes more than a matter of economics and politics. The city sustains Tewksbury. Cities sustain me as well. But I know what he means. My nourishment is here, here in this high country, along these cold, fast streams. Here in these highlands that refuse to be broken, I am reminded each time I gain a commanding ridge and look in any direction of mankind's apparently ruthless and unlimited appetite to alter, rearrange, ruin, even destroy his environment for the most picayune economic and political gains.

How does a man save a special piece of land, a stretch of landscape still touched by wildness? By becoming part of it, knowing it, letting it get under his skin, completely. By refusing to ignore it or turn his back on its beauty and solitude and what its wildness means to his well-being, the enrichment not only of his life but of the lives of others. "When I'm old," says Tewksbury, "I want to remember this, all of this. Above all, these mountains and their streams and their trout, every sensation, every shadow, every sound. These days. Always, I want to remember these days."

Tewksbury loves mountains and mountain trout. He also loves Carlotta. He mentioned her name for years before he told me much about her. We were fishing a fine run of Slickrock Creek and he turned toward me and said, "She introduced herself to me as St. Dympna."

I was rigging up my rod, fumbling with line and flies.

"Who did?"

"She did," he said.

"She who?" I asked.

"Carlotta," he said.

"And she's a saint?" I asked. Conversations with Tewksbury are like rubbing prayer beads, you never know what the next one will bring. Numbing surprise is possible at any moment.

"Well," he said, "she does take contributions and perform miracles, at least for me." There was a coyness to the words and a tinge of true excitement. "By the way, the miracles are fifty dollars to a hundred dollars and are worth every penny."

Sunlight broke full and hard through the thinly layered clouds. Tewksbury has luck the way shills have luck, that is, he seems to manufacture his own which keeps pouring into his bloodstream. In a moment's time, he had a trout on and, to celebrate, he let loose a long string of rhymes by distinguished dead poets, rhymes he peppered with his own verse, giving them new meanings, meanings that were as inviolate as Saturn's rings. Finally, he muttered something I understood, something about angling putting a man face-to-face with the great lie of invincibility.

"She's as perfect as sleep," he said.

"Who is?"

"Why, Carlotta," he said. He seemed irritated that I had forgotten about her so quickly and didn't mention her again until the next morning when we met along U.S. Forest Road 416 near the Horse Cove campground. We drove up to Jenkins grocery and loaded up on chili, tea, cheese, and crackers. By midmorning we were on the trail, already past Ike Branch, deep in woods thick with poplar and sweet-smelling hemlock, birch, and copper-red maples. I was curious about Carlotta. Who wouldn't be?

"You might as well have asked me to describe the contents of an empty box," he said. He took the small stove out of my pack, added fuel, lit it. A trout broke the surface of the creek in a wide pool above us: just a shallow dimple in the calm water betrayed its presence.

"Sí, da," Tewksbury said. "Sí, da."

"See the what?" I asked. I watched the surface of the pool, wanting desperately to see the trout's shadow, the girth of it. It would be, I imagined from the splash, as long and as thick as an anvil head.

"Sí, da," Tewksbury said. "Sí, da."

"For chrissakes, see the what!?" I asked.

"That's what I wanted to know," Tewksbury said. His words were heavy with unresolved exasperation.

"That's what she kept screaming in my ear the first night I met her at Five eleven West Fifty-sixth Street, Apartment Five. Appointments only. All major credit cards accepted. The headquarters of the Apache Massage Service. They put you in a dark room. You're supposed to whoop when you're ready. Afterward, you have to whoop again to get out. The place sounds like an aviary of tropical birds in great distress.

"I was directed to one of the rooms. There was what looked like a hospital gurney fitted with satin sheets. I lay down. I had a white towel tied loosely about my waist. The bed was on wheels. No lights except the warm red glow of a stereo's dials and the undulating, thick viscid red liquid of twin lava lamps. Bob Dylan on the stereo groaning out 'The Times They Are A-Changing,' and the air conditioner rattling like mucus-filled lungs and the whole place smelling of baby oil and Tabu.

"She appeared suddenly at the door, a soft shadow. She seemed to glide over the floor, hips in sync with the lava lamps. She took the folded hundred-dollar bill tenderly from my hand.

"It was love at first sight."

The wind had changed, blew now out of the south and east, and it smelled like rain. Clouds hung low over the creek, moved listlessly as though they were great ships dragging heavy anchor chain. Brown trout delight in dull light. It is the world they prefer—a world of opaque shadows and easy hunting.

"Sí, da," said Tewksbury.

"I did see it," I said, "and a good trout it is, too."

"No, not the damned trout," said Tewksbury, "Carlotta. That's what she kept screaming in my ear. I started seeing her twice a week."

Tewksbury kept going back because he loved her tragically and because he had no idea what she was talking about each time she yelled out in undiluted passion, "Sí, da."

"I couldn't figure it," said Tewksbury. "See the what? See the what? I was going nuts. Was it the way the gurney rolled about the room like a marble in a can each time we made love? Was it how the rhythm of the lava lamps changed so that the liquid sloshed about chaotically like seas in a storm? Or how the lights of Times Square peaked shamelessly through the apartment window?

"'Sí, da,' she kept yelling, and I went on looking until at last I saw it on the ceiling."

Silence. Tewksbury calmly took up his rod, tied a plump, dark, rumpled-looking streamer to his tippet using a sturdy Duncan's loop.

I thought of strangling him, but then I'd never know what he had finally seen.

"Okay, I'm good and hooked, Tewksbury," I said. "Tell me."

"Tell you what?" he asked. His face drooped, had the look about it of absolute ignorance.

I could feel the blood rushing in mine, pounding violently at my temples.

"About the ceiling, Tewksbury, you madman. About Carlotta's goddamned ceiling!"

"Oh," he said, "it was shadows. Sleek, thin, mysterious shadows flashing madly about on the ceiling. I didn't know what to make of them. They evoked so many images. At first, they seemed like ragged pieces of storm clouds caught in heavy wind. Then they seemed to look like the silhouettes of trout, dozens of them, spooked and making some demented run, and they were dark, charcoal-looking, and caught in a black sea. It was something."

Tewksbury drew back his rod, checked his line, the streamer.

"Of course they weren't clouds or trout at all, those shadows. Those hump-backed shadows were me and Carlotta and the dark room was our stormy sea, so to speak."

"That's what she meant, then?" I said. "That's what she'd been trying to tell you all along?" I tried to imagine Tewksbury and this strange and wonderful Carlotta, and the gurney with silk sheets, and the apartment and the lava lamps and the Dylan music, and Carlotta yelling 'Sí, da' in Tewksbury's ear. "So that's what she meant . . . the ceiling?"

"That's what who meant?" said Tewksbury. His eyes were wide and fixed almost hypnotically on the upstream edge of the pool, where the creek dropped over a wide shoal of stones. Beneath the overhanging trees, the water took on a beautiful deep blue-green color.

The thought of strangling Tewksbury seemed more attractive than ever.

"CARLOTTA!" I screamed in frantic desperation. "CARLOTTA, every time she yelled 'sí, da,' 'sí, da.'"

"Oh, that," said Tewksbury calmly, looking completely inexcitable. "It's so easy you'll laugh. I knew as soon as I found out her name, Carlotta Raynoskva. Half-Spanish and half-Russian. Sí, da. There, you have it. Spanish for yes, Russian for yes. That's what she kept saying to me night after night, week after week, every time I asked if I could see her again. Passion with a tongue half-Russian, half-Spanish. Carlotta Raynoskva. That was the same night I first noticed the shadows on the ceiling, the dark fish in a black sea. 'Sí, da,' I cried out, 'sí, DA!'

"And you know what my wonderful Carlotta said? 'See the what, my pale white amigo? See the what?' as she tenderly put the hundred-dollar bill safely away in her blazing red kimono.

"I tell you, friend, it takes a special kind of woman to fathom the depths of a man's passion, apathy, and loneliness for a paltry hundred dollars.

"And I said to her, 'I love you.' And she replied, 'I know. I know.'"

Days later, before we left, Tewksbury showed me a photograph of Carlotta Raynoskva. Black hair, cut short, practical yet not without flair and beauty; wide black eyes, a black that seemed impenetrable; cream-colored skin and thin lips pinched reluctantly in a slight smile that gave nothing of her away to the camera's lens. About her supple neck she wore a simple gold chain and an unpretentious gold cross. But it was the eyes and their haunting dark geography that held you, watched you, enveloped you.

I handed the photograph back. Tewksbury was all packed, ready to go. It was an hour before full daylight and I watched the Range Rover disappear down the mountain road.

The Smokies looked blue in the fading moonlight and I picked up my pack and fly rod and walked into the cool, dark woods, and could only hear the sound of my footsteps and the rush of the creek and in that fast water the echo of a wildness. And my own laughter, too, because when Tewksbury stuck his head out of the truck and waved, yelled good-bye, this is all I could think to say—"Sí, da, amigo, sí, da!"

Mountain Stones

SOUTHERN APPALACHIA COVERS millions of acres from upland Georgia to the Virginia high country. The burly, vast national forests, dark and deep, that cover so much of these rugged highlands account for much of the region's down-and-out beauty and rich biological diversity. Although these great woods are called national forests, in the recent past rarely have they been managed with only the public good and the public interest in mind. Rather they have been managed for their resources, as though they were mere holding areas for a wealth of lumber and minerals and wild game. Despite the immensity of the Great Smoky Mountains National Park and the southern highlands, as of 1988 the whole region had but 300,000 acres of designated protected and preserved wilderness area, barely 9 percent of the region's remaining wild lands. Recent plans drawn up by the National Park Service and the U.S. Forest Service call for only an additional 30,000 acres of wilderness lands for the entire range of the southern highlands, even though use of this mountain country is up over the last decade by more than 400 percent. And while fewer wilderness tracts are being set aside in the southern mountains, more and more of their forests are being tagged for road construction and logging. By 2030 another 3,000 miles of roads will be cut through the high country as logging in the great southern national forests increases by 350 percent.

For too long our national forests have been managed resources rather than habitats and environments that we have committed to manage wisely, intelligently. We have tried and too often failed to manage and control the nation's remnant wild places as tidy units, thinking we can somehow separate forest from the mountains it covers, streams from the valleys they flow through. Isolating wild habitats severely often means the end of diversity, a loss of richness and bounty. What we need is a new awareness of the integrity of the natural world and its biological diversity, an understanding of the interdependence and interconnectedness of life, of all things. The distance between mountain boulder and the seashore's grain of sand is but a fleck of time. There is an urgent need for the sensible protection and management of wildness as well as wilderness, all manner of diverse habitats taken as a whole rather than isolated bits of nature that we fence off as though they are murals in some stunning gallery of art, places we make into solemn and solitary symbols of the earth's wild past. Even the wildest lands, if so managed, would soon enough lose whatever is unique and special about them, and their great diversity of life would quickly wither and crumble toward extinction. There needs to be a wiser and more intelligent approach toward managing public lands, an approach that favors the land more than it favors we who do the managing.

Of course, it could be said that all of this is only selfishness on my part. This is what I'm trying to say about the southern highlands, about such places as the Chattahoochee, Cherokee, Pisgah, and the Nantahala national forests: More. More wilderness. More wildness. Fewer roads, fewer logs. More acreage for the Southern Nantahala Wilderness and the Sampson Mountain Wilderness, the Kilmer Memorial Forest and the Slickrock Wilderness, more wilderness everywhere, in the park and in the national forests. More wilderness and less of everything else we can do so easily and comfortably without. It's not yet a matter of life and death, I suppose, except for the forests and the mountains, the streams and the trout, all the creatures whose lives depend on the mountains, including nervous trout anglers like me who find solace in the high country, a sense of place, a land that defines not only where they are but who they are.

Much is at stake in these mountains, a whirlwind of life so rich that it makes Appalachia one of the earth's most important remaining international biosphere reserves. Life here is not only more intense and bountiful than we know, it is more intricate and profound and fecund than we can perhaps imagine. So much is at stake, and all hanging on in these mountains that embrace at least six different environments from shadowy hardwood coves to the hard, cold, windy reaches of the high Canadian spruce forests above 5,000 feet.

There are seventy species of fish in the hundreds of miles of cold-water creeks and streams that cascade through the southern highlands, through the park's nearly 800 square miles. Down among the lattice of shadow and light that flickers across the face of the creeks grow the lush fern falls—tangles of maidenhair, cinnamon, the yellow-throated New York fern, the elegant Christmas fern, and the shy rattlesnake fern, and on the trunks and limbs of trees bold colonies of resurrection fern.

A man I know in Robbinsville calls resurrection fern revival fern. He says, "It don't never die all the way and then rise up again, it just loses a little faith when the cold weather comes. A little warm sunshine revives it again right quick. It's like a wayward soul that's been revived."

Revival fern. I like that.

Come spring I see plenty of revival going on up along Hazel Creek and Forney Creek and Snowbird Creek, and over on Abrams Creek and Twenty Mile Creek, and so many others. As the trout rise so, it seems, do little rushes of fire pinks, and pungent alumroot, stately Solomon's seal, and the shy jack-in-the-pulpit, and tiny bluets among the stones at higher altitudes, blooming out of dark cracks of black and gray rocks, looking like captured shards of summer sky.

I am not on a first-name basis with all seventy species of fish found in these mountain streams. For as long as I can remember one family alone, trout, *Salmonidae*, has held my complete attention, haunted me and de-lighted me, been the stuff of nightmare and dream, even hauled me on oc-casion to the rim of the universe. Trout are moody, complex, irascible creatures, a large family of five groups spread over three subfamilies, none of which get along with or particularly like each other, except as a potential meal. Discussion of *Salmonidae* usually include char, Atlantic and Pacific salmon, graylings, and whitefish.

This is a lot of fish and almost all of them get under my skin or leave it trembling, as though exposed to a sudden wash of icy water.

Rainbow trout (*Salmo gairdneri*) have been in Southern Appalachian streams since at least the 1930s. Anglers began introducing them into Smoky Mountain creeks and streams in the 1920s, maybe even earlier. Rainbow trout are western trout—hearty, tenacious, elusive, and adaptable. Like most trout, they are vicious and unrelenting. Although they have been stocked in most of the world's prime trout waters, the rainbow's natural range runs roughly from the high country of northern Mexico northward through California's mountain country, and on into the Aleutian Islands, Alaska, and into Russia, where it is known as the Kamchatka trout.

Rainbows are wary, suspicious, and dyspeptic, all common traits among trout. They range widely, refusing to give in to trend, fashion, or any form of piscatorial conformity. They eschew the predictable. If human they would be carnival hucksters, bootleggers, acrobats, and skilled flimflam artists.

Lake rainbow trout rarely sport the dramatic coloring or spotted decoration of stream rainbows. Indeed, lake rainbows often flash dark greens and blues and highly polished silvers. In fast mountain water, rainbows take hold of an entirely different ensemble that features heavily spotted bodies. The spots are actually random, irregular dark blotches, moldy-black. They are also found on the tail and fins. The rainbow trout takes its name from its colorful lateral bands that can be anything from bruised salmon red to cinnabar, strawberry, rubiate, or shiny chrome red. These neon swaths of red are flashed only by mature rainbows. Unlike its cousin, the cutthroat trout, another rowdy western member of the *Salmo* clan, the rainbow has no hyroid teeth (teeth found at the back of the tongue). If time permits and if there is interest enough and you're in a counting mood, there are twelve rays on a rainbow's anal fin. If you come up with thirteen or more you are in possession of a Pacific salmon.

Large or small, rainbow trout are aggressive and rapacious. I have heard of rainbow trout taken out of pristine lakes in Canada's British Columbia that weigh fifty pounds. Some fish. The rainbows in the trout streams I fish are minnows compared to this, averaging only a pound or two. In the Smokies a five- or six-pound rainbow is a fish of legend, an angler's totem, his haunting Moby Dick, a great and noble fish, equal in character at least to its Canadian relations. Like all trout, rainbows do best in cool, clean water that ranges in temperature from freezing to perhaps 75 degrees, with the most agreeable temperatures being between the mid-50s and perhaps 65 degrees. Rainbows are, for fish, rather long-lived, a trait trout anglers ascribe to their completely disagreeable temperament. Indeed, rainbows have been known to outlive the anglers who pursue them. This is because stress and self-esteem and image and things like that mean absolutely nothing to a trout.

According to the National Park Service, there are no steelhead trout in the Smoky Mountains, which leads to some confusion over exactly what to call the big silver trout anglers pull out of some of the park's mountain lakes each fall. I came across a fisherman not long ago who had laid two of these suspicious-looking bluish-steel-colored trout up along the bank of Lake Cheoah.

"Steelhead?" I asked.

He gave me a wary stare, walked slowly and carefully all around me, looked up and down the shore of the lake.

"Ain't no such fish hereabouts," he said. His voice had the firm authority of a slammed door.

"Sure looks like steelhead," I said.

"Naw, just a couple of ol' trash fish. Hard-luck bass with a bad sickness. Use 'em for fertilizer. Everybody knows there ain't no steely-head trout in these parts."

He took his big spinning rod and threw a long cast out over the dark lake water.

"Where is it, fellah, by the way?" he asked.

"Where's what?"

"The wire," he said.

"Wire?"

"You're one of them park boys, ain'tchya? All wired up to record me saying something about steelhead. Well the only steely-headed thing I knows of around here was old man Cratis Hensley who used to have a place down past the Beaver Creek Church. My daddy told me the top of Mr. Hensley's skull was a piece of quarter-inch steel. Rustproof stuff. Kept his mind from a-wanderin'. My daddy told me that a German grenade bounced off Mr. Hensley's helmet and exploded, giving his head a skylight. Mr. Hensley was somethin'. On Sundays, up at the churchyard, he would play the spoons on his noggin. Two big ol' metal servin' spoons they was. He played hymns that came out soundin' like the crack and crackle of lightning hitting a tin roof.

"Cratis Hensley. He was the only steely-headed living thing I ever knew of around here. Really."

Whereas the rainbow trout moves about with a certain boldness and flare, pulsating like dull-red neon in soft ranges of mountain light as it rises and strikes violently, viciously, at its prey, the brown trout is a good deal moodier in temperament, an altogether more introspective trout.

Browns are fairly recent immigrants, having arrived in North America in the early 1880s and thriving in this continent's trout waters ever since. Actually, two distinct families of browns arrived along the East Coast within a year of each other. In 1883 brown trout eggs from Germany (von Behr trout) were shipped to a fish hatchery in New York and later released, while in 1884–85, brown trout from Scotland (Loch Leven browns) arrived and were also released. Few trout anglers noted or cared much for the details of which brown was which. All they knew was that there was a new and especially moody trout slashing at their lures, one big and brown, mean and beautiful.

The brown's native range is from the Mediterranean basin and the Black Sea on north through Norway and Siberia. While they sometimes appear lethargic and dim-witted, they are in truth ingenious fish that have adapted well to trout waters around the globe from New Zealand to South America and Africa.

As for water temperature, the brown is Siberian in taste. It thrives in colder waters. As the water warms, it becomes melancholy, dives deeper in search of colder pockets and currents, lies in dark, deep shady pools where sunlight manages to warm only the surface of the water. Browns avoid direct sunlight and its detailed shadows, preferring instead to move about at dusk and at night or under cover of dark, thick clouds, somber days, rain-filled days, times when the light is dull and uncertain, opaque, as though the creek were one dark pool with a finish like boot black.

Browns are usually more democratic than other trout, at least in their eating and living habits. They tend to adapt and accept a wider range of environmental changes than other trout. Like their brethren, they are carnivorous and will eat just about anything they can catch.

In a family of truly handsome fish, the brown's beauty is dark, almost mercurial, an ironic beauty that is at once muted and splashed with touches of brilliant color. There are deep black, bulbous eyes set high on a head often as blunt as a stump. In body, browns are long and stout, with the dorsal fin delicately marked by between ten and thirteen unobtrusive rays and the anal fin by nine or ten. As with the rainbow, the brown's coloring is various, often changing dramatically, depending on the environment it inhabits. The most common color is a warm honey-brown body with large bronze, dun-brown, or ebony-black spots along its back, flanks, and dorsal fin, ragged spots that flash in the light, almost glow. The larger spots seem to radiate a halo of darker colors, faded golds and sober browns and blacks, which make the fish look as though it has been dragged through a slime of brooding color and light. Along the brown's sides are more spots, often irregular, of red or olive-yellow or mellow orange, explosions of colors like old stars bursting in the melanotic darkness of space, colors so sudden that they seem pure and perfect. These same starbursts of crimson and burnt orange mark the brown's dorsal and adipose fins, fringe the upper back, and seem to slide like thick runs of paint along the spine. The backs of the browns up on Slickrock Creek are the deep red of old blood, blood clotted about a wound. Often I have taken Slickrock browns that even have a smear of shallow red on their bellies, but commonly the belly of a brown is jaundice or fallow-yellow, though I have seen many Smoky Mountain brown trout whose bellies were white as the smooth gut of an oyster shell. Shades of yellow also fleck the edges of a brown's venal, anal, and pectoral fins.

Browns are persistent hunters, skilled predators, and well equipped for killing with double zigzagging rows of vomerine teeth. The only other North American trout to pack such hardware is the landlocked salmon, and even its dentistry is not quite so impressive as that of the brown trout. Brown trout are patient, obdurate, intransigent, brutish, explosive, and, when striking, mercifully quick. In high country streams, browns feed mostly on insects, both aquatic and terrestrial, as well as on crawfish, even small birds and rodents, should they fall into the water. Browns delight in swarms of stone flies, caddis flies, and mayflies and will gorge themselves shamelessly, even gulping down an occasional relative, especially a competitive brother or sister.

When it comes to tales and stories of size, browns are the stuff of legend as well as fact. Some of these piscine potbellies can easily tip the scales at thirty pounds or more. At any weight, though, they are leviathans, fierce paunchy behemoths that strike out of hell's own darkness, bending your rod down on itself and threatening to drag you down into the cold water, down under some cold dark stone while chewing on your fly with a grizzled, primeval smile, their eyes as cold and black as the sprawl of the universe. The rainbow leaps—a gymnast arched between water and sky, glinting silver, its bowed back dingy green—but the brown dives deep, down where the light fades, breaks up, dissolves, down where darkness knows no definition, a topography of blackness where it twists and turns as though the dark had an edge sharp enough to cut the nagging line, dislodge the pinching hook.

Browns started showing up in the southern highlands about 1900. While rainbow trout of say a foot to eighteen inches are considered fish of character and respect, especially in the national park's trout waters, browns, by comparison, can grow to mammoth size. I have heard stories of twenty-pound browns, as well as the reverent, almost biblical tale of the sixteen-pound brown caught in park waters, where browns started showing up in numbers in the early 1960s. Browns of two to four pounds can be common, and on one raw October day on the upper reaches of Slickrock Creek I took and released a brown the color of dull copper that went over eight pounds. I remember telling Tewksbury about the fish.

He stepped closer toward me, looking down into my eyes. His Adam's apple twitched nervously. He had on a gray basque shirt, a blue-and-white cardigan sweater, tan riding pants, and high-topped leather boots, a black seaman's jacket, and a red Balmoral cap. I noticed his eyes were laced with motes of morning light, tiny starbursts spreading slowly as quicksilver across his cornea.

"And just how'd you know this guy weighed eight pounds? Sure it wasn't maybe seven or nine?" He threw the question down like an inquisition, a gauntlet.

I shrugged my shoulders. "It felt like eight pounds or so," I said.

Tewksbury smiled. "It's hard to argue with such precision. Sounds like a valid weigh-in to me," he said. "An eight-pounder it was, then."

That afternoon Tewksbury took a nine-inch rainbow farther down the creek, scooped the small trout up with his landing net, called me near. He said, "The bastard's small but chunky. Feels like all of six pounds to me." And he sunk the net back down into the cold, fast current, and the rainbow slipped out, moving toward an arch of black stones and deeper water, and all the time Tewksbury was laughing long and hard.

Most rainbows spawn in the spring. Browns spawn in the fall, when the water is constantly cool and the light is flat and shadows are deep. Fall is the time for browns, at least for me. Fall, as brittle leaves fill the wind and the light is thin and faded and the browns are edgy and temperamental and completely absorbing, like the season itself.

Rainbow and brown trout—both outsiders—now dominate the trout streams of the southern highlands. As recently as the early 1900s there was only one trout in these high country waters—*Salvelinus fontinalis*, the brook trout. Mountain people call them "specs" because of their brilliantly speckled and mottled backs. Actually, the skittish brook trout is not a true trout at all. It is properly a member of the char family, whose differences from true trout are mostly skeletal, though there are also some differences in arrangement of teeth and scale patterns. Perhaps the most apparent difference and the most pleasing, though, is that of color and character.

Char, as a family, are somber and have an almost funereal coloring upon which there is a breathtaking and chaotic display of spots that are much brighter in color. It is a color scheme exactly the opposite of the rainbows and browns where darker spots or stripes are seen against lighter-colored bodies.

When rising, its back in the light, a brook trout seems to flash a gallery of shallow scars across the length of its back. In full light these marks are wide, often honey-colored, sometimes pale yellow, a color which makes them look like tunnels of light isolated in a black world. Wrinkles of trapped sunlight. A friend of mine who never gets enough of specs likes to believe these twisted markings are the remnants of some lost evolutionary map, turnings of the seasons and years, the inexorable movement of water. Time endlessly passing. Another angler I know, a man with a more practical turn of mind, scoffs at such nonsense.

"It's nothing but fish camouflage," he says. His voice is firm and doubtless. "Nothing but."

It's hard to take sides, especially when watching a brook trout rise in cold water, the light settling in those wormlike tracks across its black back, making them look like tiny islands of light rising on some dark sea, islands of light rising up out of the cold, fast water. Rising.

Brook trout are the southern highlands' only native trout, although the rainbows and browns have been in these waters so long it is hard to think of them as anything but family, lives that fit the mountains. But the introduction of the rainbow and brown trout, the drastic loss of habitat caused by logging, and the press of civilization have all tended to press and push the specs, where they survive, higher and higher, up above the fall lines, deep in chilly shadows and cold water.

The brook trout is, like so much that now holds on in the Smokies and Appalachia, a survivor of the last great Ice Age. As glaciers inched down across Canada, what was not trapped or what could not adapt to the cooling climate fled the grinding ice and cold. Even though it is believed that the brook trout was at one time an ocean species that thrived in arctic waters, it too moved south and eventually migrated inland, into the temperate waters of coastal rivers. Later, as the earth once again warmed and as the ice sheets melted, shriveled, and pulled back, many species such as the brook trout were cut off, left to adapt or vanish. The brook trout survived by moving up the rivers into the colder waters of mountain streams where it flourished on crawfish and minnows and an abundant supply of insects.

And the brook trout thrived until the loggers came, until the streams were stocked with rainbow and brown trout. Pressed by new competition from man and other trout, the brook trout fled, moved higher and higher. Trout find it difficult to tolerate each other's presence, especially in smaller streams and rivers. Trout are bullies. Rainbows will press and drive off specs, just as sooner or later the big browns will press and drive off the rainbows. Not too many years ago a rumor spread through the high country like the windblown fog that fills every valley, cove, and hollow. The rumor was that the Park Service, in a sudden fit of creative management, was actually considering poisoning the streams of the Great Smoky Mountains National Park in an effort to rid the park's trout waters of renegade rainbow and brown trout, thus ridding the specs of their enemies and their competition. It caused considerable discussion and comment and not a little excitement until someone chanced to ask just what kind of magic poison, what grand elixir was so marvelous, so selective and discriminating in its killing that you could taint a river with it and yet it would do away with rainbows and brown trout and not harm anything else. It sounded as though the Park Service had come up with the piscatorial equivalent of the neutron bomb—a concoction that would kill certain species of fish without upsetting the stream's ecosystem at all.

"What next?" said Tewksbury when he heard the news. He shook his head tiredly from side to side and his eyes got brighter, as they always do when he swells with good-natured cynicism. "Perhaps some device that rids the seas of everything unprofitable, leaving us great pools of lovely tuna, cod and halibut? The grasslands of everything save cows, surely the very symbols of wildness? The earth of everything save hordes of boring human beings?! Ah, technology! Better living through mindless tinkering!"

The rumor mutated into fact. A few streams were poisoned; most are now poison free, and the brook trout, or what's left of them, are still high up. Much of the park's brook trout water is closed to fishing and has been since 1975, when a moratorium was placed on taking brook trout in the park. And where angling for brookies is allowed, most of it is strictly catch and release, barbless hooks required.

Most fly fishermen I know with an unshakable devotion to brook trout dream of Labrador or some other equally exotic destination. I wish them well each time I hike up along Big Snowbird Creek, up along its headwaters, where brook trout of some size still run, native southern highland trout in pools of cold water where sunlight comes through the woods clothing the landscape in a dazzling wardrobe of shadows.

I rarely call it Big Snowbird. It's just Snowbird Creek. Like the sublime Slickrock, it runs through the splendor of the Nantahala National Forest, up around Snowbird Mountain, in Graham County. I walk in from the old Snowbird Creek bridge or along Forest Road 75. The trails wind through the wooded slopes of the Snowbird Mountains choked with giant hemlocks, sweet sassafras, oak, poplar, and maples, great tangled slicks of holly and rhododendron. More than twenty-six miles of trails shadow the creek and its tributaries through these cool, pensive mountains. Big Snowbird Trail follows the creek up along its watershed, a climb of 2,600 feet in elevation that brings you to Big Junction and the Tennessee state line. Here, on the rib of the creek basin, the Big Snowbird and Snowbird Mountain trails join again and the mountain trail continues south along the ridge. To the north is the King Meadows Trail that climbs along the ridge to Hooper Bald. All the trails link, forming a lazy, languid loop. The trout and the mountains and the way the light here moves like tides through the woods slow me down, thank the gods, letting me measure my progress in inches and feet rather than miles.

The Snowbird Mountains have a haggard look to them, a remoteness that resists compromise. When the Cherokees of the Smoky Mountains were being rounded up for removal to the West, many of those who refused to go, refused to abandon these mountains, hid out in the rugged Snowbird Mountains where shadows are thick, dark and deep.

"They were herded up, not rounded or gathered," said Bob Winterwolf Dougal, "herded up like so much cattle and pointed to the west. My family's people stayed on the trail for twelve days then escaped and returned here, joined those in the Snowbirds and told their stories of horror and no one then called it the 'Trail of Tears.' Instead it was the 'Time of Broken Bones and Broken Hearts.'

"Here they lived for a good while and they lived well and free and were not penned up on reservations and not yet dependent on welfare for life or on liquor for dreams. It was all a very long time ago."

I fish here, here where Bob Winterwolf Dougal's ancestors hid, survived, carried on. Here in these woods studded with rotted-out stumps of the grand old chestnut trees that once dominated these forests and were wiped out by blight almost a century ago. Those who live in these mountains believe the chestnut trees will come back someday. It would be nice. I hope they are right. I still find young chestnut saplings almost every year and once I found a chestnut tree ten feet tall climbing toward the sunlight even though the blight was in it and killing it.

Here where the mountain people tried and failed to make the land pay, here I fish and there are no sounds save the creek and the wind among the trees. On the lower branches of the creek there are sleek rainbow trout and fat browns. I have taken my share of both, good fish all, but it is for the brook trout that move in the cold waters above the falls that I come, walking eagerly up the trail, an edginess in my blood, a warm anticipation spreading through my muscles, for I know that the trout, too, are on the move and anxious.

Nearing Big Falls or Mouse Knob Falls, I am sometimes certain I can feel the blood pressure hard against the walls of my arteries and veins, drain into my face, run warm just under my skin. I hear the falls and my eyes widen, my stomach tightens, every cell of me swells not with expectation but rather with a purer and rarer magic, unadorned anticipation.

After all these years, I am still not certain of the length of the walk to Big Falls, the precise distance. At my stride and pace, surely it must be more than three miles. A fine walk, whatever the distance, and brook trout at the end. What then matters distance and the gauging of it? Big Falls is steep, formidable. A dead end for the ever-restless and ambitious rainbows and brown trout below, a barrier above which the native brook trout still thrive feeding hungrily, growing to what are for mountain brook trout truly impressive size, some going to sixteen to eighteen inches and weighing a pound or more. But given the unhesitant, lightning-jolt aggressiveness of native mountain brook trout, taking a one-pound spec up on Snowbird Creek on some tiny fly and delicate tippet is rather like trying to haul in five pounds of moody bluefish or barracuda with unwaxed tooth twine. And the sound of the falls in the distance always fills the blood with great excitement, a bottomless sense of fascination and wonder.

Brook trout are fierce predators and despite their size they will strike anything that looks edible, including an angler's wide assortment of fraudulent offerings, often even those poorly presented. There have been days above Big Falls when I have taken and released more than thirty fish, days when there have been trout from first light to last, the trout hitting everything from Royal Wulffs and Adams Variants to small streamers and the dependable Tellico nymph, days when specs seemed to rise in every run of water, in every pool, streams of light seemingly etched into their black backs.

Below and above the falls, down near the Little Snowbird bridge, there are still signs of the old Buffalo-Snowbird railroad that hauled load after load after load of magnificent trees from these woods. Even so, nearby stands of huge poplar and maples and hemlock make it easy to believe that these woods are wild, true wildness indeed. In the spring, when the wind is up, the air is heady with the smell of birch and cucumber tree, sweet pepperbush, and wild hydrangea.

It is a good walk up the mountain along the creek, up past the turnoff toward Sassafras Creek and Sassafras Falls, up to the falls near Mouse Knob Branch. Beyond Big Falls, perhaps a mile or so, is the creek's magnificent Middle Falls and its large, inviting plunge pool. The creek's last large falls, Upper Falls, are six miles up from the trailhead, not far from Meadow Branch and Bearpen Branch. The trail continues along the ridgeline, coming near another of man's arbitrary lines, this one separating Tennessee from North Carolina, yet the beauty of the mountains spills easily over the crest of Laurel Top (elevation 5,317 feet) oblivious to boundaries or limits, spreading wider and wider to the north, washing over the ridges of the Cheoah Mountains and Yellow Creek Mountains, the Nantahala National Forest and the Nantahala Mountains, and all rising to meet the swelling mammoth blue backs of the Great Smokies that dominate the entire highlands, the higher peaks pressed tight against the horizon.

Often, upon reaching Big Falls, I will lay my gear aside, sit up along the falls, feel the day's weather on my skin, listen to the creek. There is a comfort deep and lasting in the sound of mountain creeks moving undeniably over the backs of dark stones. The creek widens rather than narrows at the falls, giving it an almost pastoral look and feel; the woods open and the sunlight floods in, coming off the pale green waters of the falls and deep pools in wide, undulating shafts thick with galaxies of dust and dirt, bits of rotted leaves and loam, shards of mist and tattered lengths of spiderwebbing. And I sit near the falls and watch the calm water well behind the cascades for some sign of fish, feeding brook trout, trout on the move, as they almost always are, driven by their insatiable appetite. Big Falls is as good a place as any I know of to expect a miracle. What is a miracle, after all, save the sudden appearance of the unexpected, and the unexpected is surely a resident of Snowbird Creek.

It was near the falls, years ago now, that the truly unexpected caught up with me as I slipped on a loose stone, fell, and cracked my head on another and managed to drag myself to the creek bank, where I wiped away the blood and cold water from my eyes and face and tied a blue-and-white bandanna about my head. I tried to stand and couldn't, so I lay down there in the cool autumn sunlight driving in and out of dreams, dreams full of miracles—of stones with tongues, with speech and stories to tell, every one a tale of life and motion, of complexity and intricacy, profound speeches against the lie of a stone's supposed rigidity, inflexible character, its fixity. Galaxies in my head, not of stars or of light, but of stones dancing madly. Unexpected miracles. And I was among them, a stone among stones, the earth's bones.

Raising my head slightly, looking down toward the cascade near the rim of the falls, I saw light come off the water in shimmering creamy yellow sheets, like light flooding through an immense cathedral dome fashioned of stained glass. The sound of the water plunging over the lip of the falls was as lyrical as a wind blowing hard against the curve of an ocean island. The sight of the creek just then and the sounds and the range of sunlight had no measurable use or value, and so their beauty was all the more truly uncompromising and incomparable, more than mere hydraulics, physics, stream morphology. The unexpected: miracle, magic, madness, a cracked skull, call it what you will. Whatever the name, it obviates the need for philosophy, trendy or otherwise, and leaves you the sum of nerves and marrow, muscle and bone, textured memories hidden away in a sea of cells. I saw the creek more closely still as I rinsed the bandanna and watched my blood swirl in the glint of water and sunlight, sink and move, spin as though caught in an eddy. The attraction of moving water is often overpowering, as is the urge to be in it, to be completely mixed with what is totally and unquestionably alive.

Luckily, when I fell I had the little Winston rod held high overhead in my other hand. Better to risk damage to a thick head full of loose thoughts than a well-made rod, a rod full of luck and loyalty. I had brought only the little R. L. Winston that trip and two reels, some extra leaders and tippets, and one box of flies. Nothing more. The fly fisherman is lucky—all he needs can fit comfortably in his shirt pocket. Indeed, with angling, more pockets usually leads to more gear and more gear certainly leads to more complications and vexations. Fly-fishing has a greatly undeserved reputation as an altogether elitist, snobbish, and expensive form of angling when, actually, just the opposite is true. Indeed, fly-fishing is the sanest, most unassuming, and cheapest form of angling I know of, one allowing a man to invest his time enjoying the angling life rather than becoming caught up in the fits and starts of fishing.

Fly-fishing demands more brains than muscle, a tolerance for the exasperating as well as the moving, the beautiful, the profound. And sometimes, whether a cartwheel off a slick rock in a mountain stream is involved or not, there is even the occasional brush with miracles—the unexpected—undiluted and sublime. That's the part I like best: you never know where a trout stream will lead or where a hooked trout might haul you. Too, there is no pressure on the fly fisherman, at least not those who, like me, keep mostly to themselves. Some of my best days as an angler have been those when I have not wet a line or set a hook, but only sat and watched the stream and the daylight, and by day's end my senses, if not my creel, were overflowing. Angling brings with it a certain pleasurable degree of democracy, the right to hook a fish or simply pursue an especially intriguing day, one filled with soft light and a wild labyrinth of shadows. What other pastime offers such success, such reward for nonparticipation? Fly-fishing has many attributes, but none more pleasing than its ability to find and liberate the young boy that still hides within me and to let that boy live again without embarrassment or regret, sorrow or anguish. This is more selfishness on my part because I come to the mountains and to mountain streams, all this way, to let my youth rise with the trout, to feel the water and the light, to taste the high country air.

I lay there along the creek that day listening to the falls and counting my blessings, which are many. The morning's thready, uneven clouds thickened, took on the heavy, awkward look of soggy, rumpled bedding. Changing to the north, the wind turned colder and sent tiny ripples across the surface of the stream, and I knew the faded light would entice the specs to move about less cautiously, to rise boldly and hungrily. Few trout like hard, undiffused sunlight, the flat light that comes at midmorning and lasts until afternoon and betrays movements, both to their prey and to their enemies, and drives them to deep water, wherever there is cover from the harsh light.

The wind came up stronger still, pressing the clouds down along the narrow ridge of the mountains, and what warmth the day had held seemed to evaporate like moisture off warm stones. It was cold there along the creek bank, a cold that settled deep along my spine. It seemed to me, then, that the sun and its warming light are inconstant. The universe loves the cold, is a vast glacier of cold darkness and dust and isolated stars, and that life wrinkled out of cold and thrives on gathered light, borrowed and manufactured warmth, and its raw energies. Life makes do not with time, in whatever guise, but with stolen heat and energy.

By the time the bleeding from my head had stopped, it began to rain, a slow rhythmic drizzle that turned the landscape into a tapestry of soft, moist colors, and in time a fog rose up off the creek just a few feet and hung there like some newly forming atmosphere. Everything spun and whirled; even the ground seemed to produce a feathery pulsebeat: the rise and fall of easy breathing, assured release, a breathing that sucked everything into a heady whirlwind of history and myth, legend and dream, and wild, raw possibility.

The rain came stronger, a pounding like giant open hands violently slapping against the surface of the water. I reached for my backpack, got out my poncho, and slipped it on, and sat with my back snug against a wide and shaggy hemlock. I heard above the rattling trees and rushing water, the grinding of stone against stone as though, at that moment and only for an instant, far beneath the mountain where I sat the earth's massive quivering tectonic plates had shifted, moved perhaps a millimeter and changed the earth's look and feel, sending a groan like collapsing mountainsides out over the Smoky Mountains.

Sometimes it seems possible indeed to reduce the world about you, even a world of cold and pounding rain, full of the hiss and howl of a swollen mountain stream, down to the weight and feel of a single gray-green stone. The universe will fit into such a stone, fit with room to spare, and even so nothing about you will have lessened or been diminished, and yet that stone in the palm feels like the earth itself, the touch of time and motion, life on the move and without culmination. Beyond hand and stone the whole sky of mountains seems to close in, the signposts of personal geography rather than the meaningless spread of space. Often have I touched a stone and felt this binding of life and time, the blend of memory and experience sealed beneath the skin, there remembered in crisp detail despite the passing years.

In the storm, in rain and wind, the sky went gray, the powder-dust gray of crushed granite, and in every direction mountains rose up through low-slung zinc-gray clouds, peaks and ridges rounded, worn, looking mud-black with a great sea of grizzled fog drifting up from the dark forests. The small stone in my hand was smooth, slick; the rain deepened its color, gave it a deep, beryl-green shine.

A word broke loose from my throbbing head, rattled about in my mind. Orogenesis. Mountain building. It takes falling down on your head on a substantial stone to break such a word loose. Orogenesis, a word to rub against the round, smooth stones of Snowbird Creek. I thought of stones there in the rain, of mountains rising up, crumbling down, eroding away, a stone at a time. I remembered the sensation of feeling the mountain lurch beneath me, and even though I knew it was dizziness from my cracked skull, I liked the idea of the ground under me, the mountains about me, the stones like islands in the creek, being in motion, no matter how minuscule or imperceptible such movements might be. The jounce of an atom, the shudder of a molecule, a leaf trembling in the wind—everywhere the earth moves, a steady glacial creep. Everything moves, jostles, gives in, gives way, so that the planet's history seems like some madcap, random game of geologic bumper cars. All is process, potential, and possibility.

I watched the falls, mist rising up from the plunge pool like a smoky vapor. I listened to the sound of water slapping stones. The steam seemed effortless motion, evidence of the great deception—a world in constant motion that appears to be barely moving at all. Perhaps this has something to do with why I seek out streams, high country creeks: each is a synecdoche, a seam of water and light, that expresses life as a whole, resonant with its chafing energy, its endless motion.

Mountains move. Streams are testimony to this, gnawing away at a mountain's mass of stone and dirt, carrying it away, downstream, a flow of past, mingling with the present, moving toward the future, immensity reduced to grains of sand. Even the most tranquil of mountain creeks can haul away more than 1,000 cubic feet of mountain a year. Erosion will not be denied; a force of movement that wears and tears, bends and breaks, changes one thing into another. Erosion, the patient force, fueled by time and wind and storm, the innocent flow of water. How much is heaped into the average mountain, how many cubic feet of thrust-up earth and stone? Perhaps 500 billion cubic feet, a mass that seems so imposing, so undeniably permanent, and yet it is as transitory as breath and will be eroded away in the blink of geologic time, 600 million years or so. Not long. Not long at all.

Sitting there in the rain, my head bleeding, the wound oozing, rubbing the small piece of stone in my hand, I thought of the view of the mountains from the summit of Mount Le Conte or Clingman's Dome, any of a dozen peaks, how the dark ridges hanging like streamers of tattered ribbon receding toward the horizon, toward the north and east, often reminded me of a great, smooth spread of thick black cloth that had been suddenly and violently pinched and pushed in all directions, much in appearance like the folds of squeezed cloth. Orogenesis. Plate tectonics. The theory is at once simple and

intricate, full of geologic drama. The geologist or nervous angler who embraces the notion of plate tectonics believes, to some degree, that the ground
under him is about as certain as a rain-slick highway, or might as well be, because what we know as the earth's continents, what we once believed to be
inviolate expanses of the earth's crust, are forever slipping and sliding about.
The earth is a gelatin that hasn't quite set, with the edges firm but unstable
and each layer below increasingly jellied, giving way, finally, to a seething,
boiling liquid core. Continents—the lithosphere, great slabs of earth perhaps
100 to 130 miles thick—are a delightful irony because they are, geologically,
quite light and glide stiffly atop denser layers of the earth's surface.

What sets these massive continental plates in motion, moves them about?
Actually, exactly what moves the brook trout above Snowbird Creek's Big
Falls, urges the coyotes that are moving back into the mountain, down along
Buck Knob and Sugar Creek Ridge, and Soapstone Gap, brings the black
bear out into the high country balds and meadows, urges winter clouds across
the high ridge tops—the energy of heat, the earth's incredible internal heat,
rising, rising in convection currents which in turn set the plates in motion.
The movements and shapes and placement of the continents are not a matter of design, but rather just the debris of motion, no more predictable than
which of a tree's leaves will be the first to fall or the last.

The mountain upon which I sat contemplating stones is truly unique,
could not be duplicated again any more than a species of life could, including man. All may be process, but it's the process of change, of motion, of the
possible, even among stones.

Millions of years ago Europe and North America were one landmass, a
union without permanence, as the land shifted, cracked and divided. In another 100 million years perhaps these same plates again moved toward one
another, met, one giving way, sliding beneath the other: a geologic dance
called subduction. Layers of rock sheared off, peeled easily away like so much
onionskin and left piled about, heaps of stone shavings. Mountains are as
much residue as majesty. So it is with the Appalachians, crumpled evidence
of the impact of two great continental plates, Europe and North America
and the rocky stitches that once bound them.

Sitting high up on Snowbird Creek rolling the smooth creek stone in my
cold hands, I tried to imagine a collision of such force. Imagine indeed that
I was sitting at the site of a geologic crash, a hit and run of mammoth pro-
portions. I could imagine it only in profound slow motion, the two plates

caroming off each other, slowly, like scabs being torn from injured skin. What had been but an insignificant body of water, the bed of the Atlantic Ocean, beginning to tear, to rip and spread, throwing up mountains of its own and in the process tearing the massive plates of earth slowly apart, the renting taking place over more than 150 million years. It is still taking place; the Atlantic is still growing, its belly split, molten rock pouring out. Rocks found from the Rocky Mountains east to the Mississippi are between 1 and 2.5 billion years old. Those on the spreading ocean floor are but 30 million years old. The stretch marks of geologic adolescence.

The Appalachians are among the earth's oldest mountains. The earth itself is thought to be at least 4.5 billion years old; the oldest known surface stone, located in Canada, is 3.5 billion years old. Along the worn ridgeline of Appalachia, the oldest known rocks date back perhaps a billion years.

A billion years compressed in stone: time, smooth and hard-green, held in my hand, and me wondering if a man gains any wisdom at all by cracking his head open on such ancient stones compressed by epochs of time and motion and change. As I waited for the rain to pass, I thought that I might finally be beginning to understand why the theory of plate tectonics appeals to me so—because to believe in it is to accept the completely delightful proposition that little if anything about the earth is permanent, not even such apparently geological certainties as mountains. Forces, not forms, persist; energy is spent and endures; time does not tick, it flows. The earth, this collection of interstellar dust, planetesimals and photoplanets, atmosphere, gravity, and sunlight, still boils and wrinkles with the unpredictable. And as long as there is the unpredictable, there is potential for diversity, richness, the stuff of process. The earth, despite its years, still spins and moves; it slips and slides, changing with every bend of space and time, every surge of sunlight and burst of raw energy. The great certainty is that there is perhaps no great certainty, nothing we can measure, weigh, analyze, predict. Caught up in the suffocating beauty of the chaotic, we reach for security, ultimate control of the natural world, the benign sameness of comfortable mediocrity. The thought that we might be of no more importance than an insect as an expression of life is so scary that ancient man felt compelled to invent a creation that promised assurance and ascendancy, a creation in which control was a fait accompli, something heavy with purpose and meaning and completely understandable.

The rain came through the shaggy hemlock limbs hard and steady, beating down the brim of my slouch hat. Downstream, at the rim of the falls, the stream ran hard against the rocks, roared above the rain.

Geologically, the greenstone whose smooth rounded sides I rubbed held so few years, perhaps only the earth's recent history. Young stone: a child's history. In my pack I had what I was certain was a piece of Ocoee stone. Covered with thick forests and worn by the roll of irrepressible time, the Smokies, like most of the Appalachians, boast few dramatic rock outcroppings, fewer still breathtaking stone amphitheaters. So old are the rocks of these mountains that most of them hold no fossil remains of life. Only among some of the rock formations near Cades Cove, and in the Chilhowe and Green Mountains, are there scattered traces of such ancient marine fossils as ostracods, scolithus, brachiopods, and trilobites. The story of Smoky Mountain stones is more the history of the earth's great physical forces, the power and complexity of time, the history of Appalachian orogeny. Several times in deep black nights, with clouds held tight against moon and stars as I lay stretched out on the sleeping bag looking at the sky by candlelight, I have tried to hear the wrenching screech of stones grinding against stones, of land suddenly folded, uplifted, pulled, faulted, shoved, fractured, the outcome as random and startling as that of a child building castles in wet sand. Tremendous heat and pressure changing the nature of stones, metamorphosing the mostly sedimentary rock (the dominant stones of the Smoky Mountains are metamorphosed sedimentary rock), leaving behind metasandstones, slates, metasiltstones, phyllites, quartzites. Over millions of years the land was shoved higher into the sky, shadows of smoky blue light reflected from skies so long, thick, and gray, heavy with dust and shards of stone, then suddenly washed with wrinkles of pure blue light. And winds howled hard out among the ridgelines while ice and frost clutched at the rock, as did endless streams of cold, moving water, and over time the limestones and slates, the shales and phyllites, eroded much quicker than the harder siltstones and sandstones, and stubborn quartzites. Erosion sculpted the mountains, stone by stone, ridge by ridge, valley by valley, along the range's four major fault lines (Gatlinburg, Greenbrier, Oconaluftee, and Great Smoky), giving the range the appearance of a single great syncline rising from the west-southwest to the east-northeast.

The Ocoee stone in my backpack is eroded Smoky Mountain bedrock. Ocoee rock forms the great slab of stone that with metamorphic Precambrian rock and ancient sedimentary deposits form the 20,000-foot-thick hulking stone skeleton of the Smokies. Fragments of Ocoee stone are visible along ridges, eroded pinnacles, exposed cliffs—worn knobs of Precambrian stone perhaps 500 million to a billion years old, finally exposed to sunlight and wind and the full wash of time. Mingled with them are ancient schists, gneisses, granites. These are the rocks that make up the ragged crest of the Smoky Mountains, the great Thunderhead and Anakeesta formations, with metamorphosed schists and quartzites and phyllites dominant in the southeast and less severely metamorphosed shales, slates, and sandstones to the northwest.

By late afternoon the rain had calmed to a drizzle and I looked down at the two stones in my hands, the green creekstone and the old Ocoee stone. Both worn, both smooth: both capsules of time, time not spent but still in motion, Precambrian time and Cenozoic or recent time, whirlwinds of time swirling still in atoms of stone.

Underfoot nothing rests. Things shift, drift. The morning sunlight, I knew, as it always does, would spread over on a different landscape than it would linger on now for only a pensive hour or two, as the rain stopped and the clouds broke and the light came hard as floodwaters over the ridge, filling up the sky. Mountains, like the stones in my hands, only seem immutable. Luckily, they sway and change with every press of wind.

The rain ended and I stood up feeling the knot on my skull, the jagged edge of a deep cut. I looked out over the creek, and the sky was suddenly tinged with deep blues and violets, gentle light. A horseshoe rainbow arched above the frayed clouds, west to east. The ground felt unusually soft, spongy, no steadier than a bog. I swayed and eased back down onto the ground, rested again against the hemlock tree and finally slept—a deep black sleep, one that drags you beneath dreams, away from sensation, leaves you tucked safely inside the warm, numb shell of unconsciousness. It was the kind of sleep that always startles you when you wake, leaves you momentarily disassociated, scared, lost, disconnected; the kind of sleep that seems so close to what must be death's blankness. And then, suddenly, almost instantly, you are awake and struggling again for the feel of wind and sunlight, the sound of water, and you are gulping air, grasping for life's surface, pulling yourself up out of the dark, trembling slightly, even though the sleep had been sound and good and totally absorbing.

What did I see as I struggled out of that sleep's tight, warm, cocoon, opened my eyes tiredly, pushing back sleep's plush darkness and resting on the crest of consciousness, sleep still tempting me back, back down into the soft, quiet darkness?

Not the image of Carlotta Raynoskva and the dimly lit rooms of the Apache Massage Service Tewksbury had described to me so many times in painstaking detail. Not the undulating shadow of some long-dreamed-of brook trout, as big and thick as a flank of ham steak. Not the endless dark eyes of the young woman I had met along Deep Creek months before. What eyes she had, a study in the shades and geography of supple browns. Straight, sorrel colored hair pulled back and tied in a loose ponytail, bangs falling loosely just along her delicate forehead. Hair that held sunlight so that it seemed to move like seams of liquid that gave both her hair and face a warm glow. Her name was Rachael. She traveled with a full backpack and a dog that was mostly rottweiler, a huge beast the color of tarnished copper. His name was Dog. Rachael told me matter-of-factly that at a given command Dog would rip my throat out. Rachael wanted to enjoy the mountains. Dog was her assurance that her search for peace and quiet wouldn't be rudely interrupted. No, it wasn't Rachael and Dog, Rachael and her sun-soaked hair and those endlessly brown eyes. Not even the last of the day's sunlight against the sky like colored lace, soft against the distant mountain ridges.

None of these things.

Instead, teeth, or rather the lack of them. Four on top, two on the bottom, the mouth open, a smile that looked like a neglected graveyard, the tombstones weathered, broken, eroded, or gone altogether. Above the smile, the stare of weak green eyes set deep in a small head topped by a slick of blond hair brushed straight back. Magnified through a pair of thick glasses, the eyes took on the unsettling aspect of giant cells caught in the act of dividing. At least a week's worth of untended beard, like a giant field of burnt cornstalks, the black flecked with traces of gray ash. Visible breath, quick, rhythmic clouds of it, and it was spicy and sharp rather than foul and unseeming.

I crawled out of tiredness and sleep, put all the pieces together.

Arby Mulligan. The breath alone gave him away, that unmistakable blend of ice tea, mountain whisky, and spring water, the heady ripeness of homemade wine, all punctuated with trace elements of cayenne pepper, cloves, garlic, Tabasco and Worcestershire sauce, and a strong tincture of wild onions.

He turned from me quickly, as though moved by a genuine source of urgency and emergency. Hunkered down by the creek, he dipped his huge hands tracked with hard-domed calluses into the cold, shallow water, once, twice, as creek water ran down his hard-muscled forearms like tracks of old creek beds criss-crossing rainless, hard-luck country.

"Some cut," he said, lifting the blue-and-white bandanna. "And a knot with character to go along with it. Any bigger and it'd be a peak worthy of a significant name. Something right biblical.

"You could probably use some stitches in that thing," he said. After a moment of reflection, he said, "But, then, you could probably use a good many things."

"Probably so," I said. Arby Mulligan has a way with language that equals his interpretation of cranial knots. It's one of his most interesting attributes.

He went on gazing at my head thoughtfully. He had a quizzical look on his face. I had seen it before, one night when he looked up into the night sky and spotted an object he didn't recognize, couldn't explain. He looked at my head from the top and from each side. I felt his thick fingers against my skull—a gentle squeezing, like that of a savvy shopper sizing up a melon's ripeness.

I sat there quietly studying Mulligan's eyes for any sign of the unexpected. The most incidental movement might indicate a lethal discovery, the slightest twitch might signal he'd found a knot foretelling creeping bladder infection. Anything might announce a Mulligan diagnosis. A telltale fidget, a subtle squirm or shiver, the smallest quaver, could be followed by Mulligan bending down low, close to your ear, whispering that you were living off a bum heart or about to embrace a whopping good case of Washman's disease, which was the kiss of death because Millard Washman had been dead for years and no one but Mulligan had the slightest idea what Washman died of.

True, by trade, Arby Mulligan is a logger and machinist and he always carries a reliable pair of stainless-steel calipers and a machinist's rule with him, not to calibrate nuts and bolts or to measure and shape shafts and gears, but rather to calculate and investigate the fleshy knots and bumps and ridges of his patients' heads. Mulligan hasn't cut down a tree in thirty years or fixed any piece of machinery save his Chevy pickup truck and Mrs. Pottsworth's icebox in almost as many years. The Chevy, Mulligan will tell you, runs fine if you back off and leave it alone. As for Mrs. Pottsworth and her icebox, fixing the thing is an act of neighborly kindness. She lives up the creek from Mulligan and is a widow. The handle on her icebox came off and Mulligan fashioned a new one out of a bent butter knife. He was happy to do it. Mrs.

Pottsworth fed him a good meal—ham and beans and gravy and corn bread and spring water. Fresh, warm apple pie for dessert. The apples came off a gnarled apple tree that the Pottsworths planted behind their place more than eighty years ago. They put in six trees and one survived. Mrs. Pottsworth smiles and calls it her orchard, a tree that puts out enough apples to fill a town's appetite. Some always fall and rot, giving Mrs. Pottsworth's place the heady smell of decay, sweet and sharp.

After the pie, Mrs. Pottsworth sat straight up and corpse-still in an old caneback chair by the fireplace. The fire had settled deep in the hickory wood and hissed, said Mulligan telling the story, so it was the only sound you could hear, except for Mrs. Pottsworth's breathing which settled down just as soon as Mulligan let his giant fingers roam gently about her old gray head, feeling its hilly geography. Mulligan said right off that the news was good, that she was a woman of healthy body and spirit, a true Christian woman, the Lord's own child, an honest, hardworking woman who'd lived a virtuous life and would reap her reward in heaven.

That was the truth of things, according to Arby Mulligan, phrenologist. No one doubts Mulligan's consultations because the knots of a person's head never lie and everyone knows that Arby Mulligan is blessed, has the gift of reading the flesh, even healing it, decoding its lumpy messages, speaking their meanings, interpreting their portents.

Arby Mulligan had discovered he was not only a logger and machinist but a medium, a conduit for God's healing powers and a vessel of Christian magic and miracle, on a December day in 1949 when he noticed a knot coming up in Piercy Cabe's forehead, just at his hat line. Cabe raised hogs down near Boiling Springs. Mulligan took an immediate interest in Cabe's swelling, fleshy geode and one day finally reached out and touched it, laid his right index finger on it. This is what Mulligan supposedly said after touching the spreading lump on Piercy Cabe's head. "There's a spider in the outhouse, Piercy, and you know no good can come of that. Feels like a swollen bladder. Feels like trouble ahead and plenty of it."

Mulligan's first words as a phrenologist turned out to be prophetic. Two weeks after Mulligan had felt the heat of doom leaking out of Piercy Cabe's head, Cabe took sick. By that time the bump on his head was as big and round as a cue ball. When Mulligan was first called in to advise, use his wondrous fingers, Cabe had moved his cot near the woodstove. Mulligan came into the house, placed his cool palm over Cabe's forehead. Hattie Cabe,

Piercy's mother, stood at Mulligan's side. She had set out cups of hot tea laced with thick mountain honey on the room's simple wooden table.

"Wart?" said Hattie Cabe.

"Corn, then? Infected pimple?" Her voice was soft, the kind of whisper weighted down by dread and despair.

"Cyst?" she said.

"Bunion, carbuncle, boil, white mole, blister?"

Mulligan shook his head dejectedly, removed his hand from Piercy's head.

"It's putting out death's warmth, Miss Hattie," he said. He shook Piercy's hand and said, "Chickens today, brother, feathers tomorrow," and Piercy Cabe nodded thankfully. Mulligan took a long pull of the warm tea and honey and left.

Piercy Cabe was dead in less than a month's time. The word got out about Arby Mulligan's power, how he could read the head's terrain, all manner of cranial distensions. People began showing up at Mulligan's place on Hanging Dog Creek west of Owl Creek Gap. They came by mule and horse, by cart and car and truck. Many walked. They stood in line, hats and bonnets in hand, heads bowed, waiting for Mulligan's telling touch, those fingers that could sense their fate.

Being a sought-after phrenologist turned out to be a full-time job, especially after Mulligan also started his Church of Universal Harmony. So he laid down his chain saw and his tools, except for the calipers and machinist's rule. When he isn't interpreting cranial topography, Mulligan uses the stainless-steel rule to measure the trout he catches in these mountain streams.

So naturally I kept a close watch on his eyes as he palmed my head.

He sighed. "What happened," he asked, "Tewksbury give you a stock tip and your legs went to rubber?"

"No," I said. "Tewksbury pulled out weeks ago."

Mulligan stood straight up, stepped back toward the creek, into gathering shadow.

"Should of known. I stopped by Oron Estes' place last week and while I was reading what the bumps on his head had to say I heard some guy on the television say the stock market had taken a sudden wild upturn. Knew then old Tewksbury was back in the city."

"Well?" I said.

"Well what?" he said.

"The verdict, Mulligan, the verdict!"

"Oh. A deep cut that'll knit and a swollen bruise that'll ache for some while, I suspect. Put a little time and trout slime on both and they'll heal fine."

The sky had cleared and the mountains seemed etched in a cold copper-colored light.

Mulligan carries his fly rod with him as faithfully as he totes about his Bible, leaflets proclaiming the good news of the Owl Creek Gap Church of Universal Harmony.

He took his rod, worked out some line, walked well up along the creek, began to fish. He had tied on a small streamer that flashed in the soft red light as he cast upstream into a wide pool of calm, deep water.

I took the little Winston rod and worked the bottom pools just above the falls. Against the flat sheets of sunlight coming off the surface, the creek water looked darker, more brooding, deeper. The wet stones had a polished look, like patent leather freshly shined.

The world went silent, save for the gurgle of the creek, the hiss of the falls. There was just that—the sound of moving water, water rushing over the backs of eroded stones, edging down the mountain—and nothing else, not even the sound of one bird singing.

I worked the pool half in dream until I saw it, the shadow of the fish, and my pulse throbbed so that I could feel it pushing hard against my temples. It was some trout, the length, I guessed, of my forearm, its muscled flanks working against the pull of the current, keeping its nose upstream, keeping it hanging there at the far edge of the pool in the dove-gray shadow of stones where the current bent and where the trout could easily feed on whatever the creek brought its way. I could see its jaws, its dark head, suspicious eyes, its back, a tapestry of wormy-looking markings, each one holding sunlight. It flicked its tail and took an insect off the surface of the creek, a move so graceful and sudden that the surface showed no sign of disturbance, almost no hint of presence, no wrinkle of portent. The brook trout took the third cast, when luck stayed with me and the dry fly bent naturally with the current, twitched near the islands of stone, and the fish rose violently and swallowed it, hook and all. It fought fiercely, the fight that is its blood, the all-out fight for existence, survival. Its weight on the line was more than fish; rather it was pure force, undiluted and fundamental. It was, I often imagine, what life feels like—elemental energy, raw and wild, the force of the trout's blood, a surge of boldness and savagery. It tired just as the last of the day's light began to ease from the sky, dissolve beyond the mountains, so that both moon and sun were visible for a time in the moldy blue-black sky, and I pulled the trout near me carefully, sunk the landing net under it, and let it rest there. It was a trout of years and substance, nearly eighteen inches long, huge for a Smoky Mountain brook trout. I did not touch it, though, as always, the temptation was great, almost overpowering, that old feeling I'd learned from fishing with Elias Wonder, the old Sioux who lived down the creek from my grandfather's place in the Ozarks: that if you touched a wild thing that you loved, then that life would fill your own, mingle with your blood, restore it, make you whole and vital again, leave you content with earth and wind, water and sky. I worked the fly out of the brook trout's jaw with a simple, efficient, painless fisherman's tool, and sunk the net deeper so that the trout hung free in the creek. It stayed there briefly, swaying gently until it flinched suddenly, dropped its head and was gone, leaving me with only the glow of sunlight in its dark eyes, sunlight glowing deep red like embers mixed in a bed of cave-black coals.

It was some trout. The trout of a lifetime, perhaps. No matter where I am, what my situation, no matter what time of the season, the press of the weather, all I need do is close my eyes and it is there, that shadow giving way to details of light, that wildness of trout and fast water and mad energy, all of it here in memory like a steady drip of spiritual nourishment keeping an edge to my blood and temperament.

I told Arby Mulligan about the trout and he smiled.

"I knew there was a good fish in your future," he said, "but why spoil the thrill, lessen the wonder by telling you? Bumps and knots never lie. The one on your head now speaks plainly of good trout.

"That's one thing about having the gift that troubles me—knowing sometimes what's coming before it comes. It kind of takes the surprise out of life. I guess that's why I've never laid hands on my own head. Knowing what you or Hippolyte Dulles or Tewksbury are in for is one thing, but I don't want to know what's in the cards for me until I draw them."

Like most mountain people, Arby Mulligan is anything but ornamental. He's no more predictable than thunder.

Night settled in cold with a spray of stars flung wide across the sky. I started up the camp stove, set out cheese crackers and trailmix and cool spring water. Mulligan added cold chicken, apples, pumpkin bread, and apple brandy, vintage ninety days.

Mulligan sat down on the far side of the little stove, told me he had seen Tewksbury down on Slickrock Creek weeks before, fishing and talking to himself.

"Had on lederhosen and tennis shoes and a broken-down silver-bellied cowboy hat. Kept on singing something that sounded like 'Carlotta see da mountains, Carlotta see da trout, Oh Carlotta don't you see what I dream about.' I'm telling you, brother, the man's elevator don't go all the way to the top."

We divided a half-dozen hard-boiled eggs. As he peeled one, he told me his mother's middle name was Glück.

"That's German for luck, ya know," he said with no air of snobbery but rather in the soft voice of sober humility. After all, it was just plain good fortune to actually have luck as your birthright.

"My mother couldn't read heads," Mulligan said, "but she could get gospel and verse out of chicken bones and the moon. She'd stand out on the front porch at dusk studying the sky and all of us waited for her pronouncement so we could plan our days and nights accordingly. Sometimes, on certain nights full of moonglow, I can still hear her racing about the old place wide-eyed, her face moon-white, throwing her small hands up and down over her head, and rhyming in that cold preaching voice of hers that never rose above a raspy whisper, 'I see the moon, the moon sees me. The moon sees somebody I want to see.'

"Never did find who it was she was wanting to see and her rhyming put knots on my daddy's head. I took one look at 'em and knew he was going moony, too, especially when he started in to rhyming with her: 'Pale moon doth rain, Red moon doth blow, White moon doth neither rain nor snow . . .' Toward the end he took to singing a little ditty of his own composing, 'Glück, Glück, meant to be luck. Instead laid me low before my time, killing me with insanity's rhymes.'

"True, brother. Lord's eye on it."

In giving up steady work to heal the worried, ease their frayed spirits, Arby Mulligan has shed most of his worldly possessions. He still has the old house down on Hang Dog Creek near Owl Creek Gap. It's a small clapboard house. There's no door. Instead of rooms, there is only one big room with small windows at each end. An old iron woodstove occupies the center of the room. Nearby is a wooden table and three wooden chairs and a bed. The bed's rumpled mattress rests not on box springs but on a rigid latticework of rope.

There's a wool blanket folded neatly at the foot of the bed. No pillow. On a wooden shelf near where the door isn't sits a Coleman lantern. The outhouse is out near the unkempt garden. There's no door on the outhouse either. Mulligan is uncomfortable with doors, with anything that might close a man in.

The house fits Mulligan well. It is small, square, sturdy, reliable, a rough structure that harbors no pretense. Arby is rarely home and these days mostly uses the place only for occasional meetings of the Owl Creek Gap Church of Universal Harmony. Members and converts knew the place by the lucky iron mule shoe nailed over where the door isn't.

I first met Arby Mulligan on the upper reaches of Abrams Creek in Cades Cove on the Tennessee side of the Great Smoky Mountains.

I had gotten up at first light and fished the creek with little luck and stopped after midmorning, put my rod down, crawled up on a big, flat stone bathed in full May sunlight, hoping it might change my luck, and lay there like a reptile letting the sunlight warm my skin, stir my blood.

The bite of icy creek water running down my head and face, dripping off my chin, came an instant after the stranger's small body threw a chilly shadow across my face and his voice rang out above the sound of the creek's low rumbling among the stones and the clatter of the wind among the trees.

This is what the small man said loud and clear above the sound of the creek as he poured a cupful of mountain trout water over my head: "Fear not death, young man. It's but a good night's rest . . .

"Blessed be this cold mountain water. Taste it with thy lips, friend, and know the Father's surcease . . .

"In this water time knows no division or boundary. It and all things come and go, come and go."

I took my bandanna, wiped the cold water from my eyes and face, sat up on the big, flat stone, and saw in full detail this little man dressed in bib overalls, boots, and a tattered brown fedora. He had one huge hand lifted toward the sky, while in the other he held a tin coffee cup, creek water still dripping from its metal lip. I smiled broadly remembering that one of the great allures of the mountains is that among them life's novelty has yet to completely fade and disappear. Where else could a trout angler down on his luck coil up on a warm stone and wake up being anointed with cold creek water by an innocent lunatic?

"Rise up, pilgrim, stand in the stream of things as they are, life forever renewed . . .

"Rise up and expand. You are more than you know, feel, or even suspect. Up here a man's likely to seep beyond the limits of his mind, the capacity of his skull . . .

"Come, brother, empty yourself until you're as loose as a potato sack, then fill your skin with these mountains."

He took an old handkerchief, wiped out the cup, tucked it inside an old rucksack he had laid down on the slab of stone where I sat. Groping about in the sack's black insides he pulled out a folded sheet of oilskin and took from it a white leaflet and a cheap white business card.

This is what the card looked like and said:

Arby G. Mulligan
Preaching Friar & Pulpiter & Dr. of Phrenology
Hang Dog Creek, N.C.

"A man's whole life is foretold upon the head's terrain."

The leaflet, a half sheet of the same cheap white paper, had this to say: "Mountains Bind Us All. Join Us, Brother, At The Owl Creek Gap Church Of Universal Harmony, Hang Dog Creek, North Carolina, Where Every Day Is An Epiphany."

When I looked up from the leaflet, Arby Mulligan had a wide and friendly smile on his weathered face. There was a fire in his eyes, a haunting conflagration of sunlight mixing with his dark eyes. I sealed that strange range of light away in my memory, for among my memories is a fine collection of remembered ranges of light.

Arby Mulligan offered me his hand and we shook and he said with great and true enthusiasm, "Brother, it's a pleasure to welcome you into the Owl Creek Gap Church of Universal Harmony. What have we, by the way, to lay out for supper?"

We had grape Kool-Aid and spring water, candy bars, apples, peanut butter, plum jam, and white bread—a fitting creekside feast, said Mulligan, to celebrate my joyous if unexpected rebirth.

"And it didn't harm you none, did it?" Mulligan asked. "And there ain't no strings to it either. I mean you go on into Bryson City or Asheville and pick any church you please and get yourself saved and see if there aren't real suddenlike, obligations a-plenty heaped on you. None of that with the

Church of Universal Harmony. The way we see it is that if God's around He'll see to it you're taken care of by and by. Anyway, anglers get a leg up on all religious matters once you get out of the flatland. God loves a man that smells of trout water and mountain meadows. That's true, son. The Lord's eye on it."

We ate and rested on that giant piece of stone near a redbud tree. Up the bank was pawpaw and hepatica, spent bloodroot, dogtooth violets, and the low-hanging leaves of mayapple, spread as wide as great green umbrellas, and the smell of mountain laurel on the wind. I slept deep and hard and did not wake until late afternoon and Arby Mulligan was gone. He left a note, hastily scribbled on the back of the church leaflet.

"Go up the creek another half mile. There the trout water is profound."

I tucked the leaflet inside my shirt pocket knowing somehow I'd not seen the last of Arby Mulligan.

The sunlight came off the creek in bright angles, a refracted pale yellow that went deep green as it dissolved among the thick woods, just right for spawning visions and revelations.

I was right about Arby Mulligan. As it turned out, he was as legendary as an unsolved crime. Most everybody in these mountains either knows Arby Mulligan or knows of him.

He had spent years happily walking the mountains of North Carolina and Tennessee from Mount Le Conte south to Grape Creek and north and east to the Qualla Cherokee Indian Reservation, sprinkling cold mountain creek water over the heads of anglers, hikers, campers, hunters, poachers, lovers, outlaws, trappers, loggers, farmers, rangers, lawmen, housewives, canoeists and kayakers, and children of every age. And as he tipped the cup over the head of each of them, he welcomed one and all into the warm and cordial embrace of the Church of Universal Harmony where about anything they wanted to believe was okay just as long as it didn't harm the mountains or anything else.

Mulligan saved Tewksbury four years ago along Slickrock Creek, sneaking up on the tall, lanky Tewksbury from behind, taking him unawares. Mulligan believes it's best to dip converts like that, by surprise, believing the cold water runs through the soul like a sudden jolt of high-voltage electricity.

On the day he saved him, Mulligan recalls that Tewksbury had on a bright red fez. "I had my cup full and ready, so I gently bumped the cap from his head and let him have it, poured the elixir of life on top of his head. I bet he jumped two, maybe three feet straight up."

Mulligan was laughing now, remembering how Tewksbury had screamed "Madman" while casting, hooking the red fez as it drifted downstream, sinking slowly.

"You know what I said to him?" said Mulligan. "Welcome, friend, you are renewed." And he shouted back, "No, you lunatic, I'm damned well soaked and likely to die of pneumonia before tucking myself in tonight in Bryson City. Murderer."

The way Mulligan tells it he finally got Tewksbury calmed down and they spent an engaging afternoon together on the creek discussing theology and trout angling. Mulligan offered Tewksbury a religion free of guilt and redemption. Tewksbury offered Mulligan hot vichyssoise, Cornish hen, pita bread, a variety of blintzes, and hot Turkish coffee laced with Irish whiskey.

While he went hungrily after the Cornish hen, Mulligan asked Tewksbury, "What would you wish above all else?"

Tewksbury said, "Mountain rivers, trout, a good lunch, and a relaxing nap. The simple life. And you?"

Mulligan said, "I wouldn't mind a stroll through downtown Katmandu. That and just the freedom and health to be what I am, a man of the mountains reading the fortunes writ large on the heads of my fellowmen and roaming along these beautiful streams proclaiming my simple message."

"Message?"

Mulligan shoved two pieces of pita bread into his rucksack, laid a leaflet and business card at Tewksbury's side, and began humming "Amazing Grace" as he headed back for the trail. The day was slipping by and there might be others along the creek to warn, calm, save, and reassure.

Tewksbury told me he yelled loudly after him: "Message, you say. What message?"

Without looking back, Mulligan yelled back as he gained the trail, "There's no such thing as the idyllic life, my friend. If it's not in you to do much good, at least try to do no harm. Remember your church's motto, "Everything Comes and Goes. It All Comes and Goes."

"He's as goofy as they come," Tewksbury said of Mulligan after that day on Slickrock Creek, "but harmless, I suppose, and I'll say this for the old madman, he knows human nature almost as well as he knows trout. I just wish he'd stop poking about my head. It gives me the willies."

"He's got more knots on his head than a horned toad and everyone of them feels of good luck and treasure," Mulligan said. "The man's a walking totem. Okay, he wears funny clothes and eats strange food, but he's honest and innocent, so far as I know, of treason or any other crime other than lying about trout. And how can you not like a man, even a city fellah, who talks to trout when he fishes and has never been successfully prosecuted for being a public nuisance, and like a child is afraid of the dark, or was."

"Was?" I pictured Tewksbury dead along Slickrock Creek, having been caught there after twilight, the dark strangling him to death.

Mulligan said, "I found the right knot on his head, you might say, and chased away his hobgoblins, destroyed his bogeyman."

When Mulligan found me sleeping along Snowbird Creek with a whopping new knot on my head to feel and read, he was coming back from Hippolyte Dulles's place where he hadn't been reading heads or gathering souls at all but checking on the health and spirits of the high country's black bear population and drinking a new vintage (May 1989) of Hippolyte's "Mountain Remedy."

"Saw plenty of them bears," he said. "A couple quarts of Hippolyte's Mountain Remedy does wonders for a man's senses. Everything improves, my boy. Everything. Even so, the bears have got man and dogs and wild hogs bedeviling them. Old Hippolyte says it's getting bad up there. Poachers ain't shy. When there's money to be made, a family to be fed, a man will take up the challenge, even if it means trafficking in bear bladders and paws. On the last night up in the high country, we went up to the pinnacle that looks out toward the Smokies and first we prayed mightily and then we filled the wind with sacred dust that Hippolyte got from some root doctor down in Cherokee. It's supposed to protect the bears, put a magic spell on them. And then we just rubbed the hell out of the horse chestnuts we carry to keep the haints at bay and put them in my baptismal cup and rattled them hard and coated the whole countryside in a cure that was half-Christian, half-savage. I tell you, boy, we put some powerful hoodoo up in them mountains. Enough to send a Baptist running for the closest dance hall and liquor store."

We lay down up the ridge from the creek and invested the night hours in talk until Mulligan rang the little bell he had pinned to his rucksack and called the Owl Creek Gap Church of Universal Harmony to order. His face was hidden in shadow.

He talked as though the woods were filled with friends and neighbors, every stranger and acquaintance he had baptized along the mountains' streams. I thought of him along so many trails, alone but never lonely. Overhead there was a great dome of stars in a blue-black night and the rushing creek sounded like a quartet of woodwinds, long, languid notes rising like thin echoes above the creek.

And Arby Mulligan spoke, a great rambling monologue on anything and everything that came to mind, a spontaneous soliloquy on the verities of trout, the troubles of man, the hard beauty of the mountains.

A wild monologue about how life thrives on sunlight, on energy, and cared not what came or went, whether it was an insect or man, a mountain or sea. He had a blue wool blanket pulled tight about his square shoulders. His voice came bugling out of his chest rather than his throat, giving his speech a sharper sound, that blend of mountain English that to me sounds almost Elizabethan, round and smooth, graced by wit and irony and harmless honesty.

He talked about how the Cherokee used to celebrate the mountains' bounty each year with their great Green Corn Dance. I could see his shadowy outline among the trees. He pulled the blanket up tighter around his neck, and went on telling me the dance, as he understood it, seemed to be a way of tempering greed and celebrating the earth. They burned most everything they had during the celebration to welcome the abundance of the new year, the new harvest.

"Come late spring," he said in a soft, almost distant voice, "let's get together down at Owl Creek Gap and do the Green Corn Dance."

He lay down again, all of him somehow tucked under the heavy wool blanket.

"You know what Hippolyte wanted?" he said. "Wanted a hole in his roof, right over his bed. Not a big hole. Just a hole, about the size of a fist. I stood on his table and cut it for him with an old antique handsaw he had laying about the place. Made a tidy hole."

"Why?"

"Why what, friend?"

"The hole, Mulligan," I said. "Why did Hippolyte want a hole in his roof?"

"As escape hatch for his soul once he's passed over. Hippolyte has it in his head he's dying, says it's time to set the chairs on the wagon. The hole in his roof seemed to ease him some and it's a small hole and harmless. Once it was done, we fished and he took some specs. He took to hollerin' over supper how he'd had a good life and wouldn't trade none of it, not even for a sound house, a good woman, and twenty acres of pregnant hogs. This is what he said to me: 'Brother Arby, I got me more than a man can say grace over. I got me a pot to piss in and two windows to toss it out of and a hole in my roof so that my soul can get out into the open mountain air.'

"And it's just a little hole and it makes the old man happy to think that his soul won't be cabin-bound once he's stone dead."

"Did you read his head?" I felt compelled to ask.

"Sure and told him his soul is sailing in nothing but fair weather. No harm in an innocent lie. Hippolyte won't last the winter most likely. Got a cough like death's rattle deep down in his chest."

I thought about Hippolyte Dulles's soul sailing through fair weather, the hole in the roof of his shack being the outlet into the Appalachian high country. What a pleasing thought on a cool mountain night—the idea of sailing on time, spending every inch of sailcloth on its winds, every inch completely rising and falling on swells of light and shadow, no course set, everything adrift. Because it seems so plentiful, so available, time also seems as cheap and inexhaustible as Bob Winterwolf Dougal's supply of toy plastic tomahawks. There in the dark, I confessed to how poorly I had spent time and made use of it, forever trying to either mend the past or plan the future while the bristling, insistent, unique, doomed present burns at my fingertips, mostly ill-used and ignored.

"I couldn't see the point of a religion in which you have to up and die before you get a chance to live," said Mulligan, his voice soft and low, a voice that went well with the night. "Too, me and the minister has some slight differences of theological opinion on such issues as dancing, drinking, cussing, passion, trout fishing, harmless lying and such. So that's when I up and started the Owl Creek Gap Church of Universal Harmony in which everything goes as long as it don't harm anyone. And everyone is included." I could vouch for that. Mulligan's congregation included everything from bone-reading soothsayers to Zen motorbike gang members, dermatologists, interplanetary travelers, morticians, dentists, astral seers, even a Zoroastrian from Muleshoe, Texas. "But the church ain't no radical fringe religion," said Mulligan in a whisper; "the Baptists have got me all wrong—I'm no more a threat to them or God than a child's nursery rhyme. You know that."

He was laughing now as he talked about how he had ridden down the mountain with Tewksbury once to Robbinsville and how Tewksbury had called up his apartment in New York City just to hear the message on his answering machine that said he was in the mountains trout fishing. "While he called to see if he was really gone, was really here in the mountains," said Mulligan, "I walked over to the post office and sent off the church's annual donations for food, shelter, clothing, and education to Murphy, Hiwassee, Hayesville, Andrews, Grape Creek, Bryson City, Robbinsville, Milltown, Peachtree, Dillsboro, Cherokee, and so on, and so on." He recalled on the way back up to the creek Tewksbury said his room in town had a Gideon Bible in it and he admitted finding comfort in its pages.

And, he said, they found a tree with shade and drank and napped and drank some more and how Tewksbury told him Carlotta's eyes were black, smoky black, like the light coming off the mountain ridges. A kind of deep, moody black. He told me that Tewksbury had told him that Carlotta wanted to stop taking his money but that he wouldn't hear of it. There are ethics, he said, even in her line of work.

Then Mulligan turned toward me in the bruised darkness and said, "Tewksbury thinks trout are like Hindus and live in cycles of existence. What a mouthful. Yet it seems true to me somehow. Only trout, of course, don't have as peaceful a nature as most Hindus. Even Tewksbury knows that. After he lost that big brown on Slickrock, Tewksbury sloshed out of the creek, sat himself down on a big gray stone. I joined him, asked what was for lunch. Pilgrim, this is what the man said to me: 'After a day on this trout water, let's have angst on whole wheat.' I had to beg off, though. Whatever I eat has to be on white bread and covered with mustard. Later that day, before he got ready to walk out of the woods, he said, 'Arby, you know what I tell the people I work with in the city? If you think you're in good hands with Allstate, go for Eden, and put yourself on a Smoky Mountain trout stream with Arby Mulligan. Your head and its knots will indeed be in capable hands.'

"Imagine that," Mulligan said loudly, proudly, "converts in New York City! God bless Tewksbury, I suppose."

"Yes. And us. And while we're at it," I said, "God bless God as well."

I was still looking up at the brilliant night sky. "Which way's heaven, you suppose, Mulligan?" I said.

Mulligan didn't even pause for the wind noisily rattling among the leaves. "Follow the trail and keep close to the stream."

So I thought then of all the creeks and streams I have known, of the high country I have spent so much time in. These mountains have been something of a confessional for me, which is what I get for sometimes talking to myself as I fish. Mulligan thinks this is a healthy thing. Odd would be the trout angler who doesn't talk to himself. I confess to mountain sunsets and the soft light of winter, to rising trout, and the sudden spill of cascading water over ancient stone, and counsel comes in tongues of sound and form and sunlight. However, I feel more than I hear or understand.

The night's cold wind skirled high among the tree limbs and I had finally closed my eyes and drifted toward the edge of sleep wondering why it is easier to deny reality, ignore what appears to be real, than it is to bury dreams, forget them. A trout rose in my imagination, a shadow taking shape in shallow water soaked in light the color of iodine. And with it sleep, calm and bottomless, a sleep where hawks circled on warm winds, wolves tracked through cool forests, and trout were thick in icy mountain streams.

"Good night, brother. Have faith in temporal salvation," said Mulligan. There was a tint of sadness in his voice. "Why would a god damn a man for loving mountains or some other piece of this earth? I just thank the Man for this blue planet, this green world.

"And Merry Christmas."

"Arby, it's November, for chrissakes," I mumbled.

"'Tis. Oh. Well, what the hell. Any day's worth honoring. So celebrate."

"Yeah. Celebrate."

Deep Creek Time

W HEN MULLIGAN AND I parted company the next morning, he said I ought to go on into Bryson City and get some stitches in my head. ❧ Instead, I told him I thought I might hike back down the mountain and go on over to Deep Creek. I had an old worn and wrinkled topographic map of the upper reaches of Deep Creek spread out on the ground. A winding blue line noted the course of the creek. A clutter of hastily drawn little red arrows marked the creek well. Each arrow is a cairn, a spot where I have taken a fine trout over the years.

"I see," said Mulligan. "Back on the road to Eden, then, are you? Kicked out, never to get back in, though we can get close, like children staring at candy through a shop window. Forget the map, son. Maps are a piss-poor substitute to the land's hard facts. Like old Hippolyte, I travel as both map and mapmaker."

Arby Mulligan doesn't care for maps or put much trust in them.

He handed me a half-full bottle of Hippolyte's Remedy. "Say, I think I've settled on at least one saint for the church. Ephraim Seward, a man who was true to these mountains all his life. It was a passion that cost him most everything he had. Mountains can ask much of a man. Perhaps too much. With Ephraim, eventually they got his wife and four children, even his little place above Grandview. Still, he stayed on, never went down to the flatland. Ended up building a shack near what we used to call New Hope Creek and he caught a trout or two a day and grew tomatoes and beans and corn, and he lived like that until the winter of 1973 when he froze to death. When they found him he was stiffer than an ironing board and he had this gray smile on his face as wide it seemed as a slice of moon."

I handed the bottle back and he shook it away, refused to take it.

"Drink that stuff daily, son. As long as you do you'll be fine. Stop, though, and you'll be deader than Ephraim Seward in a week's time. It's a tonic and good for the system, part whiskey, part creek water, and all faith, even though, really, in the end, such things don't matter much. Life gets us in the end. It got Ephraim. It's got its hand on Hippolyte, and it's reaching for me. That's the truth of things. The Lord's eye on it. There's more than one Trail of Tears in these mountains.

"Keep care, you hear. Keep care."

I heard him for a long time as I headed down the mountain full of early morning doubts. On this morning, the valley was clogged with huge rafts of fog, just the right kind of Icelandic weather for wondering whether earth, the minor little planet that is my home, is headed for any place particular, if it is following any particular course. At that moment, it seemed that I and my planet were both more or less directionless. I should have asked Mulligan about God's course, what bearing the earth followed.

Movement seemed somehow easier through the fog. There was the sensation of slightly uncontrolled motion, like ice melting on a warm stove. And I remembered what Mulligan had told me and Tewksbury and who knows how many others: "Give life the benefit of the doubt, and try not to cause any harm." And then there was always that telling shrug of his square shoulders, a pause, and this, "After all, what else is there to do? Tell me, what else?"

Tewksbury believes Arby Mulligan is some kind of sublime mountain idiot savant, a man who is a failure at everything except living simply, honestly, kindly, a man who does no one any harm, no one at all.

In the late spring, under warming sunlight, clouds of mayflies hatch over the cool, fast waters of Deep Creek. When it comes to mountain streams, I am a shameless adulterer, a man unable to remain faithful to any single stretch of trout water.

My passion for fast-moving, high country trout water is restless, completely undisciplined. Some trout streams haunt me; some ease me, soothe me; some delight me; and others challenge me. All of them haunt me, and a few of them have seeped into my blood. Snowbird Creek stays with me, as do

Slickrock and Hazel creeks, and always there is Deep Creek mingling with muscle and nerve, probing endlessly through mind and imagination, as though it were a totem of every trout stream I have known.

There is a restless energy that comes off Deep Creek as it rushes hard down past Thomas Ridge, Stateline Ridge, and the spine of Noland Divide, as it tumbles relentlessly down toward Bryson City and the Tuckaseigee River. Unlike most of the wilder Smoky Mountain streams, Deep Creek is, thanks to man, both accommodating and remote. The angler, depending on his commitment, temperament, stamina, and desire can either hike down the length of the creek from Clingman's Dome or hike up the creek from Deep Creek campground off U.S. 19 at Bryson City. From the campground, the Deep Creek Trail laces up the creek for more than two miles. It's a nice walk, a lovely stretch of water. I've never fished it. Indeed, I never wet a line until I am well up the trail, at least three or four miles from the campground. Back-country campsites are well spaced along the creek, including one at Bumgardner Branch, McCracken Branch, the old Bryson place, which is more than six miles up the creek. Higher still is Pole Road Creek and the deceitful beauty and calm of the Left Fork of Deep Creek. At Thomas Ridge, near Newfound Gap Road, more than thirteen miles up from the campgrounds, the elevation is more than 4,000 feet.

At my pace, it's a day's walk to Bumgardner Branch, if I hurry it a little. I rarely do. The creek is in no hurry, neither are the mountains. Nor am I. I walk slowly, stopping often to study stones and lichens or slime mold under a hand lens, to listen to warblers deep in the woods and the big creek's roar, to nap in a sudden luxurious pool of warm sunlight pouring over a nice bed of exposed rock.

More selfishness on my part, wanting to stop every few feet, filter each moment through my senses. Fortune has been kind to me: I seem to have a head that thrives on wonder of any kind, no matter how exotic or seemingly insignificant.

Taking a trout on the creek above Bumgardner Branch an hour before sundown, I let it go, watch it flash once in the still water near the creek's edge before it vanishes in the current, life as motion. The sensation of motion often overwhelms me as I fish. Once I feel a strike, feel the weight of a trout on my line, whatever structure the day has had is lost and collapses into a whirl of motion. Experience is all. I am surrounded by it, a sponge of muscle and nerve endings mopping up details and energy. The struggle of the fish, the feel of creek and the wind, slippery stones beneath my feet—all of it is like the pull of some undeniable magnet that draws me deeper and deeper into the wash of time. Taking a trout in a swift-moving mountain stream seems to erase the divisions of time. There is only the dance of particles and waves, cycles of energy. Sometimes I will hook, bring in, and begin to carefully release a fish before the full sensation of setting the hook has even fully burned in my mind. I find myself standing in the creek, and there is no sound save that of the creek and the wind in the trees. There is no great welling of emotion as the trout sinks in deeper water, no surge of loss or regret, only the prick of exhilaration and a rather selfish twitch of satisfaction at having so completely spent time that I cannot even remember its passing, except in my senses, and in the exhaustion of muscle and bone which turns it into memory. Sometimes at night in the high country when I am stretched out and only waiting for sleep to come and listening to the night sounds prickling through the woods, experiences I am not even certain I've had rise in my mind, explode in my imagination, pure moments of remembered time that race through my blood like adrenaline, a tide of past and future, incorruptible as moonglow.

A man consumed with trout rarely finds himself bound to fixed notions of time. Trout whirl boldly, constantly, and sooner or later the angler is caught in the maddening flow of time and there are no clear boundaries between feelings. Vexation and ecstasy seem but two slants of the same light. Same chemicals, different mix.

Two springs ago, I hiked up Deep Creek, hurriedly dropped my bundle of gear at Bumgardner Branch, and walked on up the creek another half mile. The air was cool and sweet and I noticed the spread of the sky not by looking up, but rather by studying its reflection off a smooth pool of water caught among a gallery of boulders. On that shred of calm water the sky was reflected, a dome of blue, a gathering of the shades and limits of the color blue, and I stood at the periphery and saw my own shadow edging across the reflected sky like a shard of cloud: the observer not only becoming the observed, but somehow changing it. Rather than startling or chaotic, such changes are most often as seemingly unapparent as a drift of shadow across a pool of water, its surface as smooth as hand-rubbed glass, the unexpected rise of trout to dry fly, or the touch. Tewksbury once told me of Carlotta Raynoskva: "For a hundred dollars," says Tewksbury, "you can buy all the change a man can handle."

The day on Deep Creek I studied the sky drifting across a small pool among the stones was the same one that Rachael and Dog showed up in my life again. They were on their way down from Clingman's Dome and had been along the creek for some time.

Rachael wore brown hiking shorts, cut above the knee, and a lightweight blue sweater. Her light brown hair was tucked loosely under a soft, gray felt hat. She carried a full backpack. She had tied a red bandanna about Dog's thick, furry neck. Dog seemed bigger than I remembered. In the late evening light his fur was the dingy red of unpolished copper. Dog's eyes are as endlessly black as Rachael's are endlessly soft brown. Dog sat nonchalantly at Rachael's feet eyeing me suspiciously, waiting patiently for me to make a move that would cause Rachael to utter the command freeing him to tear my throat out.

Every time I have seen Dog he seems to be holding back a knowing smile. It's there in the wrinkle of his thick, wet lips, his heavy, muscled jaws, the slightly yellowed gleam of his teeth.

Rachael shed her pack down at Bumgardner Branch, set up a little camp stove, put on a pot of stew. Dog sat along the edge of the creek eyeballing my every move, drooling uncontrollably.

I fished while the light lasted and caught one tiny rainbow trout. It jumped once, arching for a second in the soft purple light of dusk. Dog saw it and yowled and yapped and ran madly back up the creek bank and into the deeply shadowed woods.

I let the little trout go, looked over at Rachael. The creek water was cold against my knees.

"Okay," she said, "so you found his Achilles' heel. He's a seventy-five-pound man-killing lunatic who takes no crap from anyone or anything, but just happens to be terrified of fish. They just don't make sense to him. Don't seem natural. They give him the heebie-jeebies."

I said, "So as long as I smell of trout, I'm safe?"

"Naw," she said smiling, "you have to be a full-fledged fish. Scales, fins, smell, the whole thing. Dog's pilot light may be dim, but he isn't stupid."

I tried for another fish of any size, thinking it would be nice to have one outside the tent, a talisman to keep Dog at a safe distance.

No such luck.

By then Dog had regained his composure and returned, taken up his place at Rachael's feet, smiling that Darwinian smile and patiently waiting.

We had warmed tortillas with the stew and warm root beer. Rachael is a student at Berea College in Berea, Kentucky. The Appalachian Mountains are her major. She wants to spent the rest of her life studying and preserving what is left of Appalachian culture. She believes passionately that it is as much a part of these mountains as wild dogwoods and ginseng, as trout streams and hemlock trees. She has given herself a heavy burden, but she carries it well.

Night came unannounced, cool and pleasant. A thin layer of clouds pressed down along the ridge, into the valley. What light there was in the sky seemed dim and distant, like lantern light burning behind thick, leaden windows.

There were two candles burning between us and we talked of the mountains—mountain places, people, customs, mountain ways of doing things. As she talked, she smiled expressively, and I could see the candlelight reflected in her brown eyes. I somehow got lost for a time in that reflected flame of shimmering gold and found myself wondering as I looked into Rachael's young face bristling with energy, enthusiasm, and promise, why, given so many years, the sprawl of youth, and what seem to be great reaches of time, we come to the end one day with so little to show for the journey? So little gained, so little learned. So few risks taken. So few enduring loves. So many distractions, the piling up of things instead of the gathering in of experience, the probing of passing years. I remember being caught in a sudden snowstorm high up on Deep Creek, just a few miles below Thomas Ridge. I crawled into the blue sleeping bag inside the small green tent and crawled out two days later with a heap of scrap paper on which I had scrawled some of one life's leavings and distractions, the statistics of living. This is what I scribbled as the snow came down and turned the mountains white:

Schools attended from first grade through graduate school, 21. Number of cars owned, 4. Number of cars, apartments, houses lived in since graduation from college, 18. Pairs of hiking boots, 3. Life insurance policies, 1. Yes, I'm worth more dead than alive. Number of fly rods owned, 9. Reels, 12. Fly lines and flies, too many. Number of outstanding international, national, or local achievements, 0. Contributions given to worthy organizations last year, $807. Children, 2, both boys. Number of fly rods they own, 0. Number of computers they own, 3. Love found, too little. Number of functions I have attended that required a coat and tie, 5. Coats and ties owned, 1 of each. Number of cats owned, 3. Dogs, 3. Love found, too little. Number of hats scattered about my place, 82. Number of psychologists visited, 0. Demonstrations participated in, 0. Petitions signed, 17. Number of environmental and conservation groups of which I am a member, 19. Magazine subscriptions, too many and they keep expiring. Books read since 1985, 462, 16 of which have taken firm root in my imagination. Parents living, 1. Siblings, 1, my sister. Her hair is brown and cut short. She is married to a line officer in the U.S. Army and they have four children, all born in different places around the world. Miles flown in the last five years, 609,795, all of them bounded by Portland, Maine, and Santa Fe, New Mexico. Miles flown happily, cheerfully, 0. Church membership, none. Church affiliation, Owl Creek Gap Church of Universal Harmony. Friends whose addresses and telephone numbers I remember, 7. Number of friends without a telephone, 3; without an address, 1. Number of afternoon naps taken since I started counting, 115. Trout caught in the high country in 1988, 82. Number kept, 0. Dreams involving mountain streams, the high country, at least one fly rod, trout, and a mysterious beautiful woman who turns out to be a better trout fisherman than me, 11. Number of the same dream without the angling, 42. Number of mountain sunsets filed away in my head. Too many.

Not much of an inventory, really. A life whose shelves are pretty bare. I guess that's what I was thinking about as I looked at Rachael and listened to her rich voice and saw the candlelight in her eyes, all that energy bent on setting the world straight. She went on talking of her quest, her studies, and I slipped back away, out of the candlelight, and took note of the clouds moving slowly across the night sky and thinking why I hadn't used time more and worried about it less. Fished more, loved more, risked more, spent less time trying to mend the past, undo old mistakes, regretting lost friends, trying always to exceed what is expected of me, breaking musty resolutions, making new ones, making a living instead of just living. Everything comes and goes, comes and goes. It seemed to me then, in that flood of candlelight, that the sound of Deep Creek, the wide mountain night, Rachael's bright smile and endless stories, even the cold stare of Dog's black eyes, were worth any number of television sets, car stereos, plush carpeting, slipcovers for a tattered old green sofa.

I felt sure that evening on Deep Creek that I could see the shadow of time on Rachael's face, in the high cheekbones, the thin lips, the skin smooth and tight, the sun-tinged hair, and those deep brown eyes.

Rachael's last name, by the way, is Settles. Dog stays near her as though he were a moon, a grateful and faithful captive of her gravity. He is a lot of dog, even in candlelight. Head big as a water bucket.

Rachael went on talking about her research. She's busy working on a paper about Appalachian culture, specifically about mountain folktales and storytelling. This is one of her theories: that the trails that crisscross these old worn-out mountains are like runestones, stories linking generation to generation, cabin to cabin, ridge to ridge, ridge to cove, cove to towns. When you walk them it is like drawing a bow across a violin. Each one is full of song, bristling with human voices and natural sounds, each one with a story to tell. Rachael says these trails are tracks of song and dance, trails of misery and joy, paths of friendship, devotion, love and death, roads of myth and history, stone conduits for mountain magic, where dreams and spirits drift like fog among the great woods.

It's not a new theory, of course. Human beings have always, or at least until the advent of the Technological Age, depended deeply on storytelling, on myth and harmless magic, fact and dream, to pass on their lives, their history, the marks they made in the soft mud of time. It is nice to think of these mountains as choirs of voices whispering stories on the cool night air.

I thought of Arby Mulligan out in the mountain night, out on some trail as though he were a needle on some old Victrola and speaking in some strange crackling voice, shouting out some fine mountain story. Arby Mulligan. Also alone but never lonely.

When had I seen him last? Last week, last month? Altitude does something to a man's need to measure or even keep track of time's passage. The convenient measurements of hours and days mean little up here, here where it is all stone and shadow, sunlight and forest, and moving water. Trying to take time's pulse in the high country seems a frivolous notion: a waste of time. time has a way of defining its own symmetry and fulfilling its own rhythms. Days are days, though, and are best used by spending each one fully, nothing saved. For years I tried collecting time as though it were precious stones, certain that if I gave myself completely to earning a living fifty weeks a year, I could wrench a year's worth of solace, solitude, relaxation, joy, and fulfillment out of two weeks' vacation. It never worked. I never felt better, only empty and exhausted. These days I try not to divide time but only use it, use it all, as it comes, living through it all like fire moving through dry grass leaving only ashes. Because things come and go. Come and go.

Rachael Settles is at ease with mountain people, especially the old ones. She spends most of her free time with them. She admires them and their way of life, what's left of it. She says they are part self-reliant pragmatists and part shaman.

"They tread on both sides of reality," Rachael said through the candle-light, her voice suddenly a low whisper rippling on the night wind.

Perhaps it was as Arby Mulligan said, "Sure, there's God. But we got creek water and sunlight, too, and a trace of stardust in this old saggy flesh of ours as well. Got to remember that. Man's a curious creature. Curious."

As the candles burned down, Rachael drifted in and out of flickering shadow, flashes of orange glow. I imagined her trekking through these mountains gathering her stories. A fine image. Then I imagined her as moorless as stellar dust. Another fine image. One broken only by the intermittent smack of Dog's slobbering chops.

And Rachael talked on and on, telling me mountain stories as the night deepened and widened.

Rachael Settles is a Shaker who believes this about life: Live and let live. Her voice is as soft as rain on silk.

"Live and let live," says Rachael Settles, and every time she says it, her voice sounds like rain on silk.

I woke up the next morning thinking of death. Well, not death exactly, but extinction. Tewksbury and I had gotten into a discussion of extinction on Slickrock Creek two months before. It was a fascinating talk punctuated by trout. Every time Tewksbury raised his voice to emphasize a point, a brown trout struck violently at his wet fly. After hooking and losing three trout, Tewksbury took to whispering, tossing out gasps of barely audible sentences. He was talking about death, about how he just couldn't figure it out, theologically. According to what he had learned as a boy death was the price man paid for his fall from grace, being kicked out of the Garden. It was okay, he supposed, as far as explanations went, but something about it bothered him.

Another trout struck and Tewksbury set the hook as the brown bent the rod tip into a bow, then began taking line as it raced downstream. Holding his rod high, not going to the reel yet, Tewksbury walked deeper into the cold creek, and there was no more talk of death's mysteries until well after twilight when he brought the subject up again over dinner—hot potato soup, beef jerky, and cracked-wheat bread.

He dipped a chunk of bread into the small silver bowl of steaming soup and kept on talking as he ate, mixing bites of jerky with bread and soup.

What troubled him, he told me, even as a young man, even as he sat in the soothing, rich candlelit interior of St. Patrick's Cathedral in New York City, was the whole idea of extinction.

Extinction could not be so easily dismissed, even by the most passionate theology. If a man embraced the idea of extinction, then it seemed only logical to Tewksbury that he had also to embrace the idea of existence before the Garden and the idea of a death more complete and irreversible than he cared to imagine.

Arby Mulligan, who showed up for dessert—pound cake and hot coffee—managed to rub the chill from Tewksbury's soul.

This is what he said, "It all comes and goes. Comes and goes."

Tewksbury was only slightly mollified, saying we had to admit extinction kind of put a damper on such ideas as destiny and final glory. In the end, there seemed to be only the end.

"Some significance," said Tewksbury woefully.

"Whistle while you work," said Arby Mulligan chuckling softly to himself. "It helps. Believe me, it helps."

I had already spread out the sleeping bag and crawled in and was intent on watching a meteor shower flash wildly across the sky, a long smear of dim orange and yellow pulses of light at the edges of the night sky. It was some show up there along a ridge of thick forest and old stones, my belly full of potato soup, and a head full of the day's hours along Deep Creek, the trout spooky and reclusive. Now, near midnight, tracks of meteors across the sky, threads of ephemeral light. There is rich bounty indeed along a high mountain stream. It is not so much what you gather in, even what you see, as it is a matter of letting the mountains alter your way of looking at things.

The night seemed mine, all that blue-black sky and starlight, the howl of a coyote in the near distance, Mulligan and Tewksbury still up, huddled about the stove talking of trout and death. Their voices seemed like whispers at the edge of a distant universe and I lay there undistracted, remembering part of a problem from a college physics class in which the class was instructed to reduce to three days the time needed to create the cosmos as we know it. Reduced to this scale, the question was how long would the average human life span be? I still remember the answer: ten seconds. Ten.

Curiously the figure did not shock me. It seemed like a fair amount of time. Surely enough time to experience joy and horror, fall in love, come up with a decent thought or two, perhaps even a profound one. Time enough to conceive, assure the next generation of its ten seconds. Time to lament, regret man's potential good and potential brutality. Just enough time, perhaps, to appreciate that man is, like the atom, a microcosm that embraces, even anticipates, the macrocosm: life drifting with time. Emerging.

Meanwhile, Arby Mulligan was fuming about there being too many roads in the mountains and wouldn't Tewksbury like to enlist in a conspiracy he was always trying to hatch against the pernicious spread of what he called "the asphalt people."

Mulligan's anger had an edge on it that night. Hippolyte Dulles had died the week before. Mulligan had found him out by the woodpile behind his shanty and hauled him inside and laid him down on the old slumped bed below the small hole Mulligan had cut in the roof for Hippolyte Dulles's soul to escape through.

"Just a sack of stiff skin and heavy bone he was," said Mulligan sharply. "I'm a man that's seen plenty of death and still it always surprises me, like someone sneaking up on you, grabbing you suddenlike. I mean just think about it now, really. One second you got this warm, human being who can sing and trout-fish, feel pain, show love, cry, laugh, and the next it's all gone. No songs from the dead's gray lips. No sounds at all excepting those of leaking gases. Just dead weight, a lump of stuff no more lifelike than a bag of rocks."

What was it I had decided about miracles? That they were often only the sudden appearance of the unexpected. Death, or at least the variety described by Arby Mulligan, seemed to certainly qualify. Sort of a miracle in reverse. Apparently, death had caught Hippolyte Dulles completely by surprise.

Mulligan spread the wool blanket on the ground. Down the trail came the sound of Tewksbury's Range Rover moving steadily off in the distance toward Bryson City.

"Sure hope it was big enough," said Mulligan thoughtfully, his words tinged more with uncertainty than remorse.

"What was big enough?" I asked, only half thinking as I lay there trying to let my mind absorb the entire night sky.

"Why the hole in Hippolyte's roof," said Mulligan. "I like to think of his soul going free, slipping out into the cool air, riding the wind sort of."

I liked the idea, too—the thought of Hippolyte Dulles as some new unseen energy on the wind, a sudden rush along the creek, pushing water hard against stone and roots.

The next morning I slept well past sunrise and almost resolved to sleep the day away. The wind was soft and cool. Tucked away in my sleeping bag under the shade of the trees just above the creek, it felt as though the entire mountainside were one deep, lush hammock swaying rhythmically, hypnotically in the pale morning light.

Mulligan had been up and about for hours and had already taken two fine rainbow trout, both on a No. 18 Adams dry fly.

I could see him in the creek, the cold water up past his thighs. He suddenly put his rod under his left arm, bent down close to the surface of the creek, and with his right hand splashed creek water over his face. He looked like an old Hindu bathing contentedly in the sacred waters of the Ganges. The low, early sunlight came off the water and Mulligan's face, glints of light caught for a moment in the streams of water running down the hollows of his cheeks, the sharp point of his chin. In the distance, along the ridge, electric lines and telephone poles stood neatly, avenues of power and light and sound connecting Cherokee and Bryson City.

By midmorning Arby Mulligan had headed down the creek while I hiked up to the Left Fork of Deep Creek.

The Left Fork of Deep Creek is a liquid Prospero, a wild rush of water and light, thick forest and galleries of stone and fata morgana pinched into a narrow, shadow-filled gorge. Far back along the creek and the steep mountainsides are virgin stands of timber, hemlocks that loom above the creek like shaggy wooden leviathans. Light seeps through the choking tangle of vegetation, falls in thin pools and seams on the forest floor. It is difficult country and given to violent, drastic and dramatic swings of mood and temperament. It is a place of wild water and stubborn trout and cool sunlight. There are two practical exits from the Left Fork: one is to climb out, a nearly vertical climb up from the creek to the ridgeline and the trail out. The climb is grueling and exhausting. Or, if the climb doesn't appeal to you, you can backtrack out, rejoining the main Deep Creek Trail near where the waters of the Left Fork join those of Deep Creek.

The Left Fork is known as much for its solitude as for its trout. The silence there is beyond measure. It is hard to resist either the quiet or the trout, despite the place's difficult nature and inhospitable character.

The day I left Mulligan, I reached the cutoff to the Left Fork well before sundown. I hid my gear well off the trail, stowing everything save my rod and reel, and a day pack filled with water, cheese, and crackers, dry flies, extra line, leaders, and tippet material. I did not begin fishing the creek until I had hiked past the old sill, and then I began working the fast water and pools upstream, using the creek's current, its own energy, to present my fraudulent little temptations fashioned from fur and colored thread and feathers. As it always does, the gorge of the Left Fork seemed soaked in an almost eucharistic silence. What light fell among the stones and trees and along the creek bank seemed frayed and faded. It lay on the water as gently as layers of mist. There was a faint wind among the trees, then, suddenly, a surge, a sudden gust from the north and east coming down the mountainside that bent saplings to the ground, shredded loose bark and leaves, snapped limbs, set loose eddies of loam and flecks of stone. Overhead, what had but a moment before been a harmless expanse of sky now roiled with swelling clouds, clouds boiling higher and higher into the sky. The clouds went from gray to a sea of apocalyptic blackness that enveloped the high ridges and erased the horizon.

The wind came harder and colder, so cold each breath seemed to scrape sharply at the soft lining of the lungs like jagged bits of glass. The sky went blacker still, a seamless black. Like the rantings of a mad choir, the wind yowled through the scraggy gorge and the creek rose up, spewing waves and foam, smashing hard against gray-black stones.

With the wind's deep growling came the rain. No tame drizzle or purring shower, but sheets of water flung desperately against the ground, striking like blasts of nails pelting the ground, gouging ragged holes in the earth, slapping relentlessly at stones, tearing at the surface of the creek as though it were a great bolt of cheap black cloth.

When I had walked into the creek and made my first cast, the water was at my calf. Now, in what seemed but a moment's passage, it pulled urgently, ceaselessly at my thighs, a rising wall of storm-tossed water, slashing at boulders and trees.

And the sky went blacker still. I got to the far bank, tried crawling up the mountainside, but the ground had gone to mud, a mush of dirt and bits of stone, broken limbs, and shredded leaves. I clawed at it hoping for any shelf of solid ground, a grip that would not give way.

Where was Ambrose Noel and his prayer wheel when a man needed them?

The creek rose on and on, grinding harder at the suddenly tenuous walls of the gorge, striking out desperately at its own confinement. I slid down the slope again, tripped, and came to rest on a wide, flat stone just inches above the tumbling water. The rain had gone slack and I noticed something on the rising creek, something bobbing in the near distance. My day pack. The creek lapped over the stone, sucked hungrily at my feet, and I jumped again for the muddy bank, grasping for mud and stones, limbs and vines, and finally, somewhere in midair, decided I would roll the dice, forget about trying to scale up the boggy slope and instead climb high among the trees, there to wait out what fortune the rising waters might have in mind.

The rain came hard for another hour and the swollen creek raged—a frightening bulge of raw, wild power gnashing insistently against the constricted gorge. It was like an aneurism ballooning threateningly in a helplessly clogged artery. Something had to give. I clung to the middle branches of a sturdy maple perhaps twenty feet above the once dreamy, placid creek turned pummeling river, churning mercilessly down the mountain. I was soaked, cut up, shivering, clutching the thick branches, pressing my face hard against the maple's trunk.

The sky dripped blackness and I leaned my head slightly down, watched and listened to the creek as it lashed and cracked and groaned through the gorge. Even stones seemed to shudder.

Sixteen hours later the water had dropped enough for me to climb down. My hands were numb. My feet were numb. My handsome Winston rod was lost, no doubt heaved by waves against the rocks, smashed. My fingertips were raw and bloody from trying blindly, madly, desperately to climb up the mountain.

A pale light washed the sky and there were slants of bright morning sunlight along the fringes of gray clouds moving fast across the sky from southwest to the east. The creek purred gently and harmlessly. I walked out of the narrow gorge, back to the main channel of the creek, and found my stash of gear that I had hidden well above the creek bank, and strung a makeshift clothesline between oak trees and hung out my soggy clothes. I mixed up a bowl of chili, boiled water for hot tea, and was thankful for one dry pair of long underwear and socks, a damp pair of jeans, and a T-shirt. While the chili warmed, I got out my extra rod, put on a reel loaded with 3-weight line, tied on a good dry fly, size 18, and cast.

The sun was high in the sky and its warm light felt good against my face.

Two days later when I got down the mountain to Hattie Gareth's place, Arby Mulligan was sitting on the porch in a red-and-yellow lawn chair.

"I thought you'd bought it for sure up there on the fork in that storm," he said, "and I was out here sitting peaceful like and already trying to ship you over into the past tense inside my head."

Miss Hattie had come to the open door. She stood there laughing, half in shadow. A light wind pressed against the folds of her long blue gingham dress, caught it as if it were slack sailcloth.

Hattie Gareth's place is outside Bryson City on a small branch of Deep Creek in a fine cove of hardwood forest. It sits well off the highway, a quarter mile up a dirt and gravel road, past a rusted-out 1949 Ford truck with its hood up and its engine long gone. It sits in scrub and poison ivy vines, a sculpture of decay and irreversible endings, the way things come and go. Come and go. Miss Hattie says that the Ford, in its prime, was a fine jalopy.

The Gareth home place is not so much an expression of any particular architectural theory as it is a tribute to the triumph of common sense and practicality. Like the old dog that hangs about the place, it is a mongrel of sorts, a mix of curious features, traits, characteristics, all of them more functional than ornamental. The place looks woebegone, troubled, and caught up in misery, which is too bad because its pained look detracts from its tenacity and stubborn loyalty. The Gareth place is more home than house. It hangs on. There's always a lantern glowing in the front window, through the silky shadows that spread across the wooden porch. The porch slopes uncertainly to the left, down toward the highway. Miss Hattie says the porch threatened to give way altogether on a March day in 1957 when a posse of Methodist revivalists showed up at her door looking not to save her soul but to question her about a roving band of renegade Calvinists who were rumored to be in the mountains sowing blasphemy and handing out gold-fringed Bibles, high-toned church music, and no-risk redemption.

"The head preacher kind of pushed his fellow Methodists aside," Miss Hattie said using her long, wide pale hands to animate the story, give it image and power, "and began stomping real violent-like, driving his black boots hard against the porch boards and then the whole thing teetered and swayed the way a sinking boat fumbles about like it's going under. And the air was full of risen Methodists, fellahs leaping, hopping, jumping, tossing themselves off the porch and toward solid ground.

"Never did find out if they ever caught up with them Calvinists."

Miss Hattie's place still has the shakes; it shudders with every footstep. Half of Miss Hattie's roof is gone, exposing a rusted simple metal bed frame, a rotted pine dresser, and a cracked blue-and-white enamel chamber pot. Miss Hattie calls this her guest room. I've lain on its floor looking up into the mountain night many times, leaning my head against the soft backpack, listening to the low, muted sighing of the creek in the distance until I seemed to drift effortlessly in the night, at ease in that seemingly liquid blackness that seeps through the woods, up the mountainside.

A night at Miss Hattie's comes complete with a mountain breakfast—the smell of hot sausage, ham and eggs, freshly baked bread, steaming grits, mountain jams and honey, coffee laced with apple brandy or mountain whiskey. Arby told me years ago that Mr. Beamis Gareth died in the room without a roof. It was their room then and the roof was firm and tight. That was the winter of 1962. He was sixty-one years old and had worked for years up in Bryson City and other small mountain towns as a janitor and fix-it man for several Baptist churches.

"He cleaned up after saint and sinner alike," Mulligan said sighing audibly. "Even after me. I was a member then, though not a very loyal one. I drank. I danced. I trout-fished all the time. I dreamed of falling in love with three women at once. I loved the mountains as much as I loved God. The preacher came to me one Sunday after the early service, put his hand on my shoulder, and whispered in my ear, 'Arby, God loves you and so do I. We say to you, get right with the Lord or get you brother to the borders of hell.' I spent a week up on Deep Creek. Some hell.

"Beamis Gareth came and got me, brought me here to his place. Every night he left a Bible open on my pillow. Otherwise, he kept to his own business mostly. Always joking how he was polishing and mopping and sweeping his way to paradise."

Beamis Gareth took a chill after the late service at the old Cold Springs church. He walked home in a hard snow. The chill settled into a fever; the fever took hold and wouldn't break. The winter storm had the mountains in its grip. In three days the storm and Beamis Gareth passed over. That spring a slashing thunderstorm peeled the roof off the back section of the Gareths' house, leaving the room where Beamis had died open to wind and rain, cold and warming sunshine. Hattie Gareth moved a cot into the kitchen by the stove and let the roof go. On a shivering March night, she took Beamis's keys, opened an old tin box that Beamis kept under their bed, poked about, and came up with the five-dollar gold certificate which she used to light a fire in the woodstove.

This is what she told Arby Mulligan: "I needed the heat more than I had use for the money."

Arby Mulligan gave that story to Rachael Settles and now it is told along mountain trails and paths and logging roads from Lauada and Hogback Gap to Dillsboro and Sylva, from the Cowee Mountains and Rainbow Falls down on the Nantahala River, where the trout barely outnumber the kayakers, canoeists, and whitewater rafters, to Otter Creek School, and on north to Sassafras Gap and Meetinghouse Mountain.

Arby Mulligan had met Rachael Settles in the spring of 1987 up at the old Blue Wing Church along Soco Creek in the Smoky Mountains. Rachael supposedly turned and took one hurried, terrified glance at the bedraggled man with the bent, smooth hickory walking staff and the cheerless eyes coming up the road toward her and screamed the word that freed Dog to tear the approaching stranger's throat out.

By the way, this is the command: Abattoir.

Abattoir is just another word for slaughterhouse, yet it has a sound to it, at least when said by Rachael Settles, as cheerful as the ringing of tiny bells.

Dog charged, slobbering wildly, great dark eyes fixed madly on the figure of Arby Mulligan, but he stopped short, Rachael Settles told me later. He drew back, paused, as if to study this obviously downtrodden, luckless human being, sniffed him cautiously, then turned suddenly, padding confidently back toward Rachael Settles as if to assure her that all was well, that this bundle of middle-aged man with the walking stick and fly rod was certainly one harmless human being, a man who, although curious, seemed to be as kind and temperate as balmy weather, as innocent as summer rain. Dog had a sad look about him, Rachael said, and why not? After all, Rachael had opened the slaughterhouse and he had found nothing inside worth ripping to pieces, nothing but the laughable figure of Arby Mulligan walking down the old road humming loudly.

This is what he was humming so cheerfully—Hymn No. 1, in fact the only hymn, of the Owl Creek Gap Church of Universal Harmony:

> What Goes Around, Comes Around
> Rocks and Trout
> You and Me
> What Goes Around, Comes Around
> Mountains to the Seas.
>
> Taste Life Fully
> Feel All You Can
> Cause It All Comes and Goes
> Like Shifting Sands.

Arby Mulligan wrote this hymn himself. He says he wrote it one night while sleeping in Miss Hattie Gareth's guest room under a roof of cold mountain starlight. He woke suddenly, he says, sweating and trembling, shivering and shaking, his body full of emanation and revelation. This was the revelation: Things come and go. Come and go. So right then and there, Arby Mulligan decided to give up everything but reading the bumps on people's heads, trout fishing, and ushering converts into Owl Creek Gap Church where everyone could be a member as long as he had been doused with cold mountain creek water and as long as he believed in doing man and earth as little harm as possible.

After a good day on Slickrock Creek, a day when all of us had taken at least one handsome, hard-fighting, uncompromising, red-backed Slickrock brown trout, we were walking back toward the highway where Tewksbury had parked his green Range Rover. The wind had fallen to a whisper among the trees and the sun was low in the sky, seeming to hang precariously on the darkly shadowed ridges rising in the western sky. The light at our feet seemed at once sluggish and contumacious, fractious, as thick and uncontrollable as veins of thick slabs of lava sliding down a volcanic mountainside. One instant the light looked madder crimson and the next zinc orange. Pools of oranges and dull golds, a swelling tide of reds moving through the woods in waves of fading daylight. And I went on talking to Tewksbury about New York City, his work, his life there.

"What's your great ambition?" I asked almost nonchalantly.

"To be totally ambitionless," Tewksbury answered.

Arby Mulligan started humming, and the light went softer still, and I started thinking of the day on the creek, the hours spent, exhausted, gone. The roll of time seems to inexorably push forward, yet at that moment it seemed to me that a man is mostly molded by what he keeps, holds on to, from his past, the real and the imagined. Out of this constant mingling flows the present and intimations of the future.

The day had been a good one, I believed, a day that had filled me, left me all sense and sensation. In the day's debris was life's debris—joy and sadness, regret and longing, success and failure, pain and triumph, and, always, the endless possibilities of each passing moment. The day had added more to me than it had taken. It had left a prickling residue soaked in the feel of life, of living.

Tewksbury had taken a hotel room in town. Mulligan and I would be spending the night in Miss Hattie's guest room. I thought of that old gray-

and-white house on the hillside, half in ruin, tilting dangerously, looking like a sailing ship heeled to its portside gunnels by strong winds and rough seas, a ship flirting with disaster. In the mornings, though, Miss Hattie's place rose above layers of soupy fog like something rising through a tear in the firmament, and by noon wide streams of sunlight seemed to bind the walls.

Inside that part of the house that still has a roof, the wooden walls are papered with tombstone rubbings. Besides being a hard-working Christian janitor and general handyman, Beamis Gareth had been an accomplished stonemason and graveyard poet. His words eased many a soul into heaven and comforted the living. My favorites are tacked just above the table in the kitchen where Miss Hattie spends her mornings drinking sassafras tea mixed with ginseng: a concoction she swears keeps her bones knitted together.

"I Ain't Dead, Just Permanently Out of Town" and "The Dead Aren't So Much Lost As Suddenly Found," and "Fear Not, Life Goes On, Even Beneath This Stone."

"You can sure feel it here," said Arby Mulligan looking around the dimly lit room. "Death is near. It's got a real feel to it like maybe tree bark or shed snakeskin. And it's close enough to touch."

"How close?" I said.

"Just around the corner," Mulligan said smiling and pointing to one of the rubbings on the wall. "You know what mine's going to say?" 'He Came and He Went.' That's all. That's enough."

Arby Mulligan walked over near Miss Hattie's bed, looked up toward the roof, studied the ceiling as though he were figuring the best spot to saw a tidy hole in the roof directly over her head.

I kept on looking at the tombstone rubbings and thinking of Mulligan's self-imposed epitaph. Whatever tombstone marked his life should say this as well—that in passing through, he had harmed neither man nor earth along the way.

Going to Town

AFTER ARBY MULLIGAN WHISPERED his epitaph to me in Hattie Gareth's house, we went out to the guest room, spread out our bedrolls, lay down under a dome of stars with the mountain night pulled close and tight over us, a quilt of starlight, foggy shadows, and the endless liquid clatter of the creek.

That night I dreamed of the last trout I had taken on Deep Creek the day before, on a handsome stretch of water about three miles above the Deep Creek campground.

In the dream, I was both observer and angler, somehow outside my body watching as I hooked the fine trout, as I worked it and it worked me. I was smiling at myself smiling, evidently thankful at how spontaneous fly-fishing is, how natural it seems, as though it were as much as part of a trout stream's character as oxygen, swift water, and aquatic insects. Nothing about fly-fishing appeared consciously artificial or contrived. There was not a dollop of hubris to it, at least not as it unfolded, in my dream. In the dream, fly-fishing repelled pretense the way sailcloth sheds rain.

After I had hooked the trout its run became a mad dance, arabesques of motion and light, wrinkles of energy wrenched into flowing time. All was not only process but probability, a physics not of absolutes but of tendencies, not of the hard or the inflexible, but of the inviolate nature of probing beyond even the language of mathematics.

The trout went deeper and took me farther into the creek. I could feel the cold creek water against my belly, and the creek itself was soaked in a rich, gold organic light that seemed to consume the deep woods, leaving even the mountainsides without definition, and even the black stones along the creek refused to be absolute.

It was a dream that was at once thrilling and frightening, as confusing as a Tibetan mandala. It was a dream of unencumbered experience. Instead, there was feeling and sensation only and the sway of that golden light and the sound of the creek; the tug of the trout on the line; cool shadows against my skin; smooth stones underfoot. All of this came not as words, not as language, but as images of light and matter. A dream about high country trout fishing is apparently no place for predictable linear thinking. More often than not my dreams of high country trout seem like flashes of pure experience, something felt that eludes exact expression.

Perhaps this is why Arby Mulligan always says, every time Tewksbury taunts him about the trout he's caught and the mountain streams he's fished, "I can't put it into no damned coat of words. Not enough pockets." It happens to me, as well, and to Tewksbury, these moments beyond speech.

Here's another of my recurring trout-fishing dreams. I've caught a huge brown trout and am in a dimly lit bar in town, frantically, desperately trying to tell the story of my encounter with this noble fish. My mouth opens but nothing tumbles out. No words, no sounds of any kind. Suddenly, an old man smelling of flat beer and whiskey hands me a sheet of blank paper and a box of crayons.

Guess what happens next? I open the box and all the crayons are beige. The next morning, at breakfast, I told Mulligan of the dream. Between mouthfuls of coffee and griddle cakes, this is what he said: "Can't undo trout, not even in a dream. That's a fact. They'll make you crazy if you try and make sense of them. The Lord's eye on it."

I walked out onto the porch and into a chilly morning light, one that seemed to fill the cove in supple layers of light drifting on the wind like soft clouds of fog shaded cadmium yellow. Such a smooth light, calm as a pool of fallen rain. And the morning widened and the sunlight in the cove by Hattie Gareth's house went from pale and pinched yellows to warm rising slants of sunlight the color of overripe apricots.

Mulligan joined me on the porch. We sat on the wooden steps watching the light flood the dark woods. Crows squawked noisily from out along the highway and the wind coming off the ridges grew colder. Mulligan took his pocketknife and whittled a hickory twig to a good sharp point, worked a piece of bacon from between his few remaining teeth.

"New knot on Hattie's head," he said softly, calmly. "Has a bad-news shape to it, real bad. She'll be under the green quilt with Beamis before summer comes on full."

"Did you read this knot or is this just a professional guess?" I asked. I did not want to lose Miss Hattie or the guest room with its stunning appointments. There is so much these days I'd rather not lose.

"Sure," said Mulligan. "Read the knot on her twice just in case she wanted a second opinion. It's a death knot for sure. Each death knot is different. Hippolyte's was stone hard and had a bumpy ridge to it. This one's soft as mattress stuffing and black as mud. I touched it gentle-like and it bled as though I'd put my knife to it. And it's feverish. It's death's calling card all right. And she knows it, too."

Miss Hattie yelled from inside. "There's a helping of cakes and honey left. Get it now or it goes to the dog and crows."

Her voice trailed off like a distant echo, then came to life again, spilling out of the dark doorway.

"Mulligan," said Miss Hattie, "I want you to get back up this way come May so I can go to town and pick me out a headstone."

She had walked to the doorway, stood there, took an envelope from her apron pocket, and slipped out a piece of yellowed paper.

"This here's what Beamis wrote for my stone.

HATTIE FOSTER GARETH
AS GOOD AS ANY WOMAN GETS"

Mulligan headed down the mountain toward the Nantahala Gorge. I loaded up my backpack, hiked to my car at the Deep Creek campground, and headed for the town of Cherokee.

Bob Winterwolf Dougal had invited me to come see him after the first rib of warm weather moved among the mountains.

"That's the best time to watch the snowflakes," he said. Dougal calls white men snowflakes. "They come by the thousands, let me tell you. By the herds, fat and docile, every one of them ready to empty their wallets for the sight of a real, no-shit, pure-blooded Indian walking about in a loincloth, a bloody knife in one hand and a bottle of hooch in the other. Yessir. As long as there is wampum and wigwams, they stand in line to lay their money down."

So I gave in to curiosity and checked into the Cherokee Holiday Inn. I took a hot shower and had a hot shave, and slept between warm, thick blankets, my head on a soft, white pillow. There was a television in the room, but I didn't turn it on. Distraction, especially in large doses, tends to be habit forming. City people seem to thrive on distraction the way monks thrive on meditation or anglers thrive on things piscatorial. I knew if I turned on the television and picked up the telephone, dialed room service, I might never get out of bed.

The residents of Cherokee and the Qualla Reservation are fine mountain people, steadfastly practical, even in their theology. Having had little exposure to excess, they tend to disdain it. Life here is hard even when it is kind. You might even describe their character as Victorian, were it not for their love of good sipping whiskey, dancing, music, and wit that is as caustic as it is rowdy, and, naturally, their respect for mystery and magic, and their belief in the power of mountains to heal as well as bewitch. Their prickly, sometimes aggressive, absolute self-reliance is tinged with kindness and compassion.

I spread a map of the Smoky Mountains out on the cool, damp ground, light a candle, watch the yellow light flicker and sway over the map, illuminating the places like Cherokee, that stay with me, clutter up my memory.

Brasstown, there on the map where I traded three fresh rainbow trout for a warm root beer and a loaf of white bread; Friendship, where a man in a brown fedora held a dull jackknife to my throat and asked for exactly $12.35 to pay overdue taxes. His hand trembled as he talked and the knife's smooth blade dug harmlessly into my Adam's apple. Indian Grove Gap, where wrapped inside the blue sleeping bag's warm cocoon of down I waited out a sudden ice storm stretched out on the front seat of the car. That was the time I dreamed of the day I caught the big eight-pound brown trout on Hazel Creek on spidery 5X tippet. When I brought the big brown trout close to me, I found a piece of tippet and a bent hook lodged firmly in its jaw. It was a trout that appeared, it seemed, in more than one angler's dream. I dreamed of the trout's weight, its eyes, as endlessly intriguing as Rachael Settles's. And after I had dreamed of the big brown trout, I dreamed of Arby Mulligan, the day he took two brook trout on Snowbird Creek with one fly on one cast. It was some night there at Indian Grove Gap, a night full of snow and ice and mountain dreams. Andrews, the town where I was suddenly taken by a fit of philosophy and hiked up to Snowbird Creek where I determined only to fish and meditate. And Sylva, where I spent two days shivering and rattling in the backseat of the car full of fever and piscatorial hallucinations brought on, I think, by a can of sardines gone bad. The sardines had been my supper that day, along with crackers and cheese and bread. The sardines were packed in some kind of spicy mustard. Stuff potent enough to unhinge even the tenacious grasp of a gooseneck barnacle. Someone with liquid-blue eyes and a soft gray beard got me out of the car, threw me on the seat of a faded green John Deere tractor, and took me to the local doctor, a nervous man of middle age who kept taking my pulse and feeding me cherry-flavored cough syrup.

Once, near Paint Town, I fell asleep at the wheel; I sank into a blue-black depression in an old run-down motel near the Nantahala River and slept for three days straight down in Highlands, where I met the beautiful redhead with royal blue eyes and full lips. I looked at her standing on the corner at the traffic light on the main street and fell instantly in love. "Are you from here?" I asked. A thick wad of bubble gum appeared between rows of yellow teeth. This is what she said: "For fifty dollars, bub, I'll be from any place you like." Even in the blissful mountains, love can be tragic.

I have found comfort, too, on occasion, in Cherokee and Gatlinburg and Pigeon Forge, though often all I can recall of these towns—almost all towns—are road signs, blinking lights, pushy crowds, too much noise, the sharp smell of gas stations, sidewalks and gutters crammed with a dazzling array of aluminum cans, plastic cups and forks, buckets of half-eaten fried chicken. City life seems forever caught in the carboniferous bog of routine. Too much routine leaves my senses feeling as though I've been injected with heavy doses of Novocain. After I spend time in a town or city, especially large ones, almost everything eventually seems humdrum and uneventful, no matter how truly ridiculous, bizarre, or brutish it might be. Sooner or later city living persuades you, wrongly, that you exist inside a hermetic bubble that lets the fits and starts of living slip and slide off you as though your skin were coated with a layer of Teflon. The easier the slide, the less stressful the ride: everything is a matter of self-preservation.

Gatlinburg, Cherokee, and Pigeon Forge are regularly pilloried for their blatant lack of dignity, style, class. They are chided for being more like carnivals than real towns, road shows offering not life in any real sense but rather facsimiles of life, the fake rather than the real.

"They are cash registers connected by motels, junk-food houses, and highways," says Arby Mulligan. "Towns that cater to our seamier nature, if you will."

The side, I suppose, that feels the urge to rush off and play Adventure Golf, Haunted Golf, Fantasy Golf, and finally the greatest miniature golf challenge of them all, Hillbilly Golf. The side that now and then gets the itch to gawk at the limp entertainments served up at places like Dollywood or the desire to suit up and try indoor skydiving. The side that occasionally wants to drop by the Elvis Museum and look at X rays of the King's fingers or see his underwear. The King had a thing for the fishnet style, brightly colored. All that talent and no taste; that's what Tewksbury says.

Crowds move through these mountain towns like surging tides. If a man can get lost in a thick wood, he can become invisible in a crowded city, just another tourist waiting to be amazed, dazzled, thrilled, humored, well fed, and completely cared for. Crowds are a soothing paradox, proof, after all, that there are plenty of human beings just as lonely and desperate as we are. There is no drug as powerful as loneliness. It can compel a man to do just about anything.

Pigeon Forge is good old American free enterprise, the gloves off, anything goes, whatever the traffic will bear, as long as there is a profit in it. Whatever sells, from homemade fudge to theology. Everything's for sale or lease. Even God. See America's number one religious attraction, Christus Gardens. Admission, $5. It is life lived in bursts as quick as a huckster's pitch.

But it is all harmless, if you don't take it too seriously. Indeed, in many ways, Gatlinburg fancies itself something of a trendsetter. It is one of the South's most popular honeymoon destinations. It is also one of the few cities where one can actually find hotels and motels and resorts, complete with fireplaces, that are willing to lease firewood, with an option to burn it, if the night gets chilly enough. The brilliance of modern merchandising.

The mountain wind takes on a different character in town. It even smells differently. Early in the morning, at first light, before the town begins to stir, the wind seems sour and heavy and tired. It smells of exhaust and rotting fish, stale popcorn, cheap after-shave, flat beer, inexpensive wines, sweet perfumes. The heady smells of a different kind of adventure.

Tewksbury and I stayed in Gatlinburg the night before I planned to take him up the beautiful Alum Cave Bluff Trail, which begins nearby in the Great Smoky Mountains National Park. There are only three entrances to the park, Townsend, Cherokee, and Gatlinburg. The Alum Cave Bluff Trail begins 8.5 miles up Highway 441 from the Sugarlands Visitor Center and Park Headquarters. The trail covers more than ten miles round trip and climbs 2,560 feet up Mount Le Conte. Alum Cave is not a cave, it's a great, 100-foot-high, brooding, overhanging bluff, a fine example of the mountains' great Anakeesta rock formation, full of minerals and the tainted glow of pyrite—fool's gold. The Anakeesta and Thunderbird rock formations form most of what is the crest of the Smoky Mountains. The Alum Cave Bluff Trail is a beautiful hike, especially in early spring or in early October when colors run down the thickly wooded mountainsides like paints mixed madly by a nervous artist. It is a good trail, one that takes you into the bone and muscle of the Smoky Mountains. So much raw beauty and so close to town.

I wanted Tewksbury to fish Abrams Creek in Cades Cove, and Collins Creek, and the wild waters of the Panther Creek as yet unshadowed by trails of any kind, and a stretch of the Cataloockee River down through Cataloockee Cove. To the north of the cove is Mount Sterling, to the west rises the great dark domes of the Balsam Mountains, and to the southwest is the humpbacked spine of the Cataloockee Divide.

The day we arrived in town, Tewksbury saw the sign for the Forbidden Caverns and wanted to go. COME SEE "UNDER THE SMOKIES" the sign said. OPEN IN ANY WEATHER. As it turned out, the Forbidden Caverns aren't that forbidden. Just a simple system of limestone caves now made to earn their keep. Caves as big business, one-hour tours starting every twenty minutes. Come on down. It's always 58 degrees or cooler, no matter the season.

"The tour should have started where it stopped," said Tewksbury as we walked along Parkway Road, the main road through Gatlinburg, passing up burger places, pizza, submarine sandwiches, German food, Chinese food, British food. Over at the town's convention center, wildflower lovers from around the world were gathering for the annual Smoky Mountain Wildflower Pilgrimage. Small knots of people wearing bush hats, carrying field guides and hand lenses, milled about whispering words that drifted on the wind like bits of confetti—lady's slipper, trilliums, Solomon's seal, Fraser's sedge, jack-in-the-pulpit, Turk's-cap lily, showy orchids, spring beauties and fire pinks, mayapple and bloodroot. We thought about going into The Guinness World Records Exhibition Center and the World of Illusion, but decided we were already giddy enough. We fought back the temptation to buy tickets to the Kingdom Story at the Kingdom Resort, which bills itself as AMERICA'S LARGEST OUTDOOR DRAMA DEPICTING THE LIFE AND TIMES OF JESUS CHRIST ON EARTH! All this within sight of Clingman's Dome and the headwaters of Hazel Creek and Deep Creek.

We bought an ice-cream cone and sat on a bench near the Little Pigeon River, which runs through town, watching the crowd joggle by. Tewksbury didn't seem all that impressed, not even by the Space Needle, Ober Gatlinburg, and the 8,000-foot Alpine Slide, or Ogle's Waterpark, but then what can you show a man who lives in a city where anyone with access to a telephone can connect himself with City of Sluts, The Skin Line, Condom Sense, Wrestling Fantasy Girls, the Tarot Card Reading Line, Spanish Dial-a-Porn, Dial-an-Insult, 970-PAIN, and I Confess? Where such scintillating fare is common, even a peak at Elvis's underwear must seem like tepid excitement indeed.

It wasn't until the Savoir showed up at our bench along the Little Pigeon River that Tewksbury looked up from his Rocky road ice-cream cone, a gleam of renewed interest and enthusiasm in his eyes. The Savior had on a pair of tan, baggy chino pants, no shoes, a red wool cap, and a bright blue sports jacket. Tight about his waist was a frayed brown belt onto which was fastened a polished silver change machine. The Savior stood perhaps five feet tall and weighed at least three hundred pounds. There was a small pewter peace symbol hung about his neck on a piece of green shoestring. He had a gray goatee that he had let grow into long wisps of hair to his chest. His eyes were blue and gray: the right one was blue and the left one was gray. To his credit, the Savior had all his teeth, some freshly capped. These had the look of hand-rubbed ivory.

The Savior carried a handful of small handbills. At the top of each one was printed in huge block letters, PRAYER REQUESTS.

He handed each of us one, saying, "Your deepest wishes and desires can come true through me." He had a soft voice, kind and harmless as a whisper.

"And a bargain," he said, "at a mere two dollars a prayer. Read them over, brothers, study them. Surely there are concerns and needs in your desperate lives, areas where God through me can help."

Tewksbury was already studying the handbill. He leaned close to me, said in a low voice, "I wondered when something interesting was going to happen. Now we're getting someplace."

The Savior assured us his powers were considerable, imposing and impressive indeed. Tewksbury seemed genuinely moved by just how far a couple of bucks and prayer could get an angler cast adrift in Gatlinburg. The Savior's prayer sheet was divided into neat columns with small boxes at the side of each possible category. It looked something like this:

❐ Greater stamina in lovemaking.
❐ Smiting one's enemies.
❐ Blessing one's friends.
❐ Relief from depression.
❐ Easing a spastic colon.
❐ Ditching a lousy job.
❐ Praising an employer.
❐ Damning an employer.
❐ Relieving suffering and pain.
❐ Ending starvation in (insert state, country, etc., here. Each country .25 cents extra).
❐ Being merciful to the merciless.
❐ Eradicating Tooth Decay.
❐ Prayer for the Death Penalty.
❐ Prayer to end the Death Penalty.
❐ Prayer against war and obesity.

And so on. Prayers for the oppressed, the shivering, the tormented, those with ulcers and kidney stones, hemorrhoids, bad feet, obsessive guilt, hiccups, and all such disorders of the body and spirit were on sale that afternoon, two dollars apiece.

"Can you raise trout?" asked Tewksbury. He was still looking studiously at the handbill.

The Savior lifted his long, pale hands to his chest. "As though I were a swarm of mayflies, brother," he chimed modestly.

Tewksbury got up, fished out a five-dollar bill, pressed it gently into the Savior's hand, and said, "Then pray for us, my friend, five dollars' worth. We'll take the raising-trout prayer once a day for three days."

We walked back toward the hotel. Great shadows came seeping down from the dark slopes of the distant mountains and eased over the town's noisy, narrow, crowded streets.

We fished hard the next three days up and down Abrams Creek in Cades Cove and on Collins Creek and Panther Creek, and along the Chataloockee River. Except for two small trout on Panther Creek, we didn't raise a single fish and were tempted to stop in at the Indian Campground & Trout Farm northeast of Gatlinburg on Route 321, where, the sign taunted, there were RAINBOW TROUT. WATCH 'EM, FEED 'EM, CATCH 'EM. STOCKED POND. NO

LICENSE REQUIRED. NO CATCH, NO PAY. NO LIMIT. All this and a SWIFT MOUN-TAIN STREAM, LARGE, SHADED SITES FOR TENTS AND RVS, SWIMMING POOL, WATERFALL, LAUNDRY, GAME ROOM, STOVES, AND HOT SHOWERS.

Instead, we pressed on toward Cherokee because Tewksbury was determined that if he couldn't catch trout at least he could go into Cherokee and try again to get the best of that town's most infamous fowl—the swaggering chicken that plays—and rarely loses—tic-tac-toe.

Tewksbury played for an hour and never even came close to beating the chicken. Its eyes cold and dispassionate, staring mercilessly at Tewksbury, the chicken waited for the money to drop, the next game to begin. Tewksbury lost again and moaned as the chicken strutted victoriously about like a matador who had just slain the bull, driven it to the ground in defeat. The trick to it, of course, is that the chicken always gets the first move and it always takes the center square. The snowflakes don't stand a chance.

The chicken is something to see, really. It seems to yawn wearily at the sight of yet another tourist stepping up to challenge its supremacy at the subtle profundities of tic-tac-toe.

I looked around the swelling crowd for the smiling face of Bob Winterwolf Dougal. When a white man was being kindly and courteously flimflammed, Bob was usually close at hand beaming with pride at his people's industry and hard work in getting ahead and at their economic shellacking of the white man. I looked carefully but did not see him. Meanwhile, the gloating chicken had taken yet another game from Tewksbury. I felt sorry for Dougal. He was missing one of his people's finest hours as Tewksbury plunked down another dollar, saying, "Okay, featherbrains. This time I get the Xs!"

Riding toward the Smoky Mountains, through Sevierville and Pigeon Forge and finally Gatlinburg, you sometimes get a nervous sense of parallel worlds—the mountain, honest and wild, rough-edged, persistent, life forever on the move, and towns, landscapes altered, designed, and fabricated by man, with few natural blemishes. Every inch in use, a place of concrete, Mylar, polyurethane, acrylate, pressboard. At night the valley is a seam of light, an urgency and fever of neon, the rapid pulse of a place turning a tidy profit. An atmosphere of rich commercial bedlam, a delirium of business. And business is good, very good.

Compared to acid rain and a great many other serious environmental problems that face the Great Smoky Mountains, Gatlinburg is an almost insignificant annoyance. Indeed, it is hardly even that. It is harmless enough. And when it all gets to you there is always that invisible boundary at the end of Parkway Street, right past the gas station, the market, and the Burning Bush restaurant, that boundary where the city ends and the national park begins, where the chaos of gimmick and illusion and sleight-of-hand gives way to what is vital.

I used to carry a tent into the mountains, but I rarely used it. Eventually I quit carrying it around. I really didn't like it much and was glad to be rid of it. Being inside it reminded me of hermetic motel rooms, of offices, of crowded cities. What's the point of mountain wildness if, sooner or later, you don't propose to sink yourself into it? Too much time lying about comfortable tents is as habit forming as becoming too content with city life. Besides, leaving the tent behind lightens the load.

Summer nights in Gatlinburg and Pigeon Forge are cool and there is often on the wind a mad choir of gospel music, the shriek of honest but slightly out of tune rock 'n' roll, and the sentimental wail of country and western songs mingling with the wild-eyed fiddling of bluegrass music. The streets are clogged with cars and big, polished motorbikes, undulating groups of men and women and children. The crowd embraces them all—drifters, the newly wed, the newly divorced, exiles, fugitives, the old and young, con men and madmen, the veteran at traffic light Number 9 showing off the dull blue tattoo on his now distended belly that says bravely KILL 'EM ALL AND LET GOD SORT 'EM OUT. The words have a long, hideous red-and-black snake with a rotted-out skull's head running through them. There's a jug band down by the river and up on the ridge come the sounds of a German waltz. Above the sound of the rushing river is the odd mix of accordions and tambourines.

The little town seems to run on the rush of excitement, an excitement that has an insatiable appetite. It's no cheap high, but as I say, innocent enough, I suppose. Supposing is a human affliction. A trout can't suppose; it knows. An insect knows. A brown recluse spider knows what it needs to know. That's why I sent the one in my sleeping bag on its way back into the dark loam of the forest floor after it bit me on the forearm. It was my fault; that's what I get for turning over on it in the middle of the night while it was hunting, trying to stay alive. We know just enough to know that we know little, if anything. Therefore, we are doomed to speculate, to stumble about from one dilemma and perplexity to another, be it along mountain trout streams or in well-manicured cities and towns.

Dougal showed up just as Tewksbury finally admitted defeat to the Cherokee chicken. Standing in the McDonald's in downtown Cherokee, you can hear tourists from Iowa and Ohio giggling among themselves, trying to get up the nerve to walk up to the counter and ask for "buffalo burgers" or throw beads down and ask if the place accepts wampum. Once I overheard a young man from Kansas ask one of the cashiers at the Cherokee McDonald's if their burgers were "genuine red meat." And there was the guy in the big purple van with Kentucky plates that yelled into the drive-through speaker, "Hey, in there, real Indians don't eat McNuggets, do they?"

Dougal shrugs when he hears such things and laughs and explains how glass beads, hatchets, liquor, and Bibles simply took Native Americans by surprise and made them giddy.

He says, "How could we resist? It's like Tewksbury and the chicken. The game was rigged. We never had a chance. And at the time, a barrel of good liquor for a little land seemed like a good deal."

Dougal was eating a fish sandwich and lamenting the fact that he hasn't traveled much, especially to the north. Before he dies, though, when he's well fixed, when his economic battle is won, he says he wants to go to the Far North, up among the Eskimos of Alaska and Canada.

"I'd like to get up there when the nights don't end, when they just go on and on, and get me a sweet Eskimo woman and crawl into a warm cabin and spend the season with her, the both of us buried under a pile of parkas and mukluks."

We walked from McDonald's down toward the bridge to Big Cove Road, the bridge across the Oconaluftee River. We walked to the walkway over to Saunooke's Trading Post. Out front, on the river side of the highway, were two Native Americans, both decked out in war bonnets and buckskins and moccasins. The one in front of the tiny wooden teepee carried an ornate peace pipe. The dress was grand, but a fashion Cherokees never wore.

"We get this stuff out West. We get it half price from our brothers the Sioux, Crow, and Cheyenne," explained Dougal. "The snowflakes love it and dig deeper into their pockets. The one by the tent is Chief Joe. Not quite as charming and photogenic as Chief Henry, but a nice enough fellow. Chief Henry says he's the most photographed Indian in America and he probably is. He has a fine business mind and a keen understanding of advertising and merchandising. None of the other chiefs seem to be able to catch him. Once the tourist season opens, everyone's a chief. No shit. Anyway, Joe here helps shuffle the snowflakes over the river and into the shops and attractions across the bridge. Sort of an Indian shepherd and a damn fine one, too. Thanks to Joe we make a healthy profit here and the snowflakes go away smiling because they have been among real savages."

Dougal looked at the growing crowd, smiling broadly.

"It's great to be young and on the reservation, huh?" he said. "What a country! What opportunity! The white man's capitalism has taught us well! Take no prisoners!"

The second chief was Jonathan Slygo. He stood well to the left of the bridge to Saunooke's Trading Post. He was of average height with slumped shoulders and small, terrible scarred hands and forearms. He wore no elaborate headdress, just a single fake eagle feather tied loosely to his long, black, braided hair. The feather shuddered in the wind. A single black bear's claw hung about his neck. He chain-smoked Camels and finally sat on a small blue Coleman cooler full of crushed ice and cans of Dr. Pepper.

Dougal introduced us.

"The name's Many Scars," said Jonathan Slygo.

His voice was soft and distracted, edged with boredom.

Many Scars Slygo lives up to his name. He insisted that I gaze in curious awe at the stitchery of pinched and purple scars that marked his slender forearms and hands. "Vietnam?" I asked, turning to Dougal.

Many Scars Slygo, who went on staring blankly at the steady press of tourists filing past Chief Joe and onto the little bridge over the river, suddenly raised his small head up close to mine.

"Nope," he said, "the Wet Whistle club down in Dallas, Texas. What's it now? More than twenty years ago. White men, five, Cherokee, one. Me. What a night, I'll say. Had 'em, too, until the short fat one come at me with a busted long-neck beer bottle and the others finally got me tangled up so I couldn't move. Cops finally come and broke it up, hauled me in. Thought I was some Apache off the reservation, bent on revolution or something. They took my wallet and said what kind of Indian has a name like Jonathan Slygo. Cherokee, I told 'em. Took me to a doc who sewed me up. A hundred and six stitches. Then they kicked me out of the patrol car out on the interstate, northbound, told me Dallas don't like Indians and to stay the hell out."

Jonathan Many Scars Slygo went back to staring at the crowds. Dougal told me that Many Scars was one spiritual Native American, a man of many blessings. Before things went bad for him at the Wet Whistle, he'd been a brilliant automobile mechanic.

Dougal said, "His wisdom is still great." His wisdom, it turned out, was his ability to keep a 1960 Chevy pickup on the road and running without interruption since the summer of 1961. Dougal said that Many Scars was as close as they had to a living legend. Many Scars spent most of his days on the porch of his ramshackle house along the river leading friends and neighbors through the chaos of automotive mystery and intrigue. They came with their questions about sticky valves, thrown rods, cracked blocks, unaligned front ends, stubborn chokes, and he would tell them the way to repair it all cheaply, easily.

On weekends, come the spring, he liked to leave the greasy world of cars behind and come to town, sit here by the bridge and watch the snowflakes. Native American children dressed in Ocean Pacific shirts, Bugle Boy pants, and high-top Nike shoes gathered about Many Scars Slygo. One of the older boys handled the odds, taking and covering the bets. As I discovered, Many Scars Slygo had yet another special talent—the uncanny ability to match each passing tourist with his or her state without moving from the blue Coleman cooler under the shade of the trees.

"Missouri," he said, his voice still flat, assured, yet emotionless. The oldest boy ran quickly to a lady and man passing Chief Joe. The man had on Madras shorts, blue socks, and brown wing tips, thick black glasses, and a straw hat. He had mottled red arms and milk-white legs. His wide, blunt nose was covered by a wild trellis of indigo-blue veins.

The boy politely stopped the man. We watched. A few words and smiles were exchanged and the boy ran back, smiling, saying, "Hannibal . . . Hannibal, Missouri! That's a double, right? Pay up now and no loafers."

And so it went as Many Scars sucked down Dr Peppers and divined where each of the happy tourists walking about town had come from. He never missed, at least not while I was there.

"South Carolina . . . Ohio . . . Florida . . . Illinois . . . Minnesota . . . New Jersey . . . Indiana."

When he said, "Indiana" I suddenly spoke up and said, "Wait, now. How can you know where that woman is from? She looks like the girl next door; she could be from anywhere."

This is what Many Scars Slygo said: "Maybe, but she reminds me of Jane Pauley and Jane Pauley's a Hoosier."

Then he went on looking. Suddenly he clenched his fists until the flesh of his hands turned white when a fat man in a black Stetson with a rattlesnake hatband walked past Chief Joe. The metal toes of his smooth snakeskin boots kicked up chunks of loose rock.

"Well?" said the boy who was keeping the bets. His voice was filled with economic urgency. "Well, come on, man, where's the dude from? Say it so I can collect. Come on, man, don't choke now."

Many Scars Slygo said nothing, though. Nothing at all.

I wondered later if Many Scars Slygo could adapt his remarkable talents toward a more fruitful enterprise—like divining the presence of trout. Bob Winterwolf Dougal laughed hard and loud when I made the suggestion. He took a small jar of tacky-pink salmon eggs from his jacket pocket, pressed it tightly in my hand, saying, "Here, white man, let me share with you the sacred Native American secret for scaring up trout."

I enjoy spending time with Dougal, fishing with him, wading in the cold trout waters of Raven Fork, listening to him tell me of how the Indian can get it over the white man. He is more than a little nervous about going to the Wharton School of Business. This is what he told me as he worked a nice rainbow trout he hooked on the Raven Fork with a fat, wiggly cricket.

"It could happen, ya know. I go up there and turn white and stay that way for keeps. It could happen. That's the fear that stays with me, that it could happen. That I'll go white. I don't mind giving up some of my mind, but I'm not about to let my heart or my soul go white. What misery. Having your soul go white, that would be bad medicine. The worst."

Dougal treats this fear by spending his time coming up with surefire schemes to benefit himself and his people. His latest idea is to start a tour business called Cherokee Trails. He's already got his eye on an old school bus for sale over in Bryson City. He's going to paint it red and blue and sell seats to his fellow Cherokee, take them on a grand tour of the Indian reservations of the West. He says a day among the weary and downtrodden Sioux at Pine Ridge will surely lift his people's spirits, let them know that as Native Americans, they are among the handful of lucky tribes, those few with at least a little hope in their otherwise empty pockets.

"Our luck is bad," he says, "but not tragic. It could be worse for us, gringo." His voice cracked as he spoke and his eyes searched the woods along the river as though he expected the Cherokee's good fortune to evaporate at any moment.

The last time we went into Gatlinburg, Tewksbury convinced me that we should check into the Park Vista Hotel. It sits up high on the brow of a ridge overlooking the town, not far from the entrance to the national park. He told the clerk to give us a room on the tenth floor looking out over the valley of the Little Pigeon River. We stood out on the room's narrow balcony and watched the last of the day's sunlight bleed out of the sky and a full moon hung low over the mountains. Below, the city lost clear detail and definition, became a seam of lights, miles of lights, like a great string of fireworks that had all exploded at once.

Tewksbury said he didn't think Gatlinburg was all that seedy. Sure it couldn't lay claim to being any grand and eloquent resort city, but then it didn't pretend to be. It called itself "Good Natured" Gatlinburg, which as mottoes go, is harmless and seems to fit. Tewksbury took a long pull on a glass of bourbon and water and said the place wasn't any worse than Coney Island. So it didn't have a polished genteel image, wasn't soaked in unblemished dignity and class. It was, we agreed, what it was: good, old-fashioned heavy-duty American free enterprise juiced up to full throttle, offering whatever got the wallet out and open. And it all was harmless enough, as long as you didn't take it too seriously, mistake its clichés of mountain life for the hard realities of bankruptcy and loss that existed beyond the reach of the bright lights and laughter. The lights outlined a vein of prosperity surprisingly short and narrow, like a modest seam of gold. Riches for some, but hardly enough to end the legacy of mountain poverty, the heady mountain mix of hard times and infinite beauty.

Still, sometimes it felt good to get into town, become part of the crowds. All the sleight of hand, the fun, the illusion, the substitution of the imagined for the real, the bizarre for the brutal. Too, towns can take the edge off a man's anger and loneliness and bitterness. After all, no one is drawn to Pigeon Forge and Gatlinburg for their excellent international cuisine, for their art galleries, for their great displays of mountain culture. Most come to simply kick back, relax, cut loose, have fun, laugh, buy a thrill, a ticket to excitement, stand in line to look at what is odd and offbeat.

Having seen most every other attraction, that evening we stood in line to get into the Ripley's Believe It or Not Museum and decided afterward that our favorite exhibit was the model of Columbus's flagship, the *Santa Maria*, made entirely out of chicken bones. It's some world, believe it or not. For those who like the wildness behind bars, there are several caged bears in Pigeon Forge. There are supposed to be five of them at the Three Bears souvenir shop.

They have sad names like Mandy and Honey. They are kept out back. It costs a dollar to see them caged, lifeless, their eyes dull and disinterested. They are not Smoky Mountain black bears. They come from other places and have been behind bars all their lives. Tewksbury and I have never paid the dollar, though Tewksbury did offer to buy all five bears so he could have them moved to a fine zoo somewhere. He thinks there is at least more space and respect in a zoo than in the cramped quarters behind a shoddy souvenir shop. Joe, yet another kept bear, stays at another souvenir shop down the highway. Joe is not a Tennessee black bear, either. He comes from Maine. He lives in a small enclosure, on a slab of concrete. He lives outside where the curious can freely gawk at him. But he rarely comes out except at feeding time. In a cage no bigger than a closet, just down from Joe's lodgings, sits Bozo, the bear that held down Joe's job for more than twenty-three years. He is stuffed now. He died patriotically on July 4, 1981. The taxidermy job was not the best. Bozo looks awkward, incredibly uncomfortable. He's sitting stiffly in the small cage, paws outstretched. When we saw him, someone had put a bottle of Coca-Cola in one of his huge paws. He stars blankly out toward the Smoky Mountains, caged and kept even in death.

As Tewksbury and I roam about Gatlinburg and Pigeon Forge, we periodically stop and stare at the mountains that rise up above the towns. This we do to keep things in perspective, to keep our minds clear, our fragile sanity intact. The great, blue-black, brooding mountains are always there, hard and merciless and inexorably real. Gatlinburg also calls itself "The Gateway to the Great Smoky Mountains." Another fine slogan. Gateways, after all, are meant to be passed through.

Tewksbury and I tried counting hotels, motels, and resorts from Pigeon Forge through Gatlinburg once and stopped, with plenty left uncounted, at 150. There must be more than 100 restaurants and fast-food emporiums. Gatlinburg and Pigeon Forge put out a lot of volts: it's an energy level that requires a lot of calories, a diet of mainly pancakes (original, wild blueberry, buckwheat, orange-pineapple, log cabin, cornmeal, Caribbean—with powdered sugar, nuts, and coconut, and bananas—raisin nut, even chocolate chip), steak, seafood (fresh Maine lobster at Maxwell's), Mexican fare, German, British, deli food, Chinese, Mandarin, Szechuan, and, naturally, plenty of just plain, good mountain food. The Smoky Mountain Trout House prepares rainbow trout twelve ways and Tewksbury and I have pledged to keep coming back to town until we have tried all twelve. Broiled, panfried, sautéed, almondine, dilly, Parmesan, greenbrier almondine, grape, lemon rice, mustard sauce, and Creole.

Our last trip we had the lemon rice. Not bad, not bad at all. And after dinner we melted into the crowd along the sidewalks, walked up and down Parkway Road going into every shop looking for the ultimate souvenir. This is mine. The Smoky Mountain Weather Rock—a small twig, cut to a point and stuck into a wooden base, a smooth block of wood. Swinging from the twig, which looks something like a gallows tree in miniature, is a piece of twine which is tied about a small piece of Smoky Mountain stone. Instructions are printed boldly on a piece of paper, glued to the base. This is how the instructions read:

> When rock is—
> WARM—SUNNY
> WET—RAIN
> WHITE—SNOW
> SWINGING—WINDY
> BOUNCING—EARTHQUAKE
> GONE—TORNADO
>
> Price, $1.95 plus tax.

We decided to pass up the Guinness World Records Exhibition Center, the Hauntings, where there's "a live ghost show every 20 minutes," even the Waltzing Waters, "a spectacular display of dancing water and breathtaking lights, all set to your favorite music, from Broadway show tunes and well-known classics to contemporary hits and patriotic arrangements." We decided not to go to the Stars Over Gatlinburg Wax Museum which has a fine assortment of stiff, jaundiced-looking figures including Paul Revere, Bob Hope, John Wayne, Marilyn Monroe, and, of course, Elvis. The one time we went to the museum, someone had stuck a note into Elvis's waxy yellow hand with a toothpick. This is what the note said: "Just saw him alive as hell over at the Pancake Pantry in booths 1, 2, & 3 having a heaping helping of blackberry pancakes covered with peanut butter and syrup. No shit." And we walked on and stopped frequently and sat and looked up beyond the town at the black-faced mountains, and we walked down along the river and listened to it move endlessly over beds of stones, hissing menacingly.

We walked along the river toward the far end of town, toward the invisible yet inviolate boundary where the national park begins. I wanted to show Tewksbury the deep hole in the river behind where the Dairy Queen had been where I accidentally caught the biggest rainbow trout I've ever hooked in these mountains.

It was a wide, deep pool on the Little Pigeon almost directly behind the Dairy Queen which was behind the Burning Bush restaurant. The Dairy Queen is gone, but the river goes on, olive-green waters under a heavy archway of trees and mottled shadows.

I caught the trout in May. It was late afternoon, almost sundown; the skies were clear, the wind balmy and light. I had just come off Abrams Creek in Cades Cove. I'd been on the creek since daylight with Arby Mulligan. We had hiked above the falls. It was some day. The trail, even that high up, had a great many tourists on it. Arby offered each of them contentment and temporal salvation, free of charge. All it took was a cup of icy mountain creek water splashed quickly over the head. Most passed hurriedly without answering, afraid even to look at what was surely a genuine Appalachian madman. Some laughed. One or two actually accepted the innocent and harmless baptism. One man from Michigan, on hearing Mulligan's offer, screamed down the trail to his wife, "Hurry on up here, Linda, I've found a real hillbilly nutcase to photograph. I mean this guy is a sandwich short of a picnic. Hurry up, babe. He's one to tell the Meyers about."

The few that stopped took one look at me fly-fishing in the creek and either thought I was part of Mulligan's flimflam or part of the park service's Cades Cove Interpretive Program. Mountain Man Fishing. Small groups of folks gathered up the creek bank, all whispering, cameras clicking. They wanted me to hold up what was surely a heavy stringer of fat trout. I'd caught only one small rainbow the whole morning and, as I nearly always do, I let it go. They grimaced, frowned, looked cheated. I felt guilty as though I had somehow let them down, marred their wilderness experience. Each time a group would break up and move on, another would gather and yell out, and I jumped nervously, wondering if this was how a deer felt when it is suddenly startled while feeding quietly at the wood's edge. I moved, the crowd followed. I cast. They applauded. I hooked a tree branch. They hooted and howled. Again, they taunted me to hold up my catch for photographs, and suddenly Arby Mulligan ran out into the creek and leapt into my arms, and there we were both soaking wet and laughing hard and listening to a dozen clicking cameras.

When the sunlight went soft and seemed to turn into a liquid mist of faded reds, we walked back to the trail, hiked down the mountainside through pools of warm violet light mixed with lacy shadows. Mulligan began moaning and groaning, low, guttural sounds rising up from deep in his lungs, as though some sharp, ragged pain was grasping and clawing at his chest.

He groaned hard again and a wide grin spread comfortably across his face.

"Best thing for stress," he said. "Truly. Moan and groan religiously for ten minutes a day. Works even better if you can do it in a locked room, lights out, windows open. It'll chase away the blues, brother."

This from the man who told me, after Tewksbury complained of bouts of depression, that the best thing for melancholy was "either to make love a lot or get a pet. If both proved impractical, the only remaining remedy was cold showers, three a day."

We walked on down the mountain. I drove back to Gatlinburg; Mulligan headed for the Elkmont campground.

When I got back into Gatlinburg there was still a wide smear of sunlight in the sky. I pulled into the Dairy Queen thinking I might be able to salvage the day with an extra thick chocolate shake. My luck changed as soon as I walked up to the small window where you place your order because the Proverb Man was on duty, mixing up ice-cream cones, hamburgers and fries, malts and shakes.

I never knew his real name. He was always just the Proverb Man. His coworkers at the Dairy Queen loved him, said he was kind, caring, a hard worker. He had shy brown eyes set deep in a moon-shaped face, and his skin was the pale white of candle wax. His face was pocked with deep acne scars. He had thick pink lips that were always pressed tightly together in a kind of pinched, uncertain smile. A pair of thick glasses continually slid down the greasy bridge of his nose.

His nails were always meticulously clean, freshly clipped, neat; hair cut, well oiled, smoothed back under his white-and-red Dairy Queen paper cap. A small gold cross hung on a long gold chain and swung aimlessly about his neck as he worked. I noticed the cross was stained with flecks of ketchup and dollops of ice-cold milk.

"He'ya," said the Proverb Man. "This world is a goose, and them that do not pick will get no feathers."

No matter what you might say, the Proverb Man always answered with some bit of proverbial wisdom. That it had nothing whatsoever to do with what you were saying or ordering meant nothing to him. Nothing much at all registered except people's orders. If anything else interested him, he never let it show. He liked to fill people's orders and put a little something extra into the sack, a harmless proverb or bit of wit, no extra charge. Have a nice day, compliments of the Proverb Man.

"A shake," I said. "Double chocolate and extra cold."

The Proverb Man took up a silver shake cup, held it high over his head, said, "Bless the bridge that carries you over."

I told him about the eerie day on Abrams Creek.

"There's no disgrace in poverty, but it's damned inconvenient."

I leaned farther inside the window, asked him how he'd been getting along.

"The world is your cow, but you have to do the milking."

I shook my head in humble agreement.

A new boy was busy dropping vats of fries. "How's the new boy?" I said. The Proverb Man said, "Dead and too dumb to fall over. The more you see some people, the better you like dogs."

The milk-shake machine whirred noisily behind the Proverb Man and I commented on the deep purple light fringing the low-slung clouds over the mountains.

"It's all downhill after the equator," he said.

The Proverb Man poured the thick, rich, chocolate liquid into a big Dairy Queen cup, saying, "The past is a bucket of ashes."

He handed me the cup. "When buying horses or taking a wife, shut your eyes tight and commend yourself to God," he said.

I smiled and paid.

There was an old picnic table behind the Dairy Queen near the river's edge under the abundant shade of oaks and maples and hickory trees in full leaf. I sat there nursing the extra-thick, icy-cold chocolate shake. Just beyond the picnic table, down the creek bank, was a lovely stretch of the Little Pigeon River, a deep pool, its waters olive-green. Dappled shadows wrinkled on the surface of the pool, moving with the slow, steady current. Above the pool, the river curved slightly, hissed and spit like an annoyed cat as it crossed that invisible boundary at the edge of town, that boundary where, once crossed, it stopped being a national park river, a river under federal protection, and became instead a mountain city river. Just below the boundary the water cascaded over a natural sill of huge stones and fallen trees and limbs. Lichens festooned the slick backs of the bigger stones and the water swirled in swift eddies about the immense stones and sunken trees before it flowed toward the lower pool in an edgy rush, then eased as it came into the wide pools of diffuse sunlight.

Such an eloquent run of water to be behind a Dairy Queen, as beautiful a spot as I had seen that day up along the wild reaches of Abrams Creek, up above the falls. Below the pool there is a small bridge where the river narrows and becomes shallower, running hard and fast over a chaos of submerged stones glowing like polished ebony in the water before racing down through a long corridor of trees arched and tangled overhead so that the sunlight comes through in thin, weak veins and the river loses its lush green complexion and goes to gray, the supple gray of a wolf's belly in winter.

I still had on my hip boots; the little Winston rod was still rigged up and stretched out in the backseat of the car. I had my Gatlinburg city fishing license and my Tennessee/North Carolina fishing license; there was still a fine mosaic of sunlight and evening shadows in the sky, a chimera of pale lavenders and sultry wine-reds fringed with yellow halos. The day hung on. As long as there was light and my licenses were in order, the pool was legal and in season. Besides, I really only wanted to wade into its deep, cold green water and sip my milk shake.

I took the rod from the car, saw that I still had a passable dry fly on, a No. 14 Royal Coachman. Tucking the rod beneath my arm, I waded out into the back side of the pool toward the cascade upriver near the park boundary. The hip boots were scant insulation; the cold water sent a shudder up along my spine, through the muscles and bones of my legs and back. My calves and feet went comfortably numb.

There I was standing thigh-deep in cold river water and silken pools of charcoal shadows, rod in one hand, milk shake in the other.

The river was open behind me, so I worked the rod and line—quick, even-tempered front and back casts, thinking I'd work on the loop of my cast, making it loose and open, then slender and tight. As a fly fisherman, my loop can always stand improvement, though the trout don't seem to appreciate my efforts to entice them, no matter how hard I polish my modest skill with rod and reel.

On one of the forward casts, I let it go . . . all that worked-out line, maybe 40 feet of it including leader and tippet and that fluttering Royal Coachman, and it all uncoiled clumsily over the surface of the river, the fly coming to rest down toward the bridge.

And that's when it struck. The reel, even with all that line out, came to life, clicking and clacking frantically like some experimental machine in imminent danger of flying apart. The initial jolt, that first snap of pure, wild, predatorial rapacity, sent globs of chocolate milk shake spattering against my face, chin, and forehead. Tiny streams of milk shake smeared my glasses, reduced my view of the river to a syrupy mix of browns and greens.

That's how it happened. The Lord's eye on it, as Arby Mulligan would say. That's how I accidentally, unintentionally, after breaking all the laws of correct fly casting and the appropriate code of dignified fly-fishing behavior (starting with wading into a trout stream holding a cup half-filled with thirty-two-ounces of chocolate milk shake), hooked into that enormous trout. Only I did not yet know it was a trout or even a fish. All I knew was that I had hooked something or something had hooked me, something big with no understanding of decorum and rules of angling and no sense of compromise, or accommodation.

I quickly put the cup of milk shake between my teeth, got the rod out from under my arm and up into the air and desperately began stripping in line, not with the reel, but with my right hand.

At the end of my line there was now no real feel or give, no sense of tiredness, only the determined strain of untempered, implacable instinct, an unbridled power and strength that were hauling me deeper into the pool, farther into the river. Icy water began to fill my hip boots, soak my jeans, wrap my skin in layers of ever deepening cold.

Then, as suddenly and unexpectedly as though the sound had risen from the river bottom, I heard "Talk does not cook rice."

The Proverb Man. Turning my head for an instant toward the right bank of the river, I saw him, or rather a smudged, smeared version of him, through my milk-shake-stained glasses. He was sitting at the picnic table idly watching me, his head cradled in his greasy hands.

I went back to the trout and could, finally, feel traces of exhaustion in its fight. The great strength was ebbing, not giving up so much as giving out. Going to the reel, I hurriedly took up the loose coils of line floating scattered on the surface of the pool all about me, reeled until I could feel blunt tension on the line and little else. Just then, the line shuddered, went limp, and I could feel the trout rising. I could feel its rise through the line and rod into the muscles and nerves of my hands and arms and shoulders. Then the fish was coming up, a surge of power, a burst of pure energy, and it came violently, breaking the smooth surface of the pool as though the water were cheap green glass. Beads of water trailed off its broad back and wide flanks, caught the light, looked like thick drops of coagulated blood. In midair the big trout jerked its head and body savagely. One last total effort to break free. No compromise. None at all.

Neither knowing nor sensing its own end, even the probability of its demise, its own mortality, knowing and feeling only the instinct of blood and muscle, it used itself up brutally, completely, willingly.

"In the old of the moon, a cloudy morning bodes a fair afternoon," said the Proverb Man, his voice, as usual, registering no emotion.

The trout seemed suspended in midair for a long moment. I remember the stare of its black eye, the flash of its belly, the irregular swipe of magenta along its sides, and the water coming off its back and fins. It hit the water hard; I yanked the rod up quickly and the rod tip bowed severely. I worried whether rod and line, leader and tippet, fly and angler could hold such a trout.

"Everything helps, quoth the wren, when she pissed into the sea."

So said the Proverb Man.

Now the trout came up, spent, its exhaustion so deep that I could see its body tremble uncontrollably as it rose to the surface of the pool. As I began carefully pulling it closer to me, I yelled at the Proverb Man to run to the car and get the arctic creel from the backseat.

Out of the corner of my eye, I saw him jump up from the picnic table, run through the damp grass and lengthening shadows toward the car. As he ran, this is what he yelled, "Every Czech is a musician."

He came running back hard with the creel in hand as I kept the big trout well in front of me, the line tight.

The Proverb Man threw the creel bag to me. The arctic creel is lined with plastic and is submersible, so I let it soak for a moment in the water and allowed it to sink as I drew the trout closer still and scooped it into the bag. It didn't fit. Too big. Much too big. I eased the hook from the trout's jaw, kept its head in the water-soaked creel, and yelled to the Proverb Man that I wanted to use his meat scale. I saw him hurry inside the Dairy Queen, then appear suddenly at the back door.

"Afflictions are sent to us by God for our own good," he said.

I tucked the rod back under my arm, and held the creel firmly with both hands as I walked patiently back over the slick, stony bottom of the pool, up the creek bank, and into the Dairy Queen.

The Proverb Man handed me a napkin and I rubbed off my glasses and put the trout on the small meat scale. I saw it clearly for the first time. It looked so inelegant in the creel bag, its body bent awkwardly. It looked as long as my forearm, from the tip of my outstretched fingertips to my elbow and then some. It weighed in at just under 7.5 pounds. It lay there on the scale, the eye facing me black and still like a black stone seemingly full of nothing and yet a world of motion, of unrealized tendencies. Eyes that were reservoirs of light and probabilities. Its heavily muscled body was scarred, cut, torn, frayed, tattered, battered. There were deep wounds along its flanks and on its belly, and a large cataract, as thick and cloudy as melted wax, completely covered its right eye.

The Proverb Man looked at the trout for a long time, then said, "Marriage is the tomb of love."

I slid it back into the dripping creel bag, ran quickly for the river, all but dove in from the bank, and slowly, gently submerged the creel and trout into the cold water. As it lay there in the sunken creel, I wondered what journey it had made, how far it must have come to be so beat up and bruised. I thought of it smashing blindly against great boulders, dragging itself over shoals of rough-edged rock, hurling itself up cascades, over falls. I thought of it moving always, through icy nights and days of pounding rain, through winter's metallic-gray waters, stones and forests covered with snow, and ice on the wind, through spring's edgy, unpredictable temper, and summer's deep warm months. Where had it come from? Where was it bound?

The light had finally gone from the mountain sky and the wind off the river was colder and stronger, rattling hard among the trees. I could hear the buzz of the Dairy Queen's lights clicking on. The creel bag was empty. The big trout had gone.

On the far side of the pool I watched the spread of the mountain night sky across the smooth, glassy water. First a wash of soft white moonglow, then, on the water, the perfect reflection of stars, specks of light wrinkling in the river's current. The night sky came up on the water as though the surface of the river were a developing photograph. Yet neither the sky nor the stars, the river nor the light was fixed, merely image. It all moved. Everything was adrift.

The Proverb Man walked out the back door of the Dairy Queen, sat down near me on the damp green grass. He smelled of french fries and sweet chocolate syrup. His grimy white apron and hat glowed in the deepening night, the soft glow of distant candlelight.

Everything comes and goes, I thought. It all comes and goes—an infinite stream that is the ever-changing texture of things as they are.

"Better to wear out than to rust out," said the Proverb Man. I noticed he was smiling and had leaned back against a tree. A long silence passed, a moment of water and darkness, and the Proverb Man said, "A dead mouse feels no cold."

My camp was back at the Elkmont campground, along the Little Pigeon River. I drove back, parked, settled down into the blue sleeping bag. I watched the mountain night and listened to the soothing rush of the river. And soon I was dreaming of the big trout, that battered one-eyed trout that had hauled me, for several wondrous moments, out of my world and into its behind the Dairy Queen.